What Readers Are Saying About
Programming Concurrency on the JVM

An excellent book! Venkat skillfully leads us through the many design and implementation decisions that today's JVM developer faces in multithreaded programming. His easy-to-read style and the many examples he provides—using a variety of current open source tools and JVM languages—make this complex topic very approachable.

➤ **Albert Scherer**
   Manager, eCommerce Technologies, Follett Higher Education Group, Inc.

If the JVM is your platform of choice, then this book is an absolute must-read. Buy it, read it, and then buy a copy for all your team members. You will well be on your way to finding a good solution to concurrency issues.

➤ **Raju Gandhi**
   Senior consultant, Integrallis Software, LLC

Extremely thorough coverage of a critically important topic.

➤ **Chris Richardson**
   Author of *POJOS in Action* and Founder, CloudFoundry.com

There has been an explosion of interest and application for both new concurrency models and new languages on the JVM. Venkat's book ties it all together and shows the working developer how to structure their application and get the most out of existing libraries, even if they were built in a different language. This book is the natural successor to *Java Concurrency in Practice*.

➤ **Alex Miller**
   Architect/Senior Engineer, Revelytix, Inc.

I found *Programming Concurrency* akin to sitting under a master craftsman imparting wisdom to his apprentice. The reader is guided on a journey that starts with the "why" of concurrency and the big-picture design issues that he'll face. He's then taught the modern concurrency tools provided directly within the Java SDK before embarking upon an adventure through the exciting realms of STM and actors. I sincerely believe that this book is destined to be one of the most important concurrency books yet written. Venkat has done it again!

➤ **Matt Stine**
   Technical Architect, AutoZone, Inc.

Concurrency is a hot topic these days, and Venkat takes you through a wide range of current techniques and technologies to program concurrency effectively on the JVM. More importantly, by comparing and contrasting concurrency approaches in five different JVM languages, you get a better picture of the capabilities of various tools you can use. This book will definitely expand your knowledge and toolbox for dealing with concurrency.

➤ **Scott Leberknight**
   Chief Architect, Near Infinity Corporation

Programming Concurrency on the JVM

Mastering Synchronization, STM, and Actors

Venkat Subramaniam

The Pragmatic Bookshelf

Dallas, Texas • Raleigh, North Carolina

Many of the designations used by manufacturers and sellers to distinguish their products are claimed as trademarks. Where those designations appear in this book, and The Pragmatic Programmers, LLC was aware of a trademark claim, the designations have been printed in initial capital letters or in all capitals. The Pragmatic Starter Kit, The Pragmatic Programmer, Pragmatic Programming, Pragmatic Bookshelf, PragProg and the linking *g* device are trademarks of The Pragmatic Programmers, LLC.

Every precaution was taken in the preparation of this book. However, the publisher assumes no responsibility for errors or omissions, or for damages that may result from the use of information (including program listings) contained herein.

Our Pragmatic courses, workshops, and other products can help you and your team create better software and have more fun. For more information, as well as the latest Pragmatic titles, please visit us at *http://pragprog.com*.

The team that produced this book includes:

Brian P. Hogan (editor)
Potomac Indexing, LLC (indexer)
Kim Wimpsett (copyeditor)
David Kelly (typesetter)
Janet Furlow (producer)
Juliet Benda (rights)
Ellie Callahan (support)

ISBN-13: 978-1-934356-76-0

Book version: P1.0—August 2011

To Mom and Dad, for teaching the values of integrity, honesty, and diligence.

Contents

Part II — Modern Java/JDK Concurrency

Part III — Software Transactional Memory

Part IV — Actor-Based Concurrency

Part V — Epilogue

Preface

Speed. Aside from caffeine, nothing quickens the pulse of a programmer as much as the blazingly fast execution of a piece of code. How can we fulfill the need for computational speed? Moore's law takes us some of the way, but multicore is the real future. To take full advantage of multicore, we need to program with concurrency in mind.

In a concurrent program, two or more actions take place simultaneously. A concurrent program may download multiple files while performing computations and updating the database. We often write concurrent programs using threads in Java. Multithreading on the Java Virtual Machine (JVM) has been around from the beginning, but how we program concurrency is still evolving, as we'll learn in this book.

The hard part is reaping the benefits of concurrency without being burned. Starting threads is easy, but their execution sequence is nondeterministic. We're soon drawn into a battle to coordinate threads and ensure they're handling data consistently.

To get from point A to point B quickly, we have several options, based on how critical the travel time is, the availability of transport, the budget, and so on. We can walk, take the bus, drive that pimped-up convertible, take a bullet train, or fly on a jet. In writing Java for speed, we've also got choices.

There are three prominent options for concurrency on the JVM:

- What I call the "synchronize and suffer" model
- The Software-Transactional Memory model
- The actor-based concurrency model

I call the familiar Java Development Kit (JDK) synchronization model "synchronize and suffer" because the results are unpredictable if we forget to synchronize shared mutable state or synchronize it at the wrong level. If we're lucky, we catch the problems during development; if we miss, it can come out in odd and unfortunate ways during production. We get no compilation errors, no warning, and simply no sign of trouble with that ill-fated code.

Programs that fail to synchronize access to shared mutable state are broken, but the Java compiler won't tell us that. Programming with mutability in pure Java is like working with the mother-in-law who's just waiting for you to fail. I'm sure you've felt the pain.

There are three ways to avoid problems when writing concurrent programs:

- Synchronize properly.

- Don't share state.

- Don't mutate state.

If we use the modern JDK concurrency API, we'll have to put in significant effort to synchronize properly. STM makes synchronization implicit and greatly reduces the chances of errors. The actor-based model, on the other hand, helps us avoid shared state. Avoiding mutable state is the secret weapon to winning concurrency battles.

In this book, we'll take an example-driven approach to learn the three models and how to exploit concurrency with them.

Who's This Book For?

I've written this book for experienced Java programmers who are interested in learning how to manage and make use of concurrency on the JVM, using languages such as Java, Clojure, Groovy, JRuby, and Scala.

If you're new to Java, this book will not help you learn the basics of Java. There are several good books that teach the fundamentals of Java programming, and you should make use of them.

If you have fairly good programming experience on the JVM but find yourself needing material that will help further your practical understanding of programming concurrency, this book is for you.

If you're interested only in the solutions directly provided in Java and the JDK—Java threading and the concurrency library—I refer you to two very good books already on the market that focus on that: Brian Goetz's *Java Concurrency in Practice* [Goe06] and Doug Lea's *Concurrent Programming in Java* [Lea00]. Those two books provide a wealth of information on the Java Memory Model and how to ensure thread safety and consistency.

My focus in this book is to help you use, but also move beyond, the solutions provided directly in the JDK to solve some practical concurrency problems. You will learn about some third-party Java libraries that help you work easily with isolated mutability. You will also learn to use libraries that reduce complexity and error by eliminating explicit locks.

My goal in this book is to help you learn the set of tools and approaches that are available to you today so you can sensibly decide which one suits you the best to solve your immediate concurrency problems.

What's in This Book?

This book will help us explore and learn about three separate concurrency solutions—the modern Java JDK concurrency model, the Software Transactional Memory (STM), and the actor-based concurrency model.

This book is divided into five parts: Strategies for Concurrency, Modern Java/JDK Concurrency, Software Transactional Memory, Actor-Based Concurrency, and an epilogue.

In Chapter 1, *The Power and Perils of Concurrency*, on page 1, we will discuss what makes concurrency so useful and the reasons why it's so hard to get it right. This chapter will set the stage for the three concurrency models we'll explore in this book.

Before we dive into these solutions, in Chapter 2, *Division of Labor*, on page 15 we'll try to understand what affects concurrency and speedup and discuss strategies for achieving effective concurrency.

The design approach we take makes a world of difference between sailing the sea of concurrency and sinking in it, as we'll discuss in Chapter 3, *Design Approaches*, on page 35.

The Java concurrency API has evolved quite a bit since the introduction of Java. We'll discuss how the modern Java API helps with both thread safety and performance in Chapter 4, *Scalability and Thread Safety*, on page 47.

While we certainly want to avoid shared mutable state, in Chapter 5, *Taming Shared Mutability*, on page 73 we'll look at ways to handle the realities of existing applications and things to keep in mind while refactoring legacy code.

We'll dive deep into STM in Chapter 6, *Introduction to Software Transactional Memory*, on page 89 and learn how it can alleviate most of the concurrency pains, especially for applications that have very infrequent write collisions.

We'll learn how to use STM in different prominent JVM languages in Chapter 7, *STM in Clojure, Groovy, Java, JRuby, and Scala*, on page 141.

In Chapter 8, *Favoring Isolated Mutability*, on page 163, we'll learn how the actor-based model can entirely remove concurrency concerns if we can design for isolated mutability.

Again, if you're interested in different prominent JVM languages, you'll learn how to use actors from your preferred language in Chapter 9, *Actors in Groovy, Java, JRuby, and Scala*, on page 221.

Finally, in Chapter 10, *Zen of Programming Concurrency*, on page 243, we'll review the solutions we've discussed in this book and conclude with some takeaway points that can help you succeed with concurrency.

Is it Concurrency or Parallelism?

There's no clear distinction between these two terms in the industry, and the number of answers we'll hear is close to the number of people we ask for an explanation (and don't ask them concurrently...or should I say in parallel?).

Let's not debate the distinction here. We may run programs on a single core with multiple threads and later deploy them on multiple cores with multiple threads. When our code runs within a single JVM, both these deployment options have some common concerns—how do we create and manage threads, how do we ensure integrity of data, how do we deal with locks and synchronization, and are our threads crossing the memory barrier at the appropriate times...?

Whether we call it concurrent or parallel, addressing these concerns is core to ensuring that our programs run correctly and efficiently. That's what we'll focus on in this book.

Concurrency for Polyglot Programmers

Today, the word *Java* stands more for the platform than for the language. The Java Virtual Machine, along with the ubiquitous set of libraries, has evolved into a very powerful platform over the years. At the same time, the Java language is showing its age. Today there are quite a few interesting and powerful languages on the JVM—Clojure, JRuby, Groovy, and Scala, to mention a few.

Some of these modern JVM languages such as Clojure, JRuby, and Groovy are dynamically typed. Some, such as Clojure and Scala, are greatly influenced by a functional style of programming. Yet all of them have one thing in common—they're concise and highly expressive. Although it may take a bit of effort to get used to their syntax, the paradigm, or the differences, we'll mostly need less code in all these languages compared with coding in Java. What's even better, we can mix these languages with Java code and truly be a polyglot programmer—see Neal Ford's "Polyglot Programmer" in Appendix 2, *Web Resources*, on page 255.

In this book we'll learn how to use the java.util.concurrent API, the STM, and the actor-based model using Akka and GPars. We'll also learn how to program concurrency in Clojure, Java, JRuby, Groovy, and Scala. If you program in or are planning to pick up any of these languages, this book will introduce you to the concurrent programming options in them.

Examples and Performance Measurements

Most of the examples in this book are in Java; however, you will also see quite a few examples in Clojure, Groovy, JRuby, and Scala. I've taken extra effort to keep the syntactical nuances and the language-specific idioms to a minimum. Where there is a choice, I've leaned toward something that's easier to read and familiar to programmers mostly comfortable with Java.

The following are the version of languages and libraries used in this book:

- Akka 1.1.3 (http://akka.io/downloads)
- Clojure 1.2.1 (http://clojure.org/downloads)
- Groovy 1.8 (http://groovy.codehaus.org/Download)
- GPars 0.12 (http://gpars.codehaus.org)
- Java SE 1.6 (http://www.java.com/en/download)
- JRuby 1.6.2 (http://jruby.org/download)
- Scala 2.9.0.1 (http://www.scala-lang.org/downloads)

When showing performance measures between two versions of code, I've made sure these comparisons are on the same machine. For most of the examples I've used a MacBook Pro with 2.8GHz Intel dual-core processor and 4GB memory running Mac OS X 10.6.6 and Java version 1.6 update 24. For some of the examples, I also use an eight-core Sunfire 2.33GHz processor with 8GB of memory running 64-bit Windows XP and Java version 1.6.

All the examples, unless otherwise noted, were run in server mode with the "Java HotSpot(TM) 64-Bit Server VM" Java virtual machine.

All the examples were compiled and run on both the Mac and Windows machines mentioned previously.

In the listing of code examples, I haven't shown the import statements (and the package statements) because these often become lengthy. When trying the code examples, if you're not sure which package a class belongs to, don't worry, I've included the full listing on the code website. Go ahead and download the entire source code for this book from its website (http://pragprog. com/titles/vspcon).

Acknowledgments

Several people concurrently helped me to write this book. If not for the generosity and inspiration from some of the great minds I've come to know and respect over the years, this book would have remained a great idea in my mind.

I first thank the reviewers who braved to read the draft of this book and who offered valuable feedback—this is a better book because of them. However, any errors you find in this book are entirely a reflection of my deficiencies.

I benefited a great deal from the reviews and shrewd remarks of Brian Goetz (@BrianGoetz), Alex Miller (@puredanger), and Jonas Bonér (@jboner). Almost every page in the book was improved by the thorough review and eagle eyes of Al Scherer (@al_scherer) and Scott Leberknight (@sleberknight). Thank you very much, gentlemen.

Special thanks go to Raju Gandhi (@looselytyped), Ramamurthy Gopalakrishnan, Paul King (@paulk_asert), Kurt Landrus (@koctya), Ted Neward (@tedneward), Chris Richardson (@crichardson), Andreas Rueger, Nathaniel Schutta (@ntschutta), Ken Sipe (@kensipe), and Matt Stine (@mstine) for devoting your valuable time to correct me and encourage me at the same time. Thanks to Stuart Halloway (@stuarthalloway) for his cautionary review. I've improved this book, where possible, based on his comments.

The privilege to speak on this topic at various NFJS conferences helped shape the content of this book. I thank the NFJS (@nofluff) director Jay Zimmerman for that opportunity and my friends on the conference circuit both among speakers and attendees for their conversations and discussions.

I thank the developers who took the time to read the book in the beta form and offer their feedback on the book's forum. Thanks in particular to Dave Briccetti (@dcbriccetti), Frederik De Bleser (@enigmeta), Andrei Dolganov, Rabea Gransberger, Alex Gout, Simon Sparks, Brian Tarbox, Michael Uren, Dale Visser, and Tasos Zervos. I greatly benefited from the insightful comments, corrections, and observations of Rabea Gransberger.

Thanks to the creators and committers of the wonderful languages and libraries that I rely upon in this book and to program concurrent applications on the JVM.

One of the perks of writing this book was getting to know Steve Peter, who endured the first draft of this book as the initial development editor. His sense of humor and attention to detail greatly helped during the making of this book. Thank you, Steve. It was my privilege to have Brian P. Hogan (@bphogan) as the editor for this book. He came up to speed quickly, made observations that encouraged me, and, at the same time, provided constructive comments and suggestions in areas that required improvements. Thank you, Brian.

I thank the entire Pragmatic Bookshelf team for their efforts and encouragement along the way. Thanks to Kim Wimpsett, Susannah Pfalzer (@spfalzer), Andy Hunt (@pragmaticandy), and Dave Thomas (@pragdave) for their help, guidance, and making this so much fun.

None of this would have been possible without the support of my wife—thank you, Kavitha, for your incredible patience and sacrifice. I got quite a bit of encouragement from my sons, Karthik and Krupa; thank you, guys, for being inquisitive and frequently asking whether I'm done with the book. Now I can say yes, and it's where it belongs—in the hands of programmers who'll put it to good use.

Need and struggle are what excite and
inspire us.

        William James

CHAPTER 1

The Power and Perils of Concurrency

You've promised the boss that you'll turn the new powerful multicore processor into a blazingly fast workhorse for your application. You'd love to exploit the power on hand and beat your competition with a faster, responsive application that provides great user experience. Those gleeful thoughts are interrupted by your colleague's cry for help—he's run into yet another synchronization issue.

Most programmers have a love-hate relationship with concurrency.

Programming concurrency is hard, yet the benefits it provides make all the troubles worthwhile. The processing power we have at our disposal, at such an affordable cost, is something that our parents could only dream of. We can exploit the ability to run multiple concurrent tasks to create stellar applications. We have the ability to write applications that can provide a great user experience by staying a few steps ahead of the user. Features that would've made apps sluggish a decade ago are quite practical today. To realize this, however, we have to program concurrency.

In this chapter, we'll quickly review the reasons to exploit concurrency and discuss the perils that this path is mired in. At the end of this chapter, we'll be prepared to explore the exciting options for concurrency presented in this book.

1.1 Threads: The Flow of Execution

A thread, as we know, is a flow of execution in a process. When we run a program, there is at least one thread of execution for its process. We can create threads to start additional flows of execution in order to perform additional tasks concurrently. The libraries or framework we use may also start additional threads behind the scenes, depending on their need.

When multiple threads run as part of a single application, or a JVM, we have multiple tasks or operations running concurrently. A concurrent application makes use of multiple threads or concurrent flows of execution.

On a single processor, these concurrent tasks are often multiplexed or multitasked. That is, the processor rapidly switches between the context of each flow of execution. However, only one thread, and hence only one flow of execution, is performed at any given instance. On a multicore processor, more than one flow of execution (thread) is performed at any given instance. That number depends on the number of cores available on the processor, and the number of concurrent threads for an application depends on the number of cores associated with its process.

1.2 The Power of Concurrency

We're interested in concurrency for two reasons: to make an application responsive/improve the user experience and to make it faster.

Making Apps More Responsive

When we start an application, the main thread of execution often takes on multiple responsibilities sequentially, depending on the actions we ask it to perform: receive input from a user, read from a file, perform some calculations, access a web service, update a database, display a response to the user, and so on. If each of these operations takes only fractions of a second, then there may be no real need to introduce additional flows of execution; a single thread may be quite adequate to meet the needs.

In most nontrivial applications, however, these operations may not be that quick. Calculations may take anywhere from a couple of seconds to a few minutes. Requests for data from that web service may encounter network delays, so the thread waits for the response to arrive. While this is happening, there's no way for the users of the application to interact with or interrupt the application because the single thread is held on some operation to finish.

Let's consider an example that illustrates the need for more than one thread and how it impacts responsiveness. We often time events, so it would be nice to have stopwatch application. We can click a button to start the watch, and it will run until we click the button again. A naively written[1] bit of code for this is shown next (only the action handler for the button is shown; you can download the full program from the website for this book):

---

1. In the examples, we'll simply let exceptions propagate instead of logging or handling them—but be sure to handle exceptions properly in your production code.

introduction/NaiveStopWatch.java

```java
//This will not work
public void actionPerformed(final ActionEvent event) {
  if (running) stopCounting(); else startCounting();
}

private void startCounting() {
  startStopButton.setText("Stop");
  running = true;
  for(int count = 0; running; count++) {
    timeLabel.setText(String.format("%d", count));
    try {
      Thread.sleep(1000);
    } catch(InterruptedException ex) {
        throw new RuntimeException(ex);
    }
  }
}

private void stopCounting() {
  running = false;
  startStopButton.setText("Start");
}
```

When we run the little stopwatch application, a window with a Start button and a "0" label will appear. Unfortunately, when we click the button, we won't see any change—the button does not change to "Stop," and the label does not show the time count. What's worse, the application will not even respond to a quit request.

The main event dispatch thread is responsible for noticing UI-related events and delegating actions to be performed. When the Start button is clicked, the main event dispatch thread went into the event handler actionPerformed(); there it was held hostage by the method startCounting() as it started counting. Now, as we click buttons or try to quit, those events are dropped into the event queue, but the main thread is too busy and will not respond to those events—ever.

We need an additional thread, or a timer that in turn would use an additional thread, to make the application responsive. We need to delegate the task of counting and relieve the main event dispatch thread of that responsibility.

Not only can threads help make applications responsive, but they can help enhance the user experience. Applications can look ahead at operations the user may perform next and carry out the necessary actions, such as indexing or caching some data the user needs.

Making Apps Faster

Take a look at some of the applications you've written. Do you see operations that are currently performed sequentially, one after the other, that can be performed concurrently? You can make your application faster by running each of those operations in separate threads.

Quite a few kinds of applications can run faster by using concurrency. Among these are services, computationally intensive applications, and data-crunching applications.

Services

Let's say we're tasked to build an application that needs to process lots of invoices from various vendors. This requires that we apply rules and business workflow on each invoice, but we can process them in any order. Processing these invoices sequentially will not yield the throughput or utilize the resources well. Our application needs to process these invoices concurrently.

Computationally Intensive Apps

I once worked in the chemical industry where I wrote applications that computed various properties of chemicals flowing through different units in a refinery. This involved intensive computations that readily benefited from dividing the problem into several pieces, running the computations concurrently, and finally merging the partial results. A variety of problems lend themselves to the divide-and-conquer approach, and they will readily benefit from our ability to write concurrent programs.

Data Crunchers

I was once asked to build a personal finance application that had to go out to a web service to get the price and other details for a number of stocks. The application had to present the users with the total asset value and details of the volume of trading for each stock. For a wealthy user, the application may track shares in 100 different stocks. During a time of heavy traffic, it may take a few seconds to receive the information from the Web. That would turn into a few minutes of wait for the user before all the data was received and the processing started. The wait time could be brought down to a mere second or two by delegating the requests to multiple threads, assuming the network delay per request is a second or two and the system running the app has adequate resources and capabilities to spawn hundreds of threads.

Reaping the Benefits of Concurrency

Concurrency can help make apps responsive, reduce latency, and increase throughput. We can leverage multiple cores of the hardware and the concurrency of tasks in applications to gain speed and responsiveness. However, there are some hard challenges, as we'll discuss next, that we have to tackle before we can reap those benefits.

1.3   The Perils of Concurrency

Right now, you're probably thinking "I can get better throughput by breaking up my problem and letting multiple threads work on these parts." Unfortunately, problems rarely can be divided into isolated parts that can be run totally independent of each other. Often, we can perform some operations independently but then have to merge the partial results to get the final result. This requires threads to communicate the partial results and sometimes wait for those results to be ready. This requires coordination between threads and can lead to synchronization and locking woes.

We encounter three problems when developing concurrent programs: starvation, deadlock, and race conditions. The first two are somewhat easier to detect and even avoid. The last one, however, is a real nemesis that should be eliminated at the root.

Starvation and Deadlocks

Running into thread starvation is unfortunately quite easy. For example, an application that is about to perform a critical task may prompt the user for confirmation just as the user steps out to lunch. While the user enjoys a good meal, the application has entered a phase of starvation. Starvation occurs when a thread waits for an event that may take a very long time or forever to happen. It can happen when a thread waits for input from a user, for some external event to occur, or for another thread to release a lock. The thread will stay alive while it waits, doing nothing. We can prevent starvation by placing a timeout. Design the solution in such a way that the thread waits for only a finite amount of time. If the input does not arrive, the event does not happen, or the thread does not gain the lock within that time, then the thread bails out and takes an alternate action to make progress.

We run into deadlock if two or more threads are waiting on each other for some action or resource. Placing a timeout, unfortunately, will not help avoid the deadlock. It's possible that each thread will give up its resources, only to repeat its steps, which leads again into a deadlock—see "The Dining Philosophers Problem" in Appendix 2, *Web Resources*, on page 255. Tools such as JConsole can help detect deadlocks, and we can prevent deadlock by acquiring resources in a specific order. A better alternative, in the first place, would be to avoid explicit locks and the mutable state that goes with them. We'll see how to do that later in the book.

Race Conditions

If two threads compete to use the same resource or data, we have a *race condition*. A race condition doesn't just happen when two threads modify data. It can happen even when one is changing data while the other is trying to read it. Race conditions can render a program's behavior unpredictable, produce incorrect execution, and yield incorrect results.

Two forces can lead to race conditions—the Just-in-Time (JIT) compiler optimization and the Java Memory Model. For an exceptional treatise on the topic of Java Memory Model and how it affects concurrency, refer to Brian Goetz's seminal book *Java Concurrency in Practice* [Goe06].

Let's take a look at a fairly simple example that illustrates the problem. In the following code, the main thread creates a thread, sleeps for two seconds, and sets the flag done to true. The thread created, in the meantime, loops over the flag, as long as it's false. Let's compile and run the code and see what happens:

introduction/RaceCondition.java
```java
public class RaceCondition {
  private static boolean done;

  public static void main(final String[] args) throws InterruptedException{
    new Thread(
      new Runnable() {
        public void run() {
          int i = 0;
          while(!done) { i++; }
            System.out.println("Done!");
          }
        }
    ).start();

    System.out.println("OS: " + System.getProperty("os.name"));
    Thread.sleep(2000);
    done = true;
    System.out.println("flag done set to true");
  }
}
```

If we run that little program on Windows 7 (32-bit version) using the command `java RaceCondition`, we'll notice something like this (the order of output may differ on each run):

```
OS: Windows 7
flag done set to true
Done!
```

If we tried the same command on a Mac, we'd notice that the thread that's watching over the flag never finished, as we see in the output:

```
OS: Mac OS X
flag done set to true
```

Wait, don't put the book down and tweet "Windows Rocks, Mac sucks!" The problem is a bit deeper than the two previous runs revealed.

Let's try again—this time on Windows, run the program using the command `java -server RaceCondition` (asking it to be run in server mode on Windows), and on the Mac, run it using the command `java -d32 RaceCondition` (asking it to be run in client mode on the Mac).

On Windows, we'd see something like this:

```
OS: Windows 7
flag done set to true
```

However, now on the Mac, we'll see something like this:

```
OS: Mac OS X
Done!
flag done set to true
```

By default, Java runs in client mode on 32-bit Windows and in server mode on the Mac. The behavior of our program is consistent on both platforms—the program terminates in client mode and does not terminate in server mode.

When run in server mode, the second thread never sees the change to the flag done, even though the main thread set its value to true. This was because of the Java server JIT compiler optimization. But, let's not be quick to blame the JIT compiler—it's a powerful tool that works hard to optimize code to make it run faster.

What we learn from the previous example is that broken programs may appear to work in some settings and fail in others.

Know Your Visibility: Understand the Memory Barrier

The problem with the previous example is that the change by the main thread to the field done may not be visible to the thread we created. First, the JIT compiler may optimize the while loop; after all, it does not see the variable done changing within the context of the thread. Furthermore, the second thread may end up reading the value of the flag from its registers or cache instead of going to memory. As a result, it may never see the change made by the first thread to this flag—see *What's This Memory Barrier?*, on page 9.

We can quickly fix the problem by marking the flag done as volatile. We can change this:

```
private static boolean done;
```

to the following:

```
private static volatile boolean done;
```

The volatile keyword tells the JIT compiler not to perform any optimization that may affect the ordering of access to that variable. It warns that the variable may change behind the back of a thread and that each access, read or write, to this variable should bypass cache and go all the way to the memory. I call this a quick fix because arbitrarily making all variables volatile may avoid the problem but will result in very poor performance because every access has to cross the memory barrier. Also, volatile does not help with atomicity when multiple fields are accessed, because the access to each of the volatile fields is separately handled and not coordinated into one access—this would leave a wide opportunity for threads to see partial changes to some fields and not the others.

We could also avoid this problem by preventing direct access to the flag and channeling all access through the synchronized getter and setter, as follows:

```
private static boolean done;
public static synchronized boolean getFlag() { return done; }
public static synchronized void setFlag(boolean flag) { done = flag; }
```

The synchronized marker helps here, since it is one of the primitives that makes the calling threads cross the memory barrier both when they enter and when they exit the synchronized block. A thread is guaranteed to see the change made by another thread if both threads synchronize on the same instance and the change-making thread happens before the other thread; again, see *What's This Memory Barrier?*, on page 9.

> ## Joe asks:
> ## What's This Memory Barrier?
>
> Simply put, it is the copying from local or working memory to main memory.
>
> A change made by one thread is guaranteed to be visible to another thread only if the writing thread crosses the memory barrier[a] and then the reading thread crosses the memory barrier. synchronized and volatile keywords force that the changes are globally visible on a timely basis; these help cross the memory barrier—accidentally or intentionally.
>
> The changes are first made locally in the registers and caches and then cross the memory barrier as they are copied to the main memory. The sequence or ordering of these crossing is called *happens-before*—see "The Java Memory Model," Appendix 2, *Web Resources*, on page 255, and see Brian Goetz's *Java Concurrency in Practice* [Goe06].
>
> The write has to *happens-before* the read, meaning the writing thread has to cross the memory barrier before the reading thread does, for the change to be visible.
>
> Quite a few operations in the concurrency API implicitly cross the memory barrier: volatile, synchronized, methods on Thread such as start() and interrupt(), methods on ExecutorService, and some synchronization facilitators like CountDownLatch.
>
> ---
>
> a.   See Doug Lea's article "The JSR-133 Cookbook for Compiler Writers" in Appendix 2, *Web Resources*, on page 255.

Avoid Shared Mutability

Unfortunately, the consequence of forgetting to do either—using volatile or synchronized where needed—is quite unpredictable. The real worry is not that we'd forget to synchronize. The core problem is that we're dealing with shared mutability.

We're quite used to programming Java applications with mutability—creating and modifying state of an object by changing its fields. However, great books such as Joshua Bloch's *Effective Java* [Blo08] have advised us to promote immutability. Immutability can help us avoid the problem at its root.

Mutability in itself is not entirely bad, though it's often used in ways that can lead to trouble. Sharing is a good thing; after all, Mom always told us to share. Although these two things by themselves are fine, mixing them together is not.

When we have a nonfinal (mutable) field, each time a thread changes the value, we have to consider whether we have to put the change back to the memory or leave it in the registers/cache. Each time we read the field, we need to be concerned if we read the latest valid value or a stale value left behind in the cache. We need to ensure the changes to variables are atomic; that is, threads don't see partial changes. Furthermore, we need to worry about protecting multiple threads from changing the data at the same time.

For an application that deals with mutability, every single access to shared mutable state must be verified to be correct. Even if one of them is broken, the entire application is broken. This is a tall order—for our concurrent app to fall apart, only a single line of code that deals with concurrency needs to take a wrong step. In fact, a significant number of concurrent Java apps are broken, and we simply don't know it.

Now if we have a final (immutable) field referring to an immutable instance[3] and we let multiple threads access it, such sharing has no hidden problems. Any thread can read it and upon first access get a copy of the value that it can keep locally in its cache. Since the value is immutable, subsequent access to the value from the local cache is quite adequate, and we can even enjoy good performance.

Shared mutability is pure evil. Avoid it!

So, if we can't change anything, how can we make applications do anything? This is a valid concern, but we need to design our applications around shared immutability. One approach is to keep the mutable state well encapsulated and share only immutable data. As an alternate approach, promoted by pure functional languages, make everything immutable but use function composition. In this approach, we apply a series of transformations where we transition from one immutable state to another immutable state. There's yet another approach, which is to use a library that will watch over the changes and warn us of any violations. We'll look at these techniques using examples of problems that we'll solve using concurrency throughout this book.

1.4 Recap

Whether we're writing an interactive client-side desktop application or a high-performance service for the back end, concurrency will play a vital role in programming efforts should we reap the benefits of the evolving hardware trends and multicore processors. It's a way to influence the user experience, responsiveness, and speed of applications that run on these powerful machines. The traditional programming model of concurrency on the

---

3. For example, instances of String, Integer, and Long are immutable in Java, while instances of StringBuilder and ArrayList are mutable.

JVM—dealing with shared mutability—is froth with problems. Besides creating threads, we have to work hard to prevent starvation, deadlocks, and race conditions—things that are hard to trace and easy to get wrong. By avoiding shared mutability, we remove the problems at the root. Lean toward shared immutability to make programming concurrency easy, safe, and fun; we'll learn how to realize that later in this book.

Next, we'll discuss ways to determine the number of threads and to partition applications.

Part I

Strategies for Concurrency

The most effective way to do it is to do it.
    Amelia Earhart

CHAPTER 2

Division of Labor

The long-awaited multicore processor arrives tomorrow, and you can't wait to see how the app you're building runs on it. You've run it several times on a single core, but you're eager to see the speedup on the new machine. Is the speedup going to be in proportion to the number of cores? More? Less? A lot less? I've been there and have felt the struggle to arrive at a reasonable expectation.

You should've seen my face the first time I ran my code on a multicore and it performed much worse than I had expected. How could more cores yield slower speed? That was years ago, and I've grown wiser since and learned a few lessons along the way. Now I have better instinct and ways to gauge speedup that I'd like to share with you in this chapter.

2.1 From Sequential to Concurrent

We can't run a single-threaded application on a multicore processor and expect better results. We have to divide it and run multiple tasks concurrently. But, programs don't divide the same way and benefit from the same number of threads.

I have worked on scientific applications that are computation intensive and also on business applications that are IO intensive because they involve file, database, and web service calls. The nature of these two types of applications is different and so are the ways to make them concurrent.

We'll work with two types of applications in this chapter. The first one is an IO-intensive application that will compute the net asset value for a wealthy user. The second one will compute the total number of primes within a range of numbers—a rather simple but quite useful example of a concurrent computation–intensive program. These two applications will help us learn how many threads to create, how to divide the problem, and how much speedup to expect.

Divide and Conquer

If we have hundreds of stocks to process, fetching them one at a time would be the easiest way...to lose the job. The user would stand fuming while our application chugs away processing each stock sequentially.

To speed up our programs, we need to divide the problem into concurrently running tasks. That involves creating these parts or tasks and delegating them to threads so they can run concurrently. For a large problem, we may create as many parts as we like, but we can't create too many threads because we have limited resources.

Determining the Number of Threads

For a large problem, we'd want to have at least as many threads as the number of available cores. This will ensure that as many cores as available to the process are put to work to solve our problem. We can easily find the number of available cores; all we need is a simple call from the code:[1]

```
Runtime.getRuntime().availableProcessors();
```

So, the minimum number of threads is equal to the number of available cores. If all tasks are computation intensive, then this is all we need. Having more threads will actually hurt in this case because cores would be context switching between threads when there is still work to do. If tasks are IO intensive, then we should have more threads.

When a task performs an IO operation, its thread gets blocked. The processor immediately context switches to run other eligible threads. If we had only as many threads as the number of available cores, even though we have tasks to perform, they can't run because we haven't scheduled them on threads for the processors to pick up.

If tasks spend 50 percent of the time being blocked, then the number of threads should be twice the number of available cores. If they spend less time being blocked—that is, they're computation intensive—then we should have fewer threads but no less than the number of cores. If they spend more time being blocked—that is, they're IO intensive—then we should have more threads, specifically, several multiples of the number of cores.

So, we can compute the total number of threads we'd need as follows:

---

1. availableProcessors() reports the number of logical processors available to the JVM.

```
Number of threads = Number of Available Cores / (1 - Blocking Coefficient)
```

where the blocking coefficient is between 0 and 1.

A computation-intensive task has a blocking coefficient of 0, whereas an IO-intensive task has a value close to 1—a fully blocked task is doomed, so we don't have to worry about the value reaching 1.

To determine the number of threads, we need to know two things:

- The number of available cores
- The blocking coefficient of tasks

The first one is easy to determine; we can look up that information, even at runtime, as we saw earlier. It takes a bit of effort to determine the blocking coefficient. We can try to guess it, or we can use profiling tools or the java.lang.management API to determine the amount of time a thread spends on system/IO operations vs. on CPU-intensive tasks.

Determining the Number of Parts

We know how to compute the number of threads for concurrent applications. Now we have to decide how to divide the problem. Each part will be run concurrently, so, on first thought, we could have as many parts as the number of threads. That's a good start but not adequate; we've ignored the nature of the problem being solved.

In the net asset value application, the effort to fetch the price for each stock is the same. So, dividing the total number of stocks into as many groups as the number of threads should be enough.

However, in the primes application, the effort to determine whether a number is prime is not the same for all numbers. Even numbers fizzle out rather quickly, and larger primes take more time than smaller primes. Taking the range of numbers and slicing them into as many groups as the number of threads would not help us get good performance. Some tasks would finish faster than others and poorly utilize the cores.

In other words, we'd want the parts to have even work distribution. We could spend a lot of time and effort to divide the problem so the parts have a fair distribution of load. However, there would be two problems. First, this would be hard; it would take a lot of effort and time. Second, the code to divide the problem into equal parts and distribute it across the threads would be complex.

It turns out that keeping the cores busy on the problem is more beneficial than even distribution of load across parts. When there's work left to be done, we need to ensure no available core is left to idle, from the process point of view. So, rather than splitting hairs over an even distribution of load across parts, we can achieve this by creating far more parts than the number of threads. Set the number of parts large enough so there's enough work for all the available cores to perform on the program.

2.2 Concurrency in IO-Intensive Apps

An IO-intensive application has a large blocking coefficient and will benefit from more threads than the number of available cores.

Let's build the financial application I mentioned earlier. The (rich) users of the application want to determine the total net asset value of their shares at any given time. Let's work with one user who has shares in forty stocks. We are given the ticker symbols and the number of shares for each stock. From the Web, we need to fetch the price of each share for each symbol. Let's take a look at writing the code for calculating the net asset value.

Sequential Computation of Net Asset Value

As the first order of business, we need the price for ticker symbols. Thankfully, Yahoo provides historic data we need. Here is the code to communicate with Yahoo's financial web service to get the last trading price for a ticker symbol (as of the previous day):

```
divideAndConquer/YahooFinance.java
public class YahooFinance {
  public static double getPrice(final String ticker) throws IOException {
    final URL url =
      new URL("http://ichart.finance.yahoo.com/table.csv?s=" + ticker);

    final BufferedReader reader = new BufferedReader(
      new InputStreamReader(url.openStream()));

    //Date,Open,High,Low,Close,Volume,Adj Close
    //2011-03-17,336.83,339.61,330.66,334.64,23519400,334.64
    final String discardHeader = reader.readLine();
    final String data = reader.readLine();
    final String[] dataItems = data.split(",");
    final double priceIsTheLastValue =
      Double.valueOf(dataItems[dataItems.length - 1]);
    return priceIsTheLastValue;
  }
}
```

We send a request to http://ichart.finance.yahoo.com and parse the result to obtain the price.

Next, we get the price for each of the stocks our user owns and display the total net asset value. In addition, we display the time it took for completing this operation.

divideAndConquer/AbstractNAV.java
```java
public abstract class AbstractNAV {
  public static Map<String, Integer> readTickers() throws IOException {
    final BufferedReader reader =
      new BufferedReader(new FileReader("stocks.txt"));

    final Map<String, Integer> stocks = new HashMap<String, Integer>();

    String stockInfo = null;
    while((stockInfo = reader.readLine()) != null) {
      final String[] stockInfoData = stockInfo.split(",");
      final String stockTicker = stockInfoData[0];
      final Integer quantity = Integer.valueOf(stockInfoData[1]);

      stocks.put(stockTicker, quantity);
    }

    return stocks;
  }

  public void timeAndComputeValue()
    throws ExecutionException, InterruptedException, IOException {
    final long start = System.nanoTime();

    final Map<String, Integer> stocks = readTickers();
    final double nav = computeNetAssetValue(stocks);

    final long end = System.nanoTime();

    final String value = new DecimalFormat("$##,##0.00").format(nav);
    System.out.println("Your net asset value is " + value);
    System.out.println("Time (seconds) taken " + (end - start)/1.0e9);
  }

  public abstract double computeNetAssetValue(
    final Map<String, Integer> stocks)
    throws ExecutionException, InterruptedException, IOException;
}
```

The readTickers() method of AbstractNAV reads the ticker symbol and the number of shares owned for each symbol from a file called stocks.txt, part of which is shown next:

```
AAPL,2505
AMGN,3406
AMZN,9354
BAC,9839
BMY,5099
...
```

The timeAndComputeValue() times the call to the abstract method computeNetAsset-Value(), which will be implemented in a derived class. Then, it prints the total net asset value and the time it took to compute that.

Finally, we need to contact Yahoo Finance and compute the total net asset value. Let's do that sequentially:

divideAndConquer/SequentialNAV.java

```java
public class SequentialNAV extends AbstractNAV {
  public double computeNetAssetValue(
    final Map<String, Integer> stocks) throws IOException {
    double netAssetValue = 0.0;
    for(String ticker : stocks.keySet()) {
      netAssetValue += stocks.get(ticker) * YahooFinance.getPrice(ticker);
    }
    return netAssetValue;
  }

  public static void main(final String[] args)
    throws ExecutionException, IOException, InterruptedException {
    new SequentialNAV().timeAndComputeValue();
  }
}
```

Let's run the SequentialNAV code and observe the output:

```
Your net asset value is $13,661,010.17
Time (seconds) taken 19.776223
```

The good news is we managed to help our user with the total asset value. However, our user is not very pleased. The displeasure may be partly because of the market conditions, but really it's mostly because of the wait incurred; it took close to twenty seconds[2] on my computer, with the network delay at the time of run, to get the results for only forty stocks. I'm sure making this application concurrent will help with speedup and having a happier user.

Determining Number of Threads and Parts for Net Asset Value

The application has very little computation to perform and spends most of the time waiting for responses from the Web. There is really no reason to

---

2. More than a couple of seconds of delay feels like eternity to users.

wait for one response to arrive before sending the next request. So, this application is a good candidate for concurrency: we'll likely get a good bump in speed.

In the sample run, we had forty stocks, but in reality we may have a higher number of stocks, even hundreds. We must first decide on the number of divisions and the number of threads to use. Web services (in this case, Yahoo Finance) are quite capable of receiving and processing concurrent requests.[3] So, our client side sets the real limit on the number of threads. Since the web service requests will spend a lot of time waiting on a response, the blocking coefficient is fairly high, and therefore we can bump up the number of threads by several factors of the number of cores. Let's say the blocking coefficient is 0.9—each task blocks 90 percent of the time and works only 10 percent of its lifetime. Then on two cores, we can have (using the formula from *Determining the Number of Threads*, on page 16) twenty threads. On an eight-core processor, we can go up to eighty threads, assuming we have a lot of ticker symbols.

As far as the number of divisions, the workload is basically the same for each stock. So, we can simply have as many parts as we have stocks and schedule them over the number of threads.

Let's make the application concurrent and then study the effect of threads and partitions on the code.

Concurrent Computation of Net Asset Value

There are two challenges now. First, we have to schedule the parts across threads. Second, we have to receive the partial results from each part to calculate the total asset value.

We may have as many divisions as the number of stocks for this problem. We need to maintain a pool of threads to schedule these divisions on. Rather than creating and managing individual threads, it's better to use a thread pool—they have better life cycle and resource management, reduce startup and teardown costs, and are warm and ready to quickly start scheduled tasks.

As Java programmers, we're used to Thread and synchronized, but we have some alternatives to these since the arrival of Java 5—see *Is There a Reason to*

---

3. To prevent denial-of-service attacks (and to up-sell premium services), web services may restrict the number of concurrent requests from the same client. You may notice this with Yahoo Finance when you exceed fifty concurrent requests.

Joe asks:
Is There a Reason to Use the Old Threading API in Java?

The old threading API has several deficiencies. We'd use and throw away the instances of the Thread class since they don't allow restart. To handle multiple tasks, we typically create multiple threads instead of reusing them. If we decide to schedule multiple tasks on a thread, we had to write quite a bit of extra code to manage that. Either way was not efficient and scalable.

Methods like wait() and notify() require synchronization and are quite hard to get right when used to communicate between threads. The join() method leads us to be concerned about the death of a thread rather than a task being accomplished.

In addition, the synchronized keyword lacks granularity. It doesn't give us a way to time out if we do not gain the lock. It also doesn't allow concurrent multiple readers. Furthermore, it is very difficult to unit test for thread safety if we use synchronized.

The newer generation of concurrency APIs in the java.util.concurrent package, spearheaded by Doug Lea, among others, has nicely replaced the old threading API.

- Wherever we use the Thread class and its methods, we can now rely upon the ExecutorService class and related classes.

- If we need better control over acquiring locks, we can rely upon the Lock interface and its methods.

- Wherever we use wait/notify, we can now use synchronizers such as CyclicBarrier and CountdownLatch.

Use the Old Threading API in Java?, on page 22. The new-generation Java concurrency API in java.util.concurrent is far superior.

In the modern concurrency API, the Executors class serves as a factory to create different types of thread pools that we can manage using the ExecutorService interface. Some of the flavors include a single-threaded pool that runs all scheduled tasks in a single thread, one after another. A fixed threaded pool allows us to configure the pool size and concurrently runs, in one of the available threads, the tasks we throw at it. If there are more tasks than threads, the tasks are queued for execution, and each queued task is run as soon as a thread is available. A cached threaded pool will create threads as needed and will reuse existing threads if possible. If no activity is scheduled on a thread for well over a minute, it will start shutting down the inactive threads.

The fixed threaded pool fits the bill well for the pool of threads we need in the net asset value application. Based on the number of cores and the presumed blocking coefficient, we decide the thread pool size. The threads in this pool will execute the tasks that belong to each part. In the sample run, we had forty stocks; if we create twenty threads (for a two-core processor), then half the parts get scheduled right away. The other half are enqueued and run as soon as threads become available. This will take little effort on our part; let's write the code to get this stock price concurrently.

divideAndConquer/ConcurrentNAV.java

```
public class ConcurrentNAV extends AbstractNAV {
  public double computeNetAssetValue(final Map<String, Integer> stocks)
      throws InterruptedException, ExecutionException {
    final int numberOfCores = Runtime.getRuntime().availableProcessors();
    final double blockingCoefficient = 0.9;
    final int poolSize = (int)(numberOfCores / (1 - blockingCoefficient));

    System.out.println("Number of Cores available is " + numberOfCores);
    System.out.println("Pool size is " + poolSize);
    final List<Callable<Double>> partitions =
      new ArrayList<Callable<Double>>();
    for(final String ticker : stocks.keySet()) {
      partitions.add(new Callable<Double>() {
        public Double call() throws Exception {
          return stocks.get(ticker) * YahooFinance.getPrice(ticker);
        }
      });
    }

    final ExecutorService executorPool =
      Executors.newFixedThreadPool(poolSize);
    final List<Future<Double>> valueOfStocks =
      executorPool.invokeAll(partitions, 10000, TimeUnit.SECONDS);

    double netAssetValue = 0.0;
    for(final Future<Double> valueOfAStock : valueOfStocks)
      netAssetValue += valueOfAStock.get();

    executorPool.shutdown();
    return netAssetValue;
  }

  public static void main(final String[] args)
      throws ExecutionException, InterruptedException, IOException {
    new ConcurrentNAV().timeAndComputeValue();
  }
}
```

In the computeNetAssetValue() method we determine the thread pool size based on the presumed blocking coefficient and the number of cores (Runtime's availableProcessor() method gives that detail). We then place each part—to fetch the price for each ticker symbol—into the anonymous code block of the Callable interface. This interface provides a call() method that returns a value of the parameterized type of this interface (Double in the example). We then schedule these parts on the fixed-size pool using the invokeAll() method. The executor takes the responsibility of concurrently running as many of the parts as possible. If there are more divisions than the pool size, they get queued for their execution turn. Since the parts run concurrently and asynchronously, the dispatching main thread can't get the results right away. The invokeAll() method returns a collection of Future objects once all the scheduled tasks complete.[4] We request for the partial results from these objects and add them to the net asset value. Let's see how the concurrent version performed:

```
Number of Cores available is 2
Pool size is 20
Your net asset value is $13,661,010.17
Time (seconds) taken 0.967484
```

In contrast to the sequential run, the concurrent run took less than a second. We can vary the number of threads in the pool by varying the presumed blocking coefficient and see whether the speed varies. We can also try different numbers of stocks as well and see the result and speed change between the sequential and concurrent versions.

Isolated Mutability

In this problem, the executor service pretty much eliminated any synchronization concerns—it allowed us to nicely delegate tasks and receive their results from a coordinating thread. The only mutable variable we have in the previous code is netAssetValue, which we defined on line 25. The only place where we mutate this variable is on line 27. This mutation happens only in one thread, the main thread—so we have only isolated mutability here and not shared mutability. Since there is no shared state, there is nothing to synchronize in this example. With the help of Future, we were able to safely send the result from the threads fetching the data to the main thread.

There's one limitation to the approach in this example. We're iterating through the Future objects in the loop on line 26. So, we request results from

---

4. Use the CompletionService if you'd like to fetch the results as they complete and rather not wait for all tasks to finish.

one part at a time, pretty much in the order we created/scheduled the divisions. Even if one of the later parts finishes first, we won't process its results until we process the results of parts before that. In this particular example, that may not be an issue. However, if we have quite a bit of computation to perform upon receiving the response, then we'd rather process results as they become available instead of waiting for all tasks to finish. We could use the JDK CompletionService for this. We'll revisit this concern and look at some alternate solutions later. Let's switch gears and analyze the speedup.

2.3 Speedup for the IO-Intensive App

The nature of IO-intensive applications allows for a greater degree of concurrency even when there are fewer cores. When blocked on an IO operation, we can switch to perform other tasks or request for other IO operations to be started. We estimated that on a two-core machine, about twenty threads would be reasonable for the stock total asset value application. Let's analyze the performance on a two-core processor for various numbers of threads—from one to forty. Since the total number of divisions is forty, it would not make any sense to create more threads than that. We can observe the speedup as the number of threads is increased in Figure 1, *Speedup as the pool size is increased*, on page 26.

The curve begins to flatten right about twenty threads in the pool. This tells us that our estimate was decent and that having more threads beyond our estimate will not help.

This application is a perfect candidate for concurrency—the workload across the parts is about the same, and the large blocking, because of data request latency from the Web, lends really well to exploiting the threads. We were able to gain a greater speedup by increasing the number of threads. Not all problems, however, will lend themselves to speedup that way, as we'll see next.

2.4 Concurrency in Computationally Intensive Apps

The number of cores has a greater influence on the speedup of computation-intensive applications than on IO-bound applications, as we'll see in this section. The example we'll use is very simple; however, it has a hidden surprise—the uneven workload will affect the speedup.

Let's write a program to compute the number of primes between 1 and 10 million. Let's first solve this sequentially, and then we'll solve it concurrently.

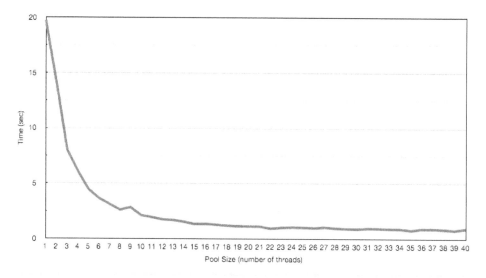

Figure 1—Speedup as the pool size is increased

Sequential Computation of Prime Numbers

Let's start with the abstract class AbstractPrimeFinder, which will help group some common methods for the problem at hand. The isPrime() method will tell whether a given number is prime, and the countPrimesInRange() method uses it to count the number of primes in a range of numbers. Finally, the timeAndCompute() method will keep a tab of the time it took to count the primes.

divideAndConquer/AbstractPrimeFinder.java

```java
public abstract class AbstractPrimeFinder {
  public boolean isPrime(final int number) {
    if (number <= 1) return false;

    for(int i = 2; i <= Math.sqrt(number); i++)
      if (number % i == 0) return false;

    return true;
  }

  public int countPrimesInRange(final int lower, final int upper) {
    int total = 0;

    for(int i = lower; i <= upper; i++)
      if (isPrime(i)) total++;

    return total;
  }
```

```java
public void timeAndCompute(final int number) {
  final long start = System.nanoTime();

  final long numberOfPrimes = countPrimes(number);

  final long end = System.nanoTime();

  System.out.printf("Number of primes under %d is %d\n",
    number, numberOfPrimes);
  System.out.println("Time (seconds) taken is " + (end - start)/1.0e9);
}

  public abstract int countPrimes(final int number);
}
```

Next, we'll invoke the code sequentially. For a sequential count of primes between 1 and a given number, we simply call countPrimesInRange() with the parameters 1 and number.

divideAndConquer/SequentialPrimeFinder.java

```java
public class SequentialPrimeFinder extends AbstractPrimeFinder {
  public int countPrimes(final int number) {
    return countPrimesInRange(1, number);
  }

  public static void main(final String[] args) {
    new SequentialPrimeFinder().timeAndCompute(Integer.parseInt(args[0]));
  }
}
```

Let's exercise the code with 10000000 (10 million) as an argument and observe the time taken for this sequential run.

```
Number of primes under 10000000 is 664579
Time (seconds) taken is 6.544368
```

On my dual-core processor, it took this sequential code, run in server mode, a little more than six seconds to count the number of primes under 10 million. It would take a lot longer if we run it in client mode. Let's see what speedup we can achieve by turning this to run in concurrent mode.

Concurrent Computation of Prime Numbers

Since this is a computationally intensive task, throwing a lot of threads on the problem will not help. The blocking coefficient is 0, and so the suggested number of threads, from the formula in *Determining the Number of Threads*, on page 16, is equal to the number of cores. Having more threads than that will not help speedup; on the contrary, it may actually slow things down. This is because it makes little sense for the nonblocking task to be paused for another thread to run part of our own problem. We might as well finish the task before taking up the next one when all the cores are busy. Let's first write the concurrent code, give it two threads and two divisions, and see what happens. We've ducked the question of number of parts right now; we'll revisit it after we make some progress.

The concurrent version for primes counting is structurally similar to the concurrent version of the net asset value application. However, instead of computing the number of threads and parts, here we'll take those two as parameters, in addition to the candidate number for primes count. Here's the code for the concurrent primes count:

divideAndConquer/ConcurrentPrimeFinder.java
```
public class ConcurrentPrimeFinder extends AbstractPrimeFinder {
  private final int poolSize;
  private final int numberOfParts;

  public ConcurrentPrimeFinder(final int thePoolSize,
    final int theNumberOfParts) {
    poolSize = thePoolSize;
    numberOfParts = theNumberOfParts;
  }
  public int countPrimes(final int number) {
    int count = 0;
    try {
      final List<Callable<Integer>> partitions =
        new ArrayList<Callable<Integer>>();
      final int chunksPerPartition = number / numberOfParts;
      for(int i = 0; i < numberOfParts; i++) {
        final int lower = (i * chunksPerPartition) + 1;
        final int upper =
          (i == numberOfParts - 1) ? number
            : lower + chunksPerPartition - 1;
        partitions.add(new Callable<Integer>() {
          public Integer call() {
            return countPrimesInRange(lower, upper);
          }
        });
      }
      final ExecutorService executorPool =
        Executors.newFixedThreadPool(poolSize);
      final List<Future<Integer>> resultFromParts =
        executorPool.invokeAll(partitions, 10000, TimeUnit.SECONDS);
      executorPool.shutdown();
      for(final Future<Integer> result : resultFromParts)
        count += result.get();
    } catch(Exception ex) { throw new RuntimeException(ex); }
    return count;
  }
```

```
    public static void main(final String[] args) {
      if (args.length < 3)
        System.out.println("Usage: number poolsize numberOfParts");
40    else
        new ConcurrentPrimeFinder(
            Integer.parseInt(args[1]), Integer.parseInt(args[2]))
          .timeAndCompute(Integer.parseInt(args[0]));
    }
45 }
```

We divided the range from 1 to the given number into the requested number of parts, with each division containing about the same number of values (lines 13 to 26). We then delegated the job of counting the number of primes in each part to individual instances of Callable. Now that we have the parts on hand, let's schedule their execution. We'll use a thread pool for that and submit the execution of these parts to the executor service (lines 28 to 31). In the final step, line 33, we total the results received from the parts.

We're ready to take this for a ride. I have two cores, so if I create two threads and two parts, I expect to get about twice the speedup (it should take about half the time as the sequential run). Let's test that by running the program for 10 million numbers, with both the pool size and the number of partitions being 2, using the command java ConcurrentPrimeFinder 10000000 2 2.

```
Number of primes under 10000000 is 664579
Time (seconds) taken is 4.236507
```

The number of primes in our sequential and concurrent runs are the same, so that's good, and the same amount of work was done in the two versions. However, I expected the runtime to be around three seconds with two cores, but we came a little over four seconds—a rather measly 1.5 times the speedup instead of twice the speedup. It's time to go back to the drawing board to figure out what we missed.

You probably have a hunch that this has to do with the number of divisions—certainly, increasing the number of threads without increasing the number of divisions will not help. However, since this is computationally intensive, we already know that increasing the threads to more than the number of cores will not help. So, it's gotta be the number of parts. Let's try to justify that and arrive at a solution.

Let's bring up the activity monitor (on Windows, bring up your Task Manager, and on Linux bring up your system/resource monitor) to see the activities of the cores. Run the prime finder in sequential mode and then in concurrent mode. The results should be similar to the one in Figure 2, *Activities of cores during sequential and concurrent primes counting,* on page 30.

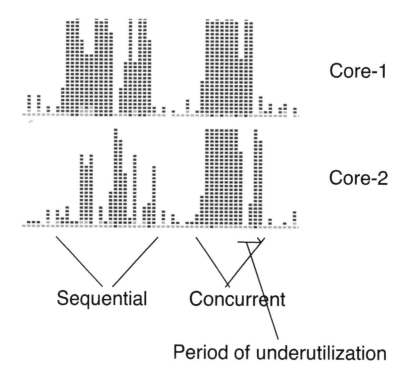

Figure 2—Activities of cores during sequential and concurrent primes counting

The cores are underutilized during the sequential run as we'd expect. During the concurrent run, however, for most part, both the cores are quite active. However, right about 60 percent into it only one core is active. This tells us that the workload across the two threads/cores is not evenly distributed—the first half finished much faster than the second. If we think about the nature of the given problem, it now becomes obvious—the effort to check a larger prime in the second part is more than the effort to check a smaller prime in the first part. To achieve the maximum speedup, we need to partition the problem across the two threads evenly.

In general, a fair distribution of workload among the parts may not be easy to achieve; it requires a fairly good understanding of the problem and its behavior across the range of input. For the count primes problem, the approach we took was to split the range into equal parts in serial order. Instead, we can try to group them into combinations of big and small numbers to get a uniform distribution. For instance, to divide into two parts, we may consider taking the first and last quarters in the range into one part and the middle two quarters into the second. The code we currently have does not lend itself to that kind of partitioning. If we change the code to do that, we will notice that the runtime reduces. The split, however, gets harder as we consider a greater number of parts—with more cores, we'd want to have more parts. Fortunately, there is a simpler solution.

The main problem with fewer parts, like two, is that one core does more work while the other cores twiddle their digit. The finer we divide the problem, more likely there will be enough slices to keep all the cores busy. Start with more parts than threads, and then as threads complete smaller parts, they will pick up other parts to execute. Some cores can work on long-running tasks, while other cores can pick up several short-running tasks. For the example, let's see how the pool size and partitions affect performance; we'll keep the pool size to 2 but vary the number of parts to 100:

```
Number of primes under 10000000 is 664579
Time (seconds) taken is 3.550659
```

That's about 1.85 times the speedup; it's not quite the desired two times, but it's close. We could try to vary the number of parts or the partitioning strategy. However, with fairly ad hoc partitioning, we're able to get a decent speed increase. The ad hoc partitioning may not work all the time. The key is that we should ensure the cores have a fairly uniform workload for good utilization.

2.5 Speedup for the Computationally Intensive App

The counting primes examples was trivial, but it showed that for computationally intensive operations a fair balance of workload among parts is critical.

We had to choose the partition size and the pool size. Let's see what effect these two factors have on the performance. I ran the program in client mode (because it takes longer to run than server mode, and that makes it easier to compare the results) on a eight-core processor. The measure of performance is shown in Figure 3, *Primes calculation in client mode on an eight-core processor: effect of pool size and parts*, on page 32.

There are a few lessons we can learn from the figure about making computationally intensive applications concurrent:

- We need to have at least as many partitions as the number of cores—we see the performance was poor for fewer than eight parts.

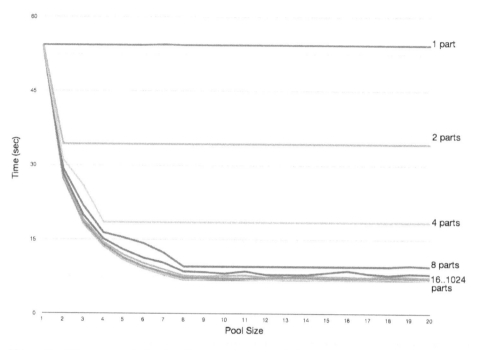

Figure 3—Primes calculation in client mode on an eight-core processor: effect of pool size and parts

- Having more threads than the number of cores does not help—we see that for each partitioning, the curve flattens past the pool size of eight.

- Having more partitions is better than having fewer, because more partitions help keep the cores busy—this is quite evident from the curves.

- After a certain number of large partitions, having more partitions has little benefit—for example, I observed that with eight cores and a pool size of eight, the time taken for 16, 64, 256, 512, and 1024 partitions was 8.4s, 7.2s, 6.9s, 6.8s, and 6.8s, respectively.

Keep an eye on the effort to divide the problem; if that takes significant computation, that's time wasted from real computations. It's critical to have a reasonable number of parts so all the cores have enough work to do. Devise a simple method to divide the problem and see whether that provides a fair utilization of all the cores.

2.6 Strategies for Effective Concurrency

On one hand, we want to ensure consistency and accuracy when using concurrency. On the other hand, we want to ensure we're getting as much performance as possible on the given hardware. In this chapter, we looked at ways to meet both these goals.

We can easily avoid race conditions or consistency issues once we fully eliminate shared mutable state. When threads don't compete to access mutable data, there's no issue of visibility and crossing the memory barrier. We also don't have to worry about controlling the execution sequence of threads; since they don't compete, there are no mutually exclusive sections to safeguard in code.

Provide shared immutability where possible. Otherwise, follow isolated mutability—ensure only one thread ever can access that mutable variable. We're not talking about synchronizing shared state here. We're ensuring that only one thread ever has access to that mutable variable, period.

How many threads we create and how we partition the problem affects the performance of your concurrent application.

First, in order to benefit from concurrency, we must be able to partition problems into smaller tasks that can be run concurrently. If a problem has a significant part that can't be partitioned, then the application may not really see much performance gain by making it concurrent.

If tasks are IO intensive or have significant IO operations, then having more threads will help. In this case, the number of threads should be much greater than the number of cores. We can estimate the number of threads using the formula presented in *Determining the Number of Threads*, on page 16.

For a computationally intensive process, having more threads than cores may actually hurt—see *Concurrent Computation of Prime Numbers*, on page 27. However, we'll benefit by having at least as many threads as the number of cores, assuming the problem can be partitioned into at least as many tasks as the number of threads.

Although the number of threads affects performance, it is not the only thing. The workload of each part and how much time each part takes to complete relative to others both affect performance. A uniform partitioning of the problem may take too much effort and may not yield better results than ad hoc partitioning. Weigh the efforts vs. the benefit. We should try to arrive at a fair workload by using a simple approach to partitioning. In any case, good partitioning requires understanding the nature of the problem and its behavior for different input. The difficulty of this depends on the complexity of the problem on hand.

2.7 Recap

Here are the ways to reap the benefits of multicore processors:

- We have to divide the application into multiple tasks that can be run concurrently.

- We should choose at least as many threads as the number of cores, provided the problem is large enough to benefit from those many threads.

- For computationally intensive applications, we should limit the number of threads to the number of cores.

- For IO-intense applications, the time spent blocking influences the number of threads we'd create.

- Estimate the number of threads using the following formula:

  ```
  Number of threads = Number of Available Cores / (1 - Blocking Coefficient)
  ```

  where $0 \leq$ blocking coefficient < 1.

- We should slice the problem into several parts so there is enough work for cores and they're utilized well.

- We must avoid shared mutable state and instead use either isolated mutability or shared immutability.

- We should make good use of the modern threading API and thread pools.

Next, we'll discuss some design options for dealing with state.

In the middle of difficulties lies opportunity.
> Albert Einstein

CHAPTER 3

Design Approaches

We can't avoid manipulating state; that's integral to programs we create. The compiler, for instance, takes a set of source files and creates bytecode, and the Mail app keeps track of unread emails, among other things.

As we gain experience with Java, we're often set in the way we design programs. Objects encapsulate state, and their methods help transition between selected valid states. I scoffed when someone said we can create significant code that doesn't change state. Later when he showed me how, I was intrigued and enlightened, like that kid in the bookstore.[1]

Manipulating state doesn't necessarily mean mutating state. Think of state transformation instead of state modification. It's a way to design state change without modifying anything. In this chapter, we'll explore ways to create programs that don't change anything in memory. Don't be tricked by the length of this chapter—it's short, but it captures some fundamental approaches to design.

3.1 Dealing with State

There's no escape from dealing with state, but there are three ways to do so: shared mutability, isolated mutability, and pure immutability.

One extreme is shared mutability; we create variables and allow any thread to modify them—in a controlled fashion, of course. Programming with shared mutability is simply the way of life for most of us Java programmers, but this leads to the undesirable synchronize and suffer model. We have to ensure that code crosses the memory barrier at the appropriate time and have good visibility on the variables. With shared mutability, we must also ensure

---

1. My kids taught me it's more fun hanging out at the bookstore than at the candy store.

that no two threads modify a field at the same time and that changes to multiple fields are consistent. We get no support from the compiler or the runtime to determine correctness; we have to analyze the code to ensure we did the right thing. The minute we touch the code, we have to reanalyze for correctness, because synchronization is too easy to get wrong. Fortunately, we have other options.

An alternate middle ground to deal with state is isolated mutability, where variables are mutable but are never seen by more than one thread, ever. We ensure that anything that's shared between threads is immutable. Java programmers will find this fairly easy to design, and so the isolated mutability may be a reasonable approach.

Pure immutability is the other extreme where nothing is allowed to change. Designing for this is not easy, partly because of the nature of the problems but mostly because of our inexperience with this approach. The language also makes this hard; it requires a lot of effort and discipline to program with immutability in Java. It's a paradigm shift and requires exploring some different data structures and ways than we're used to in Java. However, if we can realize such a practical design, the result is rewarding—easy and safe concurrency.

The method we choose to deal with state depends on the problem and our team's willingness to explore design options. Pure immutability is ideal. However, that's easier said than done, especially for programmers who've spent years mutating shared state. At a minimum, we should aim for isolated mutability and avoid the purely evil shared mutability.

We discussed three methods to deal with state. Next, we'll learn how to apply these using a single problem.

3.2 Exploring Design Options

Dealing with state is an activity that takes practice in the art of programming. What we do with the input we receive, the results of calculations, and the files we change all involve state. We can't avoid state, but we have a choice of how to deal with it. Here we'll first pick an example and in the next few sections explore different options to dealing with its state.

At a recent Java user group meeting, the conversation rolled over to the topic of collective experience among the members. I saw the young and the mature in the gathering and volunteered to total the number of years of experience. Let's explore the options I had available to complete this task.

At first thought, the net years would change as I totaled each person's work years—can't avoid mutability, it appears. There were several folks in the room, and I needed to quickly devise a way to get the total. Let's discuss the pros and cons of the three options for dealing with state.

3.3 Shared Mutable Design

Our first approach to total work years is a familiar approach: write 0 on the board and ask everyone to walk up to add their work years to that total.

Fred, who's closest to the board, jumps up to add his years to the total, and before we know it, a number of people have lined up, creating contention around the board. As soon as Fred is done, Jane gets her turn. We'll have to keep an eye to ensure pranksters don't change the entry to something impossible like infinity.

Shared mutability is at work here, along with the challenges it brings. We have to police more than one person trying to change the number at a given time. Furthermore, people have to patiently wait for their turn to write on the board as each person takes their turn. And I hope not to be that last person in the line....

In programming terms, if each person in the room were a separate thread, we would have to synchronize their access to the shared mutable variable total. One badly behaved participant ruins it for the whole group. Also, this approach involves quite a bit of blocking of threads, high thread safety, but low concurrency.

For a large group, this task could become time-consuming and frustrating. We want to ease that pain, so let's explore another way.

3.4 Isolated Mutable Design

I can walk up to the board, but instead of putting down the initial total of 0, I can put my phone number so everyone in the room can text their work years to me.

Each person now sends me the information from the comfort of their seats. They don't have to wait in line, and they're done as fast as they can punch those smartphone keys.

I'd receive the years in sequence as they arrive, but the senders are concurrent and nonblocking.

Isolated mutability is at work here. The total is isolated: only I hold this value, and others can't access it. By isolating the mutable state, we've eliminated the problems of the previous approach. There are no worries of two or more people changing the stuff at the same time.

I'd continue to total the years as they're received. My carrier took care of turning the concurrent messages into a nice sequential chain of messages for me to process. I can announce the total at the end of the meeting or as soon as I think they're done.

In programming terms, if each person in the room, including me, were a thread (actually an *actor*, as we'll see in Chapter 8, *Favoring Isolated Mutability*, on page 163), each of them simply would send an asynchronous message to me. The message itself is immutable—much like the text message, the data I receive would be a copy on my side, and there should be no way to change anything that affects the sender's view. I'm simply modifying a local well-encapsulated variable. Since I'm the only one (thread) changing this data, there's no need to synchronize around that change.

If we ensure that the shared data is immutable and the mutable data is isolated, we have no concerns of synchronization in this approach.

3.5 Purely Immutable Design

Dealing with full immutability takes a bit of getting used to. Changing things feels natural, and it's easy because we're used to that way of programming in Java. It's hard to think of ways to total the work years without changing anything, but it's possible.

We can ask everyone in the room to form a chain while remaining in their seats. Instruct everyone to receive a number from the person on their left, add their own work years to that number, and pass the combined total to the person to their right. I can then provide my own work years to the first person in the room who's eagerly waiting on me.

In this approach no one ever changes anything. Each person holds the total of work years up to them in the chain. The total I receive from the last person in the chain is the total work years of the entire group.

We were able to compute the total without changing a thing. Each person took a partial total and created a new total. The old total value they received is something they could retain or discard (garbage collect) as they wanted.

This last approach is common in functional programming and is achieved using function composition. We'd use methods like foldLeft(), reduce(), or inject() in languages such as Scala, Clojure, Groovy, and JRuby to implement such operations.

This approach also does not have any concerns of concurrency. It took a bit of effort to organize or compose this sequence of operations, but we were able to achieve the result with total immutability. If the number of people is very large, we can even partition them into smaller groups—forming a tree instead of a line—to allow greater concurrency and speed.

3.6 Persistent/Immutable Data Structures

In the pure immutable design for the net work-years example, we asked each person to create a new total. As we go through the chain of people, a new number is created while an old number is discarded—not a big deal since the numbers are relatively small.

The data we have to deal with may not be that small; it could be a list, tree, or matrix. We may need to work with objects that represent a boiler, a satellite, a city, and so on. We won't naively copy these large objects over and over because that'll lead to poor performance. Immutable or persistent data structures come to the rescue here.

Persistent[2] data structures version their values so older and newer values stay around or persist over time without degrading performance. Since the data are immutable, they're shared effectively to avoid copy overhead. Persistent data structures are designed to provide super-efficient "updates." Languages like Clojure and Scala make extensive use of these kinds of data structures. We'll discuss the design of two different persistent data structures next.

Immutable Lists

Back to the user group meeting, we've been asked to collect the names of the attendees. Let's explore how we can organize the data with pure immutability. We may use a single linked list where each node has two pointers or references. The first reference is to the person, and the second reference is to the next node in the list, as in the example in Figure 4, *Persistent list processing*, on page 40. We'll see how to work with this immutable list.

It's time to change the list because Susan just joined the meeting. We can create a node that holds a reference to her. Since the current list is immutable, we can't add this new node to the end of the list. That operation would require changing the second reference of the last node in the list, a task that an immutable node won't allow.

---

2. The word *persistent* here does not have anything to do with storage; it's about data being persisted or preserved unchanged over time.

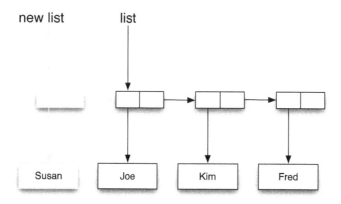

Figure 4—Persistent list processing

Instead of adding this new node to the end, we can add it to the beginning. The second reference in the new node we created can point to the head of the current list. Rather than modifying the existing list, we just got a new list. However, the new list shares all but the first node with the existing list, as shown in Figure 4, *Persistent list processing*, on page 40. In this approach, the addition takes only constant time irrespective of the list size.

Removals from the head of the list also take constant time. The new list contains one element fewer and holds a pointer to the second node (which can be obtained with a simple read) from the original list.

Since adds and removes from the head of the immutable list are constant time, we will benefit from them if we can design problems and algorithms to effectively operate on the head of lists, instead of the tail or middle.

Persistent Tries

Immutable lists give great performance while preserving state, but we can't organize operations around the head of lists all the time. Also, often data is not a simple list but more complex, like a tree or a hashmap, which can be implemented using trees. We can't get away by simply changing the root of a tree; we have to be able to change other elements to support insert or re-move operations.

If we can flatten the tree, then a change to the tree simply becomes a change to one of its short branches. That's exactly what Phil Bagwell, a researcher at EPFL, Switzerland, did by using a high branching factor, at least thirty-two children per node, to create what he called *tries*—see "Ideal Hash Trees" in Appendix 2, *Web Resources*, on page 255. The high branching factor reduces the time for operations on tries, as we'll soon discuss.

In addition to the high branching factor of thirty-two or more, tries use a special property to organize the keys. The key for a node is determined by its path. In other words, we don't store the key in the nodes; their location is their key. For example, let's use numbers for the path and keep the branching factor to three, a rather small number compared to the recommended thirty-two or more, but this makes it easy to discuss. We'll use this trie to store the list of people (Joe, Jill, Bob, Sara, Brad, Kate, Paul, Jake, Fred, and Bill, in that order) attending the department meeting, as in Figure 5, *Using a trie to store a list of people*, on page 42.

Since the branching factor we used in this example is 3, the paths in base 3 represent the index of each node. For example, the path for Bill is 100, which, in base 3, represents the index value of 9. Similarly, Brad is at path 11 and so has an index value of 4.

While Bagwell's tries were not immutable, Rich Hickey, the creator of Clojure, used a variation of them to create a persistent hash implementation in Clojure. A trie with a branching factor of thirty-two requires at most four levels to hold up to 1 million elements. An operation to change any element requires copying only up to four elements—close to constant time operation.

We can use tries to implement different data structures such as trees, hashmaps, and even lists. The immutable list we saw in Figure 4, *Persistent list processing*, on page 40 allowed us to add and remove elements only at the head. Tries remove that restriction and allow us to "add" and "remove" elements at any index in an immutable list.

For example, let's add the new member Sam to the end of our meeting list we implemented using a trie in Figure 5, *Using a trie to store a list of people*, on page 42. Sam's index of 10 translates to path 101 in base 3, so that node should appear as a sibling of the Bill node, as a child of the Sara node. Since all the nodes are immutable, in order to accomplish this task, we'd have to copy the Sara, Jill, and root nodes; the rest of the nodes are unaffected. The structure of the trie after this selective copying is shown in Figure 6, *"Changing" persistent list*, on page 43.

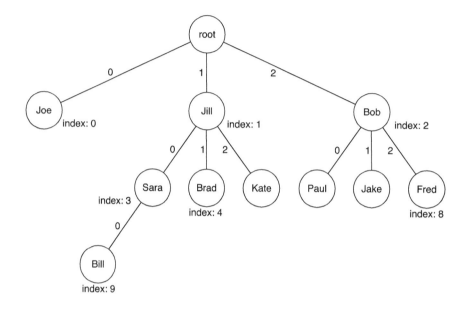

Figure 5—Using a trie to store a list of people

Rather than having to copy all elements, we had to copy only three nodes, the affected node and its ancestors. The copying itself was a shallow copy; we copied the links to the child nodes but not the child nodes themselves. As we increase the branching factor to thirty-two or more, the number of affected nodes for the append operation will still remain close to four, which is the number of levels, while the number of elements the list can hold approaches a million. So, appending to a list is a constant-time operation for all practical purposes. Inserting elements into arbitrary index position will be slightly more expensive. However, depending on the position, we will need some extra partial copying. Unaffected nodes and their descendents are shared intact.

3.7 Selecting a Design Approach

We can avoid most of the issues with concurrency by opting for isolated mutability or pure immutability. For the most part, it's easier to program with isolated mutability than with pure immutability.

With isolated mutability, we must ensure that the mutable variable is in fact isolated and never escapes to more than one thread. We also need to

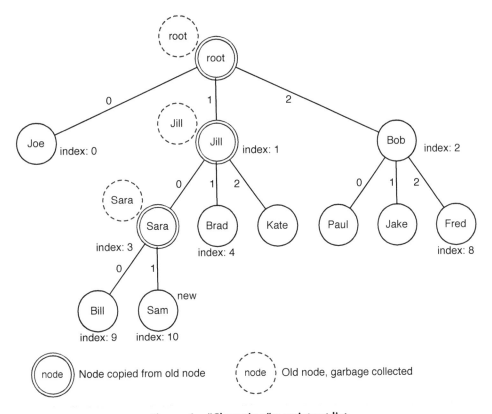

Figure 6—"Changing" persistent list

ensure that the messages we pass between threads are immutable. Use either the concurrent API provided with the JDK or one of the actor-based concurrency frameworks for message passing.

Designing for pure immutability requires more effort. It's harder to realize it in applications that use object-oriented decomposition more than a functional decomposition. We have to devise better algorithms that favor immutability, apply recursive structure or functional composition, and utilize persistent data structures.

3.8 Recap

We can't avoid dealing with state, but we have three options:

- Shared mutability
- Isolated mutability
- Pure immutability

Though we're used to shared mutability, we should avoid it as much as possible. Eliminating shared mutable state is the easiest way to avoid synchronization woes. It takes us far more effort to pick these design approaches than to pick up a library or an API. It also requires us to step back and think through how we'd design applications.

We don't want to compromise performance in order to preserve state. So, to design with immutability, we'll need to use modern data structures that preserve state and at the same time provide great performance.

We discussed ways to deal with state in this chapter. Next, we'll program concurrency using the facilities provided in the JDK.

Part II

Modern Java/JDK Concurrency

I don't know, it all happened so fast.

Turtle mugged by a gang of snails

CHAPTER 4

Scalability and Thread Safety

If you started programming in Java in the last century like I did, you've endured the multithreading and collections API that shipped with earlier Java versions. It handles threads and provides thread safety but doesn't quite consider performance or scalability. Even though threads are relatively lightweight, it takes time and resources to create them. Also, thread safety is provided at the expense of scalability—overly conservative synchronization limits performance.

So, even though it's been around the longest and is still available, the old threading API is not the right choice if we want maintainable code with better scalability and throughput.

It's a new century, and there's a newer concurrency API released with Java 5. It's quite an overhaul of the threading API, and it's better in three main ways:

- It's less painful and more efficient to deal with threads, especially thread pools.
- The new synchronization primitives offer finer granularity—thus more control—than the original primitives.
- The new data structures are scalable—thread safety with reasonable concurrent performance.

To learn the benefits and challenges of this API, let's create a disk utility that will find the total size of all the files in a directory. For large directory hierarchies, a sequential run of this program would take a long time. We'll have to turn to concurrency to speed it up.

4.1 Managing Threads with ExecutorService

To find the directory size, we could split the operation into parts, with each task exploring a subdirectory. Since each task has to run in a separate thread, we could start an instance of Thread. But threads are not reusable—we can't restart them, and scheduling multiple tasks on them is not easy. We certainly don't want to create as many threads as the number of subdirectories we find—it's not scalable and is the quickest way to fail. The java.util.concurrent API was introduced exactly for this purpose—to manage a pool of threads.

We met the ExecutorService and the different types of executors in *Concurrent Computation of Net Asset Value*, on page 21. The ExecutorService, the Executors factory, and the related API ease the pain of working with pools of threads. They conveniently separate the types of pools from the operations we perform on them.

Each ExecutorService represents a thread pool. Rather than tying the lifetime of a thread to the task it runs, ExecutorService separates how we create the thread from what it runs. We can configure the type of thread pool—single threaded, cached, priority based, scheduled/periodic, or fixed size—and the size of the wait queue for tasks scheduled to run. We can easily schedule any number of tasks to run. If we simply want to send off a task to run, we can wrap the task in a Runnable. For tasks that will return a result, we can wrap them in Callable.

To schedule arbitrary tasks, we use the execute() or submit() methods of ExecutorService. To schedule a collection of tasks, we use the invokeAll() method. If we care for only one of the tasks to complete, as in optimization problems where one of many possible results is adequate, we can use the invokeAny() method. These methods are overloaded with a timeout parameter, which is the amount of time we're willing to wait for the results.

As soon as we create an executor service, the pool of threads is ready and active to serve. If we have no tasks for them, then the threads in the pool idle away—except in the case of cached pool, where they die after a delay. If we no longer need the pool of threads, invoke the shutdown() method. This method doesn't kill the pool instantly. It completes all tasks currently scheduled before it shuts down the pool, but we can't schedule any new tasks. A call to shutdownNow() tries to force-cancel currently executing tasks. There's no guarantee, however, because it relies on the tasks to respond well to the interrupt() call.

ExecutorService also provides methods that allow us to check whether the service has terminated or shut down. However, it is better not to rely on them. We should design for task completion rather than thread/service death—focus on completion of work (application logic) instead of termination of threads (infrastructure activity).

4.2 Coordinating Threads

Once we divide a problem into parts, we can schedule several concurrent tasks in a pool of threads and wait for their results to arrive. When these tasks complete, we can proceed as in Figure 7, *Thread coordination—scheduling and joining*, on page 50. We don't want to wait for the threads to die, because these threads may be reused to run several tasks. The result of the scheduled tasks is what we really care about. We can easily achieve this using the Callable interface and the submit() or invokeAll() methods of ExecutorService. Let's look at an example.

To find the total size of all files in a directory hierarchy with potentially thousands of files, we can run several parts concurrently. When parts finish, we need to total up the partial results.

Let's first take a look at the sequential code for totaling the file size:

scalabilityAndTreadSafety/coordinating/TotalFileSizeSequential.java
```java
public class TotalFileSizeSequential {
  private long getTotalSizeOfFilesInDir(final File file) {
    if (file.isFile()) return file.length();

    final File[] children = file.listFiles();
    long total = 0;
    if (children != null)
      for(final File child : children)
        total += getTotalSizeOfFilesInDir(child);
    return total;
  }

  public static void main(final String[] args) {
    final long start = System.nanoTime();
    final long total = new TotalFileSizeSequential()
      .getTotalSizeOfFilesInDir(new File(args[0]));
    final long end = System.nanoTime();
    System.out.println("Total Size: " + total);
    System.out.println("Time taken: " + (end - start)/1.0e9);
  }
}
```

We start at a given directory and total the size of all the files, recursively drilling down the subdirectories.

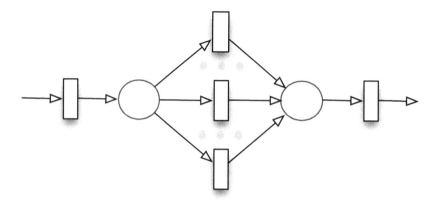

Figure 7—Thread coordination—scheduling and joining

This and other file size programs in this book will take a long time on the first run, and the time will drop down for subsequent runs performed within minutes. This is because of the caching of the file system. I have discarded the time from the first run so that all the runs used in comparison have the advantage of cache.

Let's run this on a few directories. We'll use the output to compare the performance of the concurrent version we'll create soon.

```
>java TotalFileSizeSequential /etc
Total Size: 2266456
Time taken: 0.011836

>java TotalFileSizeSequential /usr
Total Size: 3793911517
Time taken: 18.570144
```

We certainly can hope to gain an increase in speed by making this code concurrent. We can divide the problem into tasks where each task accepts a directory and returns its total size. The Callable interface is a good fit for this because its call() method can return a result when done. As we loop through each file in the directory, we can schedule the task using the submit() method of ExecutorService. We can then gather up all the partial results by simply calling the get() method of the Future object; this object acts as a delegate that will provide us with the result when available. Let's implement the logic we just discussed in a NaivelyConcurrentTotalFileSize class:

scalabilityAndTreadSafety/coordinating/NaivelyConcurrentTotalFileSize.java

```
public class NaivelyConcurrentTotalFileSize {
  private long getTotalSizeOfFilesInDir(
    final ExecutorService service, final File file)
    throws InterruptedException, ExecutionException, TimeoutException {
    if (file.isFile()) return file.length();

    long total = 0;
    final File[] children = file.listFiles();

    if (children != null) {
      final List<Future<Long>> partialTotalFutures =
        new ArrayList<Future<Long>>();
      for(final File child : children) {
        partialTotalFutures.add(service.submit(new Callable<Long>() {
          public Long call() throws InterruptedException,
            ExecutionException, TimeoutException {
            return getTotalSizeOfFilesInDir(service, child);
          }
        }));
      }

      for(final Future<Long> partialTotalFuture : partialTotalFutures)
        total += partialTotalFuture.get(100, TimeUnit.SECONDS);
    }

    return total;
  }
```

The code starts to explore a given directory. For each file or subdirectory, we create a task for finding its size and schedule it on the pool on line 14. Once we've scheduled tasks for all files and subdirectories under a directory, we wait for their size to be returned through the Future objects. To compute the total size for a directory, we then iterate over futures on line 22. We don't want to block endlessly for a result to arrive, so there's a time limit for the get() method to respond. In other words, we bail out with an error if a task doesn't finish within that time. Each time we recursively call the get-TotalSizeOfFilesInDir() methods, we schedule more tasks on the executor service pool, as long as there are more directories and files to visit.

Let's create the code to invoke the previous method:

scalabilityAndTreadSafety/coordinating/NaivelyConcurrentTotalFileSize.java

```
  private long getTotalSizeOfFile(final String fileName)
    throws InterruptedException, ExecutionException, TimeoutException {
      final ExecutorService service = Executors.newFixedThreadPool(100);
      try {
        return getTotalSizeOfFilesInDir(service, new File(fileName));
      } finally {
```

```
                    service.shutdown();
        }
    }

    public static void main(final String[] args)
        throws InterruptedException, ExecutionException, TimeoutException {
        final long start = System.nanoTime();
        final long total = new NaivelyConcurrentTotalFileSize()
            .getTotalSizeOfFile(args[0]);
        final long end = System.nanoTime();
        System.out.println("Total Size: " + total);
        System.out.println("Time taken: " + (end - start)/1.0e9);
    }
}
```

Since threads are a limited resource, we don't want to create too many of them; see Chapter 2, *Division of Labor*, on page 15 on how to estimate. Once we create the pool, we set the exploration of the given directory in motion using the getTotalSizeOfFilesInDir() method.

Let's take the code for a drive and see how it performs:

```
>java NaivelyConcurrentTotalFileSize /etc
Total Size: 2266456
Time taken: 0.12506
```

The file size reported here is the same as in the sequential version, but the speed wasn't encouraging. It actually took longer to run. A lot of time was spent in scheduling, instead of doing real work for the rather flat directory hierarchy under /etc. Let's not let our hopes fade yet. Perhaps we'll see an improvement for the /usr directory, which took more than eighteen seconds in the sequential run. Let's give that a try:

```
>java NaivelyConcurrentTotalFileSize /usr
Exception in thread "main" java.util.concurrent.TimeoutException
        at java.util.concurrent.FutureTask$Sync.innerGet(FutureTask.java:228)
        at java.util.concurrent.FutureTask.get(FutureTask.java:91)
        at NaivelyConcurrentTotalFileSize.getTotalSizeOfFilesInDir(
          NaivelyConcurrentTotalFileSize.java:34)
        at NaivelyConcurrentTotalFileSize.getTotalSizeOfFile(
          NaivelyConcurrentTotalFileSize.java:45)
        at NaivelyConcurrentTotalFileSize.main(
          NaivelyConcurrentTotalFileSize.java:54)
```

Hum...it's not quite what we wanted to see, a timeout problem. Don't panic; there's a reason I called this version *naive*.

The flaw is in the getTotalSizeOfFilesInDir() method; it clogs the thread pool. As this method discovers subdirectories, it schedules the task of exploring them to other threads (line 14). Once it schedules all these tasks, this method awaits response from each one of them (line 23). If we had only a few directories, then it's no big deal. But if we have a deep hierarchy, this method will get stuck. While threads wait for response from the tasks they create, these tasks end up waiting in the ExecutorService's queue for their turn to run. This is a potential "pool induced deadlock," if we didn't have the timeout. Since we used a timeout, we're able to at least terminate unfavorably rather than wait forever. Making code concurrent is not trivial—it's time to go back to the drawing board to fix this code.

We want to delegate the computation of size for various directories to different threads but not hold on to the calling thread while we wait for these tasks/threads to respond.[1]

One way to tackle this is for each task to return a list of subdirectories it finds, instead of the full size for a given directory. Then from the main task we can dispatch other tasks to navigate the subdirectories. This will prevent holding threads for any period longer than simply fetching the immediate subdirectories. While the tasks fetch subdirectories, they can also total the size of files in their directories. Let's put that design to work in a Concurrent-TotalFileSize and see whether it gives us better results.

As we discover subdirectories and files, we need to pass the list of subdirectories and the total size of files to the main thread. We'd need an immutable object to hold these values, so let's create an inner class called SubDirectoriesAndSize to hold that.

scalabilityAndTreadSafety/coordinating/ConcurrentTotalFileSize.java
```java
public class ConcurrentTotalFileSize {
  class SubDirectoriesAndSize {
    final public long size;
    final public List<File> subDirectories;
    public SubDirectoriesAndSize(
      final long totalSize, final List<File> theSubDirs) {
      size = totalSize;
      subDirectories = Collections.unmodifiableList(theSubDirs);
    }
  }
}
```

Next we'll write the method that, given a directory, will return an instance of SubDirectoriesAndSize that holds the subdirectories of the given directory along with the size of files it contains.

---

1. Later we'll see how the actor-based model fits really well to solve this problem.

scalabilityAndTreadSafety/coordinating/ConcurrentTotalFileSize.java

```
private SubDirectoriesAndSize getTotalAndSubDirs(final File file) {
  long total = 0;
  final List<File> subDirectories = new ArrayList<File>();
  if(file.isDirectory()) {
    final File[] children = file.listFiles();
    if (children != null)
      for(final File child : children) {
        if (child.isFile())
          total += child.length();
        else
          subDirectories.add(child);
      }
  }
  return new SubDirectoriesAndSize(total, subDirectories);
}
```

As we discover subdirectories, we want to delegate the task of exploring
them to other threads. Most of the efforts for concurrency will go into the
new method getTotalSizeOfFilesInDir().

scalabilityAndTreadSafety/coordinating/ConcurrentTotalFileSize.java

```
private long getTotalSizeOfFilesInDir(final File file)
  throws InterruptedException, ExecutionException, TimeoutException {
  final ExecutorService service = Executors.newFixedThreadPool(100);
  try {
    long total = 0;
    final List<File> directories = new ArrayList<File>();
    directories.add(file);
    while(!directories.isEmpty()) {
      final List<Future<SubDirectoriesAndSize>> partialResults =
        new ArrayList<Future<SubDirectoriesAndSize>>();
      for(final File directory : directories) {
        partialResults.add(
          service.submit(new Callable<SubDirectoriesAndSize>() {
          public SubDirectoriesAndSize call() {
            return getTotalAndSubDirs(directory);
          }
        }));
      }
      directories.clear();
      for(final Future<SubDirectoriesAndSize> partialResultFuture :
        partialResults) {
        final SubDirectoriesAndSize subDirectoriesAndSize =
          partialResultFuture.get(100, TimeUnit.SECONDS);
        directories.addAll(subDirectoriesAndSize.subDirectories);
        total += subDirectoriesAndSize.size;
      }
    }
    return total;
```

```
  } finally {
    service.shutdown();
  }
}
```

We create a thread pool of size 100 and add the given top-level directory to a list of directories to explore. Then, while there are files left to explore, we invoke getTotalAndSubDirs() in separate threads for each directory on hand. As the response from these threads arrive, we then add the partial file size they return to a total and add the subdirectories to the list of directories to explore. Once all the subdirectories have been explored, we return the total file size. For the last step, to get this code moving, we need the main() method.

scalabilityAndTreadSafety/coordinating/ConcurrentTotalFileSize.java
```
  public static void main(final String[] args)
    throws InterruptedException, ExecutionException, TimeoutException {
    final long start = System.nanoTime();
    final long total = new ConcurrentTotalFileSize()
      .getTotalSizeOfFilesInDir(new File(args[0]));
    final long end = System.nanoTime();
    System.out.println("Total Size: " + total);
    System.out.println("Time taken: " + (end - start)/1.0e9);
  }
}
```

This version of concurrent implementation took quite some effort, but when compared to the old NaivelyConcurrentTotalFileSize, the new ConcurrentTotalFileSize is a better design—it does not hold a thread for a long time. It quickly gets a list of subdirectories, so we can separately schedule the visits to them. It looks like this should give us the desired result; let's see if that's true.

```
>java ConcurrentTotalFileSize /usr
Total Size: 3793911517
Time taken: 8.220475
```

First, unlike the naive version, this version completed successfully. To find the total size of the /usr directory, it took only about eight seconds compared to more than eighteen seconds the sequential run took. Time to celebrate?

Let's review what we did in this example. We dispatched tasks to threads and then waited for their results only in the main thread. All the other threads are quick, in that they only take time to find the total size of files and, in addition, return the list of subdirectories in a given directory.

Although that design idea is quite simple, implementing it wasn't easy. We had to create a class to hold the immutable results from the tasks. It also took some effort to continuously dispatch tasks and coordinate their results.

The end result: better performance but quite a bit of added complexity. Let's see whether we can simplify this.

Coordination Using CountDownLatch

Future served in two ways in the previous example. First it helped get the result of the tasks. Implicitly, it also helped coordinate the thread with these tasks/threads. It allowed us to wait for those results to arrive before the thread proceeded with its work. Future, however, is not helpful as a coordination tool if tasks have no results to return. We don't want to have an artificial return result simply for the sake of coordination. CountDownLatch can serve as a coordination tool in situations like this.

The NaivelyConcurrentTotalFileSize code was a lot simpler and shorter than the ConcurrentTotalFileSize code. I prefer simple code that works. The problem with NaivelyConcurrentTotalFileSize is that each thread waited for the tasks it's scheduled to complete. The nice thing about both the versions of code was they had no mutable shared state. If we compromise a little on the shared mutability,[2] we can keep the code simple and make it work as well. Let's see how.

Instead of returning the subdirectories and the file size, we can let each thread update a shared variable. With nothing to return, the code will be a lot simpler. We still have to ensure that the main thread waits for all the subdirectories to be visited. We can use the CountDownLatch for this, to signal the end of wait. The latch works as a synchronization point for one or more threads to wait for other threads to reach a point of completion. Here we simply use the latch as a switch.

Let's create a class called ConcurrentTotalFileSizeWLatch that will use CountDownLatch. We'll recursively delegate the task of exploring subdirectories to different threads. When a thread discovers a file, instead of returning the results, it updates a shared variable totalSize of type AtomicLong. AtomicLong provides thread-safe methods to modify and retrieve the values of a simple long variable. In addition, we'll use another AtomicLong variable called pendingFileVisits to keep a tab on the number of files still to be visited. When this count goes to zero, we release the latch by calling countDown().

scalabilityAndTreadSafety/coordinating/ConcurrentTotalFileSizeWLatch.java
```
public class ConcurrentTotalFileSizeWLatch {
  private ExecutorService service;
  final private AtomicLong pendingFileVisits = new AtomicLong();
  final private AtomicLong totalSize = new AtomicLong();
  final private CountDownLatch latch = new CountDownLatch(1);
```

---

2. See how easy it is to fall into this trap of using shared mutability?

```
private void updateTotalSizeOfFilesInDir(final File file) {
  long fileSize = 0;
  if (file.isFile())
    fileSize = file.length();
  else {
    final File[] children = file.listFiles();
    if (children != null) {
      for(final File child : children) {
        if (child.isFile())
          fileSize += child.length();
        else {
          pendingFileVisits.incrementAndGet();
          service.execute(new Runnable() {
            public void run() { updateTotalSizeOfFilesInDir(child); }
          });
        }
      }
    }
  }
  totalSize.addAndGet(fileSize);
  if(pendingFileVisits.decrementAndGet() == 0) latch.countDown();
}
```

The mechanics of exploring directories is done, so we now need code to create the pool of threads, set the exploration of directories running, and wait on the latch. When the latch is released by updateTotalSizeOfFilesInDir(), the main thread is released from its await() call and returns the total size it knows.

scalabilityAndTreadSafety/coordinating/ConcurrentTotalFileSizeWLatch.java

```
  private long getTotalSizeOfFile(final String fileName)
    throws InterruptedException {
    service = Executors.newFixedThreadPool(100);
    pendingFileVisits.incrementAndGet();
    try {
     updateTotalSizeOfFilesInDir(new File(fileName));
     latch.await(100, TimeUnit.SECONDS);
     return totalSize.longValue();
    } finally {
      service.shutdown();
    }
  }
  public static void main(final String[] args) throws InterruptedException {
    final long start = System.nanoTime();
    final long total = new ConcurrentTotalFileSizeWLatch()
      .getTotalSizeOfFile(args[0]);
    final long end = System.nanoTime();
    System.out.println("Total Size: " + total);
    System.out.println("Time taken: " + (end - start)/1.0e9);
  }
}
```

This version has a lot less code. Let's run it.

```
>java ConcurrentTotalFileSizeWLatch /usr
Total Size: 3793911517
Time taken: 10.22789
```

The time taken is slightly more than the ConcurrentTotalFileSize version. This is because of the extra synchronization in all the threads—shared mutability requires protection for thread safety, and that lowers concurrency.

In the previous example we used CountDownLatch as a simple switch by setting the latch value to 1. We could also use higher value and let multiple threads wait on it. That would be useful if we want multiple threads to reach a coordination point before continuing to perform some task. A CountDownLatch, however, is not reusable. Once it's used for a synchronization, it must be discarded. If we want a reusable synchronization point, we should use a CyclicBarrier instead.

The performance of the code was better than the sequential version TotalFileSizeSequential. It was a bit worse than the ConcurrentTotalFileSize version but a lot simpler. However, there's an added risk of accessing a shared mutable variable—something I have cautioned against quite a bit. It would be so much better if we can keep the code simple and still avoid the shared mutability. We will see how to do that later in Chapter 8, *Favoring Isolated Mutability*, on page 163.

4.3 Exchanging Data

We will often want to exchange data between multiple cooperating threads. In the previous examples, we used Future and AtomicLong. Future is quite useful when we want to get a response from a task on completion. AtomicLong and the other atomic classes in the java.util.concurrent.atomic package are useful for dealing with single shared data values. Although these are useful for exchanging data, they can get unwieldy as we saw in the previous example. To work with multiple data values or to exchange data quite frequently, we'll want a better mechanism than either of these provided. The java.util.concurrent API has a number of classes that provide thread-safe ways to communicate arbitrary data between threads.

If we simply want to exchange data between two threads, we can use the Exchanger class. This serves as a synchronization point where two threads can swap data in a thread-safe manner. The faster thread is blocked until the slower thread catches up to the synchronization point to exchange data.

If we want to send a bunch of data between threads, instances of the BlockingQueue interface can come in handy. As the name indicates, inserts are blocked until space is available, and removals are blocked until data is available. The JDK provides quite a few flavors of BlockingQueue. For example, to match inserts with removals, use a SynchronousQueue that coordinates each insert operation with the corresponding remove operation by another thread. If we want data to bubble up based on some priority, we can use PriorityBlockingQueue. For a simple blocking queue, we can select a linked-list flavor from LinkedBlockingQueue or an array flavor from ArrayBlockingQueue.

We can use a blocking queue to solve the total file size problem concurrently. Rather than using the AtomicLong mutable variable, we can have each thread place the partial file size it computes into a queue. The main thread can then take these partial results from the queue and compute the total locally. Let's first write the code to explore the directories:

scalabilityAndTreadSafety/coordinating/ConcurrentTotalFileSizeWQueue.java

```java
public class ConcurrentTotalFileSizeWQueue {
  private ExecutorService service;
  final private BlockingQueue<Long> fileSizes =
    new ArrayBlockingQueue<Long>(500);
  final AtomicLong pendingFileVisits = new AtomicLong();
  private void startExploreDir(final File file) {
    pendingFileVisits.incrementAndGet();
    service.execute(new Runnable() {
      public void run() { exploreDir(file); }
    });
  }
  private void exploreDir(final File file) {
    long fileSize = 0;
    if (file.isFile())
      fileSize = file.length();
    else {
      final File[] children = file.listFiles();
      if (children != null)
        for(final File child : children) {
          if (child.isFile())
            fileSize += child.length();
          else {
            startExploreDir(child);
          }
        }
    }
    try {
      fileSizes.put(fileSize);
    } catch(Exception ex) { throw new RuntimeException(ex); }
    pendingFileVisits.decrementAndGet();
  }
```

We delegate separate tasks to explore the subdirectories. Each task keeps a tab of the total size of files directly under a given directory and in the end puts the total size into the queue using the blocking call put(). Any subdirectories discovered by the tasks are explored in separate tasks/threads.

The main thread set the previous code in motion and simply loops through the queue to total the file sizes it receives from the tasks until all subdirectories have been explored.

scalabilityAndTreadSafety/coordinating/ConcurrentTotalFileSizeWQueue.java

```
  private long getTotalSizeOfFile(final String fileName)
    throws InterruptedException {
    service = Executors.newFixedThreadPool(100);
    try {
      startExploreDir(new File(fileName));
      long totalSize = 0;
      while(pendingFileVisits.get() > 0 || fileSizes.size() > 0)
      {
        final Long size = fileSizes.poll(10, TimeUnit.SECONDS);
        totalSize += size;
      }
      return totalSize;
    } finally {
      service.shutdown();
    }
  }
  public static void main(final String[] args) throws InterruptedException {
    final long start = System.nanoTime();
    final long total = new ConcurrentTotalFileSizeWQueue()
      .getTotalSizeOfFile(args[0]);
    final long end = System.nanoTime();
    System.out.println("Total Size: " + total);
    System.out.println("Time taken: " + (end - start)/1.0e9);
  }
}
```

Let's see how this version performs:

```
>java ConcurrentTotalFileSizeWQueue /usr
Total Size: 3793911517
Time taken: 10.293993
```

This version is comparable in performance to the previous one, but the code is a notch simpler—the blocking queue helped with exchanging and synchronizing the data between the threads. Next we'll see how we can improve on these solutions even further with the new API introduced in Java 7.

4.4   Java 7 Fork-Join API

ExecutorService manages a pool of threads and allows us to schedule tasks for execution by threads in its pool. It is, however, up to us to decide how many threads will be in the pool, and there is no distinction between tasks we schedule and subtasks these tasks create. Java 7[3] brings a specialization of ExecutorService with improved efficiency and performance—the fork-join API.

The ForkJoinPool class dynamically manages threads based on the number of available processors and task demand. Fork-join employs work-stealing where threads pick up (steal) tasks created by other active tasks. This provides better performance and utilization of threads.

Subtasks created by active tasks are scheduled using different methods than external tasks. We'd typically use one fork-join pool in an entire application to schedule tasks. Also, there's no need to shut down the pool since it employs daemon threads.

To schedule tasks, we provide instances of ForkJoinTask (typically an instance of one of its subclasses) to methods of ForkJoinPool. ForkJoinTask allows us to fork tasks and then join upon completion of the task. ForkJoinTask has two subclasses: RecursiveAction and RecursiveTask. To schedule tasks that don't return any results, we use a subclass of RecursiveAction. For tasks that return results, we use a subclass of RecursiveTask.

The fork-join API is geared toward tasks that are reasonably sized so the cost is amortized but not too large (or run indefinitely in loops) to realize reasonable throughput. The fork-join API expects tasks to have no side effects (don't change shared state) and no synchronized or blocking methods.

The fork-join API is very useful for problems that can be broken down recursively until small enough to run sequentially. The multiple smaller parts are scheduled to run at the same time, utilizing the threads from the pool managed by ForkJoinPool.

Let's use the fork-join API to solve the file size problem. Recall the naive solution we developed in Section 4.2, *Coordinating Threads*, on page 49. That solution was quite simple, but we ran into the problem of pool-induced deadlock for larger directory hierarchies. Tasks ended up waiting for tasks

---

3.   All Java examples in this book, except this section, use Java 6. In this section, we'll use Java 7, downloadable from http://jdk7.java.net/download.html. If you're on the Mac, see http://wikis.sun.com/display/OpenJDK/Mac+OS+X+Port.

they spawned while holding threads much needed for these subtasks to run. The fork-join API puts an end to that problem with work-stealing. When a task waits for a subtask to finish, the thread that's executing the task picks up a new task to run. Let's take a look at the code for the file size problem using the fork-join API.

scalabilityAndTreadSafety/fork-join/FileSize.java

```java
public class FileSize {

  private final static ForkJoinPool forkJoinPool = new ForkJoinPool();

  private static class FileSizeFinder extends RecursiveTask<Long> {
    final File file;

    public FileSizeFinder(final File theFile) {
      file = theFile;
    }

    @Override public Long compute() {
      long size = 0;
      if (file.isFile()) {
        size = file.length();
      } else {
        final File[] children = file.listFiles();
        if (children != null) {
          List<ForkJoinTask<Long>> tasks =
            new ArrayList<ForkJoinTask<Long>>();
          for(final File child : children) {
            if (child.isFile()) {
              size += child.length();
            } else {
              tasks.add(new FileSizeFinder(child));
            }
          }

          for(final ForkJoinTask<Long> task : invokeAll(tasks)) {
            size += task.join();
          }
        }
      }

      return size;
    }
  }

  public static void main(final String[] args) {
    final long start = System.nanoTime();
    final long total = forkJoinPool.invoke(
        new FileSizeFinder(new File(args[0])));
    final long end = System.nanoTime();
```

```
        System.out.println("Total Size: " + total);
        System.out.println("Time taken: " + (end - start)/1.0e9);
    }
}
```

In the FileSize class, we hold a reference to an instance of ForkJoinPool. This instance is defined static so that it can be shared across the entire program. We define a static inner class called FileSizeFinder that provides the task execution engine by extending RecursiveTask and implementing its compute() method. In this method, we total the size of files in a given directory and delegate the task of finding the size of subdirectories to other tasks, that is, other instances of FileSizeFinder. The invokeAll() method waits for all the subtasks to finish before moving forward. However, while the task is blocked, the thread steals more work rather than idling (like the highly responsible members of a successful team). The task returns the total size of the given directory upon completing the compute() method.

Let's compile and run the code using Java 7:

```
>java com.agiledeveloper.pcj.FileSize /etc
Total Size: 2266456
Time taken: 0.038218

>java com.agiledeveloper.pcj.FileSize /usr
Total Size: 3793911517
Time taken: 8.35158
```

From the output we see that this version of the program did quite well compared to the other concurrent versions we saw in this chapter. We also see that, for large directory hierarchies, the program did not suffer the problem that the naive version had.

In the example, we recursively divided until we got a directory or a file. In general, we don't want to break down the problem too small because that may result in scheduling overhead.

The collections that are part of the java.util.concurrent package give us thread safety and act as a synchronization point. Thread safety is important, but we don't want to compromise performance. Next we'll explore java.util.concurrent data structures geared toward performance.

4.5 Scalable Collections

Collections like Vector that originally came with Java gave us thread safety at the cost of performance. All of our accesses, irrespective of the need, were thread safe but slow.

Later collections like ArrayList provided speed but lacked thread safety. Again, we traded performance for thread safety when we used one of the synchronized wrappers of the collections, like using the synchronizedList() of Collections.

The bottom line is that we had to pick between thread safety and performance. Java 5's java.util.concurrent changed all that with concurrent data structures like ConcurrentHashMap and ConcurrentLinkedQueue. These collections provide better performance, at the expense of space, but we have to be willing to accept a little change in semantics.

Synchronized collections provide thread safety, while concurrent collections provide both thread safety and better concurrent access performance. Using synchronized collections is like driving through a traffic light–controlled intersection; concurrent collection is like an uncongested freeway.

If we change a synchronized map while iterating over it, we're greeted with a ConcurrentModificationException. In essence, we're required to hold an exclusive lock, a rather pessimistic lock, on the map when we iterate over it. This increased thread safety but clearly lowered concurrency. Consequently, we get low throughput with these synchronous collections.

Concurrent collections, on the other hand, were designed to provide throughput. They let multiple operations coexist. We're welcome to modify a map, for example, while we're iterating over it. The API guarantees the integrity of the collection, and we'll never see the same element appear twice in a current iteration. It's a compromise in semantics because we must be willing to accept elements being changed and removed while we're iterating over them or getting elements.

Let's explore the behavior of ConcurrentHashMap in contrast to the older maps.

In the following code, we iterate over a map of scores in a separate thread. Right in the middle of the iteration we put a new key into the map.

scalabilityAndTreadSafety/concurrentCollections/AccessingMap.java
```
public class AccessingMap {
  private static void useMap(final Map<String, Integer> scores)
    throws InterruptedException {
    scores.put("Fred", 10);
    scores.put("Sara", 12);

    try {
      for(final String key : scores.keySet()) {
        System.out.println(key + " score " + scores.get(key));
        scores.put("Joe", 14);
      }
    } catch(Exception ex) {
```

```
        System.out.println("Failed: " + ex);
    }

    System.out.println("Number of elements in the map: " +
        scores.keySet().size());
}
```

If the map is either a plain-vanilla HashMap or its synchronized wrapper, this code will freak out—it will result in the violation we discussed. In reality, before we iterate over a synchronized collection, we'd have to lock it to prevent such violation. If the map is a ConcurrentHashMap, however, it will not suffer the wrath of ConcurrentModificationException. To see this difference in behavior, let's exercise the useMap() first with an instance of the good old HashMap(), then with a synchronized wrapper, and finally with an instance of ConcurrentHashMap.

scalabilityAndTreadSafety/concurrentCollections/AccessingMap.java

```
public static void main(final String[] args) throws InterruptedException {
    System.out.println("Using Plain vanilla HashMap");
    useMap(new HashMap<String, Integer>());

    System.out.println("Using Synchronized HashMap");
    useMap(Collections.synchronizedMap(new HashMap<String, Integer>()));

    System.out.println("Using Concurrent HashMap");
    useMap(new ConcurrentHashMap<String, Integer>());
  }
}
```

When we run this example, we'll see that the traditional maps could not handle this modification in the middle of the iteration (even from within a single thread), but the ConcurrentHashMap took it really well.

```
Using Plain vanilla HashMap
Sara score 12
Failed: java.util.ConcurrentModificationException
Number of elements in the map: 3
Using Synchronized HashMap
Sara score 12
Failed: java.util.ConcurrentModificationException
Number of elements in the map: 3
Using Concurrent HashMap
Sara score 12
Fred score 10
Number of elements in the map: 3
```

In addition to allowing interleaved reads and writes, the concurrent collections provide better throughput than the synchronized versions. This is because rather than holding an exclusive lock, the concurrent collections allow multiple updates and reads to work concurrently. Our reads will see the latest values. If the read occurs in the middle of a bulk write, our read is not blocked for the entire update to complete. This means we may see part of the change but not all. In any case, concurrent collections guarantee visibility or the *happens-before* behavior.

Let's take a look at the performance of concurrent map vs. the synchronized version. In this measure, the workload of each thread is about the same, so as the number of threads is increased, the overall workload in the process is increased as well—giving opportunity for more contention. In each thread I access a random key from the map. If the key is not found, I insert it about 80 percent of the time, and if the key is found, I remove it about 20 percent of the time. I try the previous operations first on a ConcurrentHashMap and then on a HashMap with a synchronized wrapper.

The throughput on a eight-core processor is shown in Figure 8, *Throughput of ConcurrentHashMap vs. synchronized HashMap on an eight-core processor*, on page 67. The synchronized HashMap did slightly better than the ConcurrentHashMap when the number of threads was fewer than two; that is, the synchronized version did well when there was no concurrency. As the number of threads increased, the ConcurrentHashMap clearly outperformed HashMap.

If we're willing to accept the difference in semantics of the concurrent collections, we'll benefit from their better performance compared to synchronized collections.

4.6 Lock vs. Synchronized

We've avoided explicit synchronization so far in the examples in this chapter. We can't escape it for long, however, if we're going to restrict ourselves to the JDK concurrency API—it'll show up the minute we have to coordinate changes to multiple variables or multiple objects.

In Java, we have two constructs to acquire locks—the archaic synchronized and its modern counterpart, the Lock interface. The Lock interface gives us more control for locking than the synchronized keyword. Let's discuss how.

synchronized

We use synchronized to gain an explicit monitor/lock on objects. While grabbing the monitor and releasing it at the end of the block, it also helps threads cross the memory barrier. However, synchronized is very primitive in its capabilities and has quite a few limitations.

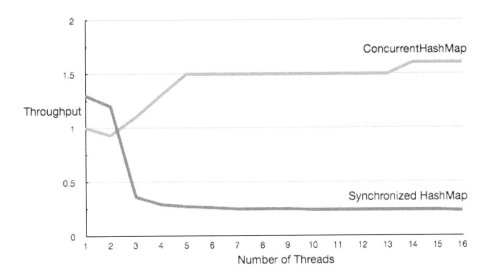

Figure 8—Throughput of ConcurrentHashMap vs. synchronized HashMap on an eight-core processor

Unfortunately, synchronized makes it possible to indefinitely block to acquire a lock. This is because there's no easy way to tell synchronized to wait for a finite time to acquire a lock.

If we attempt unit testing for thread safety, we'll find that synchronized makes it impossible. There is no effective, simple, and deterministic way, like replacing synchronized with a mock, to examine whether we're wrapping a mutually exclusive block of code in a synchronized section or block.

Furthermore, synchronized leads to exclusive locks, and no other thread can gain access to the monitors held. This does not favor situations with multiple readers and infrequent writers. Even though the readers could run concurrently, they're serialized, and this results in poor concurrent performance.

As we can see, even though synchronized is baked into the language as a keyword, it provides a rather highly conservative thread safety with little ability for us to control.

The Lock Interface

The Java 5 Lock interface gives us better control than the synchronized keyword does—see the Lock interface in Appendix 2, *Web Resources*, on page 255.

Much like synchronized, the implementors of the Lock interface guarantee that calls to their methods cross the memory barrier. We acquire and release locks using the Lock interface's lock() and unlock() methods, like so:

```
aMonitor.lock();
try {
  //...
} finally {
  aMonitor.unlock();
}
```

We perform the unlock() in the finally block to ensure a proper unlock even in the case of exceptions. Although lock() is a blocking call, we can call the nonblocking variation tryLock() to instantly acquire the lock if available. To wait for a finite time, provide a timeout parameter to the tryLock() method. There's even a variation that allows us to interrupt a thread while it's waiting for a lock.

Let's see how the Lock interface fixes each of the concerns we raised with synchronized.

With the tryLock() method, our lock requests are not forced to block. Instead, we can check instantly whether we've acquired the lock. Also, if we decide to wait for a lock, we can place a limit on the wait time.

The Lock interface makes it quite easy to unit test for thread safety; for details, see "Test Driving Multithreaded Code" in Appendix 2, *Web Resources*, on page 255. We can simply mock out the implementation of the Lock interface and check whether the code being tested requests the lock and unlock at the appropriate time.

We can acquire concurrent read locks and exclusive write locks using Read-WriteLock. Thus, multiple readers can continue concurrently without having to wait and are delayed only when a conflicting writer is active.

Let's look at an example of using ReentrantLock, which implements the Lock interface. As the name suggests, it allows threads to rerequest locks they already own, thus allowing them to reenter their mutually exclusive sections.

A bank has approached us to write code that transfers money between two accounts, where an Account class is defined, as shown next:

scalabilityAndTreadSafety/locking/Account.java
```
public class Account implements Comparable<Account> {
  private int balance;
  public final Lock monitor = new ReentrantLock();

  public Account(final int initialBalance) { balance = initialBalance; }
```

```
public int compareTo(final Account other) {
  return new Integer(hashCode()).compareTo(other.hashCode());
}

public void deposit(final int amount) {
  monitor.lock();
  try {
    if (amount > 0) balance += amount;
  } finally { //In case there was an Exception we're covered
    monitor.unlock();
  }
}

public boolean withdraw(final int amount) {
  try {
    monitor.lock();
    if(amount > 0 && balance >= amount)
    {
      balance -= amount;
      return true;
    }
    return false;
  } finally {
    monitor.unlock();
  }
}
}
```

Quite a bit is going on in the Account class; let's discuss the various pieces in it.

If two threads try to transfer money between two accounts concurrently but in the opposite order, like so:

```
thread1: transfer money from account1 to account2
thread2: transfer money from account2 to account1
```

then in this case thread1 may lock account1, and simultaneously thread2 may lock account2. The two thread are now deadlocked, waiting to acquire a lock on the other account they need, while holding their current locks. We can prevent this by making the two threads request locks on accounts in the same order. Then, one of them can proceed to acquire both the locks. The other thread can then follow after a temporary block, instead of being held by a deadlock. The Account class implements the Comparable interface to facilitate this natural order for locking (see the deadlock avoidance discussion in Brian Goetz's *Java Concurrency in Practice* [Goe06]).

We have ensured that the deposit() and withdraw() operations are mutually exclusive by acquiring and releasing locks using a ReentrantLock. In addition, operations such as transfer may have to compose multiple deposits and withdraws into one mutually exclusive operation. To allow this, the Account exposes its lock instance.

So, we're all set to write the transfer() method in an AccountService class. We first try to gain locks on the two given accounts in their natural order, which is the reason for the sort. If we can't acquire the lock on either of them within one second, or whatever duration we're comfortable with, we simply throw a LockException. If we gain the locks, we complete the transfer if sufficient funds are available.

scalabilityAndTreadSafety/locking/AccountService.java
```
public class AccountService {
  public boolean transfer(
    final Account from, final Account to, final int amount)
    throws LockException, InterruptedException {
    final Account[] accounts = new Account[] {from, to};
    Arrays.sort(accounts);
    if(accounts[0].monitor.tryLock(1, TimeUnit.SECONDS)) {
      try {
        if (accounts[1].monitor.tryLock(1, TimeUnit.SECONDS)) {
          try {
            if(from.withdraw(amount)) {
              to.deposit(amount);
              return true;
            } else {
              return false;
            }
          } finally {
            accounts[1].monitor.unlock();
          }
        }
      } finally {
        accounts[0].monitor.unlock();
      }
    }
    throw new LockException("Unable to acquire locks on the accounts");
  }
}
```

The transfer() method avoided deadlock by ordering the accounts and avoided indefinite wait (starvation) by limiting the time it waits to acquire the locks. Since the monitors used are reentrant, subsequent calls to lock() within the deposit() and withdraw() methods caused no harm.

While the transfer() method avoided deadlock and starvation, the deposit() and withdraw() methods' use of lock() may potentially cause problems in another context. As an exercise, I suggest that you modify these methods to use try-Lock() instead of lock().

This may be a departure from what you're used to doing. However, it's better to use the Lock interface and the supporting classes instead of the old synchronized construct to better manage locking.

Even though the Lock interface has eased concerns, it's still a lot of work and easy to err. In later chapters, we'll achieve a worthy design goal—entirely avoid locks/synchronization—and achieve explicit lock-free concurrency.

4.7 Recap

The modern concurrency API java.util.concurrent has improved a number of things over the older API. It allows us to do the following:

- Manage a pool of threads

- Easily schedule tasks for concurrent execution

- Exchange data between concurrently running threads in a thread-safe manner

- Gain fine-grained synchronization

- Benefit from better concurrent performance using concurrent data structures

Although the newer API helps in a number of ways, it still requires us to be vigilant to avoid race conditions and shared mutable data.

We'll discuss some of the ways to deal with shared mutability in the next chapter.

The beaten path is the safest, but the traffic's terrible!

   Jeff Taylor

CHAPTER 5

Taming Shared Mutability

I've discouraged shared mutability quite a few times so far in this book. You may ask, therefore, why I discuss it further in this chapter. The reason is quite simple: it's been the way of life in Java, and you're likely to confront legacy code that's using shared mutability.

I certainly hope you'll heavily lean toward isolated mutability or pure immutability for any new code, even in existing projects. My goal in this chapter is to help cope with legacy code—the menacing code you've soldiered to refactor.

5.1 Shared Mutability != public

Shared mutability is not restricted to public fields. You may be thinking "Gee, all my fields are private, so I have nothing to worry about," but it's not that simple.

A shared variable is accessed, for read or write, by more than one thread. On the other hand, a variable that's never accessed by more than one thread—ever—is isolated and not shared. Shared mutable variables can really mess things up if we fail to ensure visibility or avoid race conditions. It's rumored that shared mutability is the leading cause of insomnia among Java programmers.

Irrespective of access privileges, we must ensure that any value passed to other methods as parameters is thread safe. We must assume that the methods we call will access the passed instance from more than one thread. So, passing an instance that's not thread safe will not help you sleep better at night. The same concern exists with the references we return from methods. In other words, don't let any non-thread-safe references *escape*. See *Java Concurrency in Practice* [Goe06] for an extensive discussion of how to deal with escaping.

Escaping is tricky; we may not even realize until we closely examine the code that it's there. In addition to passing and returning references, variables may escape if we directly set references into other objects or into static fields. A variable may also escape if we passed it into a collection, like the BlockingQueue we discussed previously. Don't be surprised if the hair on the back of your neck stands up the next time you open code with mutable variables.

5.2 Spotting Concurrency Issues

Let's learn to identify the perils in shared mutability with an example and see how to fix those problems. We'll refactor a piece of code that controls a fancy energy source. It allows users to drain energy, and it automatically replenishes the source at regular intervals. Let's first glance at the code that's crying for our help:

tamingSharedMutability/originalcode/EnergySource.java
```java
//Bad code
public class EnergySource {
  private final long MAXLEVEL = 100;
  private long level = MAXLEVEL;
  private boolean keepRunning = true;

  public EnergySource() {
    new Thread(new Runnable() {
      public void run() { replenish(); }
    }).start();
  }

  public long getUnitsAvailable() { return level; }

  public boolean useEnergy(final long units) {
    if (units > 0 && level >= units) {
      level -= units;
      return true;
    }
    return false;
  }

  public void stopEnergySource() { keepRunning = false; }

  private void replenish() {
    while(keepRunning) {
      if (level < MAXLEVEL) level++;

      try { Thread.sleep(1000); } catch(InterruptedException ex) {}
    }
  }
}
```

Identify the concurrency issues in the EnergySource class. There are a few easy-to-spot problems but some hidden treasures as well, so take your time.

Done? OK, let's go over it. The EnergySource's methods may be called from any thread. So, the nonfinal private variable level is a shared mutable variable, but it's not thread safe. We have unprotected access to it, from a thread-safety viewpoint, in most of the methods. That leads to both the visibility concern—calling thread may not see the change, because it was not asked to cross the memory barrier—and race condition.

That was easy to spot, but there's more.

The replenish() method spends most of the time sleeping, but it's wasting an entire thread. If we try to create a large number of EnergySources, we'll get an OutOfMemoryError because of the creation of too many threads—typically the JVM will allow us to create only a few thousand threads.

The EnergySource breaks the class invariant.[1] A well-constructed object ensures that none of its methods is called before the object itself is in a valid state. However, the EnergySource's constructor violated invariant when it invoked the replenish() method from another thread before the constructor completed. Also, Thread's start() method automatically inserts a memory barrier, and so it escapes the object before its initiation is complete. Starting threads from within constructors is a really bad idea, as we'll discuss in the next section.

That's quite a few issues for such a small piece of code, eh? Let's fix them one by one. I prefer not to fix problems concurrently so I can focus on solving each in turn.

5.3 Preserve Invariant

We may be tempted to start threads from constructors to get background tasks running as soon as an object is instantiated. That's a good intention with undesirable side effects. The call to start() forces a memory barrier, exposing the partially created object to other threads. Also, the thread we started may invoke methods on the instance before its construction is complete.

An object should preserve its invariant, and therefore starting threads from within constructors is forbidden.

---

1. Class invariant is a condition that every object of the class must satisfy at all times—see *What Every Programming Should Know About Object-Oriented Design* [Pag95] and *Object-Oriented Software Construction* [Mey97]. In other words, we should never be able to access an object in an invalid state.

EnergySource is clearly in violation on this count. We could move the thread-starting code from the constructor to a separate instance method. However, that creates a new set of problems. We have to deal with method calls that may arrive before the thread-starting method is called, or a programmer may simply forget to call it. We could put a flag to deal with that, but that'd lead to ugly duplicated code. We also have to prevent the thread-starting method from being called more than once on any instance.

On the one hand, we shouldn't start threads from constructors, and on the other hand, we don't want to open up the instance for any use without fully creating it to satisfaction. There's gotta be a way to get out of this pickle.

The answer is in the first item in *Effective Java* [Blo08]: "Consider static factory methods instead of constructors." Create the instance in the static factory method and start the thread before returning the instance to the caller.

tamingSharedMutability/fixingconstructor/EnergySource.java

```
//Fixing constructor...other issues pending
private EnergySource() {}

private void init() {
  new Thread(new Runnable() {
    public void run() { replenish(); }
  }).start();
}

public static EnergySource create() {
  final EnergySource energySource = new EnergySource();
  energySource.init();
  return energySource;
}
```

We keep the constructor private and uncomplicated. We could perform simple calculations in the constructor but avoid any method calls here. The private method init() does the bulk of the work we did earlier in the constructor. Invoke this method from within the static factory method create(). We avoided the invariant violation and, at the same time, ensured that our instance is in a valid state with its background task started upon creation.

Look around your own project; do you see threads being started in constructors? If you do, you have another cleanup task to add to your refactoring tasks list.

5.4 Mind Your Resources

Threads are limited resources, and we shouldn't create them arbitrarily. EnergySource's replenish() method is wasting a thread and limits the number of instances we can create. If more instances created their own threads like that, we'd run into resource availability problems. The replenish operation is short and quick, so it's an ideal candidate to run in a timer.

We could use a java.util.Timer. For a better throughput, especially if we expect to have a number of instances of EnergySource, it's better to reuse threads from a thread pool. ScheduledThreadPoolExecutor provides an elegant mechanism to run periodic tasks. We must ensure that the tasks handle their exceptions; otherwise, it would result in suppression of their future execution.

Let's refactor EnergySource to run the replenish() method as a periodic task.

tamingSharedMutability/periodictask/EnergySource.java

```
//Using Timer...other issues pending
public class EnergySource {
  private final long MAXLEVEL = 100;
  private long level = MAXLEVEL;
  private static final ScheduledExecutorService replenishTimer =
    Executors.newScheduledThreadPool(10);
  private ScheduledFuture<?> replenishTask;

  private EnergySource() {}

  private void init() {
    replenishTask = replenishTimer.scheduleAtFixedRate(new Runnable() {
      public void run() { replenish(); }
    }, 0, 1, TimeUnit.SECONDS);
  }

  public static EnergySource create() {
    final EnergySource energySource = new EnergySource();
    energySource.init();
    return energySource;
  }

  public long getUnitsAvailable() { return level; }

  public boolean useEnergy(final long units) {
    if (units > 0 && level >= units) {
      level -= units;
      return true;
    }
    return false;
  }

  public void stopEnergySource() { replenishTask.cancel(false); }

  private void replenish() { if (level < MAXLEVEL) level++; }
}
```

In addition to being kind on resource usage, the code got simpler. We got rid of the keepRunning field and simply canceled the task in the stopEnergySource() method. Instead of starting a thread for each instance of EnergySource, the init() method scheduled the timer to run the replenish() method. This method, in turn, got even simpler—we're not concerned about the sleep or the timing, so instead we focus on the logic to increase the energy level.

We made the reference replenishTimer a static field. This allows us to share a pool of threads to run the replenish() operation on multiple instances of EnergySource. We can vary the number of threads in this thread pool, currently set to 10, based on the duration of the timed task and the number of instances. Since the replenish() task is very small, a small pool size is adequate.

Making the replenishTimer field static helped us share the pool of threads in the ScheduledThreadPoolExecutor. However, this leads to one complication: we have to figure out a way to shut it down. By default the executor threads run as nondaemon threads and will prevent the shutdown of the JVM if we don't explicitly shut them down. There are at least two ways[2] to handle this:

- Provide a static method in the EnergySource class, like so:

```
public static void shutdown() { replenishTimer.shutdown(); }
```

  There are two problems with this approach. The users of the EnergySource have to remember to call this method. We also have to add logic to deal with instances of EnergySource being created after the call to shutdown().

- We may pass an additional ThreadFactory parameter to the newScheduledThread-Pool() method. This factory can ensure all the threads created are daemon threads, like so:

```
private static final ScheduledExecutorService replenishTimer =
  Executors.newScheduledThreadPool(10,
      new java.util.concurrent.ThreadFactory() {
    public Thread newThread(Runnable runnable) {
      Thread thread = new Thread(runnable);
      thread.setDaemon(true);
      return thread;
    }
  });
```

  The main disadvantage of this approach is more code for us to write and maintain.

---

2. The Google Guava API (http://code.google.com/p/guava-libraries/), which provides quite a few convenience wrappers on top of the JDK concurrency API, also provides a method to create pools that exits automatically.

Our EnergySource just lost a few pounds and is more scalable than when we created the thread internally.

Examine your own project to see where you're creating threads, especially using the Thread class. Evaluate those situations to see whether you can use a periodic task scheduler like we did.

5.5 Ensure Visibility

The memory barrier has to be crossed at the appropriate time. Crossing it in the constructor is not good, and we fixed that problem in the example. However, we must ensure that other methods that access the shared mutable variable level cross the memory barrier. See *What's This Memory Barrier?*, on page 9 to refresh your memory about why to cross the memory barrier.

If we consider race conditions only, we may argue against synchronizing getter methods; we may get convinced that the slightly old copy of a variable's value is adequate. The motivation to synchronize or lock getters is as much about visibility as race conditions—if we fail to cross the memory barrier, our thread is not guaranteed to see the change for an unpredictable duration of time in the future.

Let's ensure that the methods of EnergySource cross the memory barrier; using the synchronized keyword is the easiest way to achieve that. Let's use that now to provide visibility and then improve on it later—I try to follow the "make it work; make it better" motto.

Each method that touches the mutable variable level to read or write needs to cross the memory barrier, so we'll mark them all as synchronized. The original version will not allow the replenish() method to be marked synchronized since it looped indefinitely. The latest version here has no such problem, since it's a short, quick method invoked from the timer. Here's the new version that ensures visibility:

tamingSharedMutability/ensurevisibility/EnergySource.java
```
//Ensure visibility...other issues pending
  //...
  public synchronized long getUnitsAvailable() { return level; }

  public synchronized boolean useEnergy(final long units) {
    if (units > 0 && level >= units) {
      level -= units;
      return true;
    }
    return false;
  }
```

```
public synchronized void stopEnergySource() {
  replenishTask.cancel(false);
}

private synchronized void replenish() { if (level < MAXLEVEL) level++; }
}
```

We marked the methods getUnitsAvailable(), useEnergy(), and replenish() as synchronized since these methods touch the level variable. Even though we'd expect only one thread to invoke stopEnergySource(), let's go ahead and synchronize it just in case it is invoked from more than one thread. After all, that's the whole point of providing thread safety.

Examine your own project and see whether all access to mutable variables, both getters and setters, cross the memory barrier using synchronized or one of the other relevant constructs. Access to final immutable variables don't need to cross memory barriers, since they don't change and cached values are as good as the one in memory.

5.6 Enhance Concurrency

I could build a moat filled with alligators around my house to provide safety, but that would make it a challenge for me to get in and out each day. Overly conservative synchronization is like that; it can provide thread safety but makes code slow. We want to ensure that the synchronization happens at the right level for each class so we don't compromise thread safety but still enjoy good concurrency.

Synchronizing instances is fairly common but has some problems. For one, its scope is the entire object, and that becomes the level of granularity for concurrency. This limits us to at most one synchronized operation on the entire object at any time. If all the operations on the object are mutually exclusive, such as add and remove on a collection, then this is not entirely bad, though it can certainly be better. However, if the object can support multiple operations, such as drive() and sing(), that can run concurrently but need to be synchronized with other operations, such as drive() and tweet(), which should be mutually exclusive, then synchronizing on the instance will not help with speed. In this case, we should have multiple synchronization points within the objects for these methods.

EnergySource managed to ensure visibility and thread safety. However, the synchronization is overreaching. There's little reason to be synchronizing on the instance in this case. Let's fix that.

Since the level was the only mutable field in the class, we can move synchronization to that directly. This will not work all the time, however. If we had more than one field, we may have to protect access around changes to multiple fields. So, we may have to provide one or more explicit Lock instances, as we'll see later.

We've determined that it would be nice to move the synchronization to the level variable. However, there's a slight problem in that Java does not allow us to lock on primitive types like long. We can get around that constraint by changing the variable to AtomicLong from long. This will provide fine-grained thread safety around the access to this variable. Let's take a look at the modified code first before we discuss it further:

tamingSharedMutability/enhanceconcurrency/EnergySource.java
```java
public class EnergySource {
  private final long MAXLEVEL = 100;
  private final AtomicLong level = new AtomicLong(MAXLEVEL);
  private static final ScheduledExecutorService replenishTimer =
    Executors.newScheduledThreadPool(10);
  private ScheduledFuture<?> replenishTask;

  private EnergySource() {}

  private void init() {
    replenishTask = replenishTimer.scheduleAtFixedRate(new Runnable() {
      public void run() { replenish(); }
    }, 0, 1, TimeUnit.SECONDS);
  }

  public static EnergySource create() {
    final EnergySource energySource = new EnergySource();
    energySource.init();
    return energySource;
  }

  public long getUnitsAvailable() { return level.get(); }

  public boolean useEnergy(final long units) {
    final long currentLevel = level.get();
    if (units > 0 && currentLevel >= units) {
      return level.compareAndSet(currentLevel, currentLevel - units);
    }
    return false;
  }

  public synchronized void stopEnergySource() {
    replenishTask.cancel(false);
  }
```

```
    private void replenish() {
        if (level.get() < MAXLEVEL) level.incrementAndGet();
    }
}
```

We got rid of the synchronized marking from getUnitsAvailable(), since the AtomicLong takes care of thread safety and visibility for access to the value it holds.

We also removed the synchronized from the method useEnergy(). However, the improved concurrency comes with a slight change in semantics. Earlier we locked out any access while we examined the availability of energy. If we found enough energy, we were guaranteed to have it. However, that lowered concurrency; while one thread took the time, all others interacting with the EnergySource were blocked. In this improved version, multiple threads can compete for the energy at the same time without holding exclusive locks. If two or more threads compete at the same time, one of them would succeed, and the others would simply have to retry. We have much better speed for reads and safety for writes as well.

The replenish() is also not asking for an exclusive lock. It grabs the level in a thread-safe manner and then, without holding any lock, increments the value. This is OK since there is only one thread increasing the energy level. If the method found the value to be lower than MAXLEVEL, it remains lower, even though the value may decrease. The increment itself is thread safe, and there is no issue of consistency.

We've left the stopEnergySource() method marked synchronized because the call to this method will be so infrequent there's no need to make this locking any more granular at this point. Later in *Creating Transactions in Java*, on page 105, we'll look at an alternative way to implement this method.

Revisit your own project and look for places where you can improve concurrency without compromising thread safety. Check to see whether there are places where you can introduce lock objects instead of synchronizing on the entire instance. While at it, ensure proper synchronization is in place for all methods that deal with mutable state, both reads and writes.

5.7 Ensure Atomicity

The previous example had no explicit synchronization in code, but any related euphoria is short-lived. We can't avoid synchronization if our mutable state has more than one related or dependent variable and we use the JDK concurrency API. Let's see how.

Our success with the refactoring efforts so far did not go unnoticed. We've now been asked to make an enhancement: to keep track of the energy source's usage. Each time the energy source is drained, we need to keep a count. This means we need to ensure that the changes to level and to the new variable usage are atomic. In other words, changes to both of them in a thread should be kept or both of them discarded. We should never be able to see change to one of the fields and not the other.

This brings back the need for explicit synchronization in code. Using synchronized is the simplest option, but that would limit concurrency among multiple readers. If we don't mind a reader blocking another reader, then we should certainly favor this simplicity. However, if we like a greater degree of concurrency and don't mind trading some complexity for that, then we may use a ReentrantReadWriteLock. This provides a pair of locks, a read lock and a write lock, that readers and writers can use, respectively. Using this lock will allow us to have multiple concurrent readers or one exclusive writer at any given instance. Let's use this lock in the example. Since we're using explicit locks, we can scale back to a simple long instead of the AtomicLong for the level field.

tamingSharedMutability/ensureatomicity/EnergySource.java

```java
public class EnergySource {
  private final long MAXLEVEL = 100;
  private long level = MAXLEVEL;
  private long usage = 0;
  private final ReadWriteLock monitor = new ReentrantReadWriteLock();
  private static final ScheduledExecutorService replenishTimer =
    Executors.newScheduledThreadPool(10);
  private ScheduledFuture<?> replenishTask;

  private EnergySource() {}

  private void init() {
    replenishTask = replenishTimer.scheduleAtFixedRate(new Runnable() {
      public void run() { replenish(); }
    }, 0, 1, TimeUnit.SECONDS);
  }

  public static EnergySource create() {
    final EnergySource energySource = new EnergySource();
    energySource.init();
    return energySource;
  }

  public long getUnitsAvailable() {
    monitor.readLock().lock();
    try {
      return level;
```

```java
      } finally {
        monitor.readLock().unlock();
      }
    }

    public long getUsageCount() {
      monitor.readLock().lock();
      try {
        return usage;
      } finally {
        monitor.readLock().unlock();
      }
    }

    public boolean useEnergy(final long units) {
      monitor.writeLock().lock();
      try {
        if (units > 0 && level >= units) {
          level -= units;
          usage++;
          return true;
        } else {
          return false;
        }
      } finally {
        monitor.writeLock().unlock();
      }
    }

    public synchronized void stopEnergySource() {
      replenishTask.cancel(false);
    }

    private void replenish() {
      monitor.writeLock().lock();
      try {
        if (level < MAXLEVEL) { level++;  }
      } finally {
        monitor.writeLock().unlock();
      }
    }
  }
```

We introduced two new fields: usage, to count how many times the energy source is drained, and monitor, an instance of ReentrantReadWriteLock, to ensure changes to the two mutable variables are atomic. In the useEnergy() method, we first acquire a write lock. We can use a timeout on the lock if we desire. Once the write lock is acquired, we change the level and the usage variables. Within the safe haven of the finally block, we release the acquired lock.

Similarly, we acquire the write lock in the replenish() method as well. This ensures that changes made by useEnergy() and replenish() are mutually exclusive.

We need to use a lock in the get methods to ensure the visibility of the fields and also that partial changes within useEnergy() are not seen. By using a read lock, we allow multiple gets to run concurrently and block only when a write is in progress.

This code provides fairly decent concurrency and thread safety at the same time. We do have to be vigilant to ensure that we haven't compromised safety at any point. The code is more complex than the previous version, which, unfortunately, makes it easier to make mistakes. In the next chapter, we'll see how we can avoid explicit synchronization.

5.8 Recap

Working with shared mutable state is a huge burden that requires us to endure added complexity and the accompanied greater chances of error. When refactoring code, look out for some common concurrency-related mistakes:

- Don't create threads from within constructors; instead, create them in static factory methods—see Section 5.3, *Preserve Invariant*, on page 75.

- Don't create arbitrary threads; instead, use a pool of threads to reduce the tasks startup time and resource use—see Section 5.4, *Mind Your Resources*, on page 76.

- Ensure that access to mutable fields cross memory barrier and are visible to threads properly—see Section 5.5, *Ensure Visibility*, on page 79.

- Evaluate the granularity of locks and promote concurrency. Ensure that the locks are not overly conservative but are at the right level to provide adequate thread safety and concurrency at the same time—see Section 5.6, *Enhance Concurrency*, on page 80.

- When working with multiple mutable fields, verify that the access to these variables is atomic; that is, other threads don't see partial changes to these fields—see Section 5.7, *Ensure Atomicity*, on page 82.

In this chapter, we saw how hard explicit synchronization can be. In the next chapter, we'll discuss how to avoid explicit synchronization altogether, an approach that's relatively new to the JVM.

Part III

Software Transactional Memory

We are governed not by armies and police but by ideas.

> *Mona Caird*

CHAPTER 6

Introduction to Software Transactional Memory

Recall the last time you finished a project where you had to synchronize shared mutable variables? Instead of relaxing and enjoying that feeling of a job well done, you probably had a nagging feeling of doubt, wondering whether you managed to synchronize in all the right places. My programming has involved quite a few such unnerving moments. That's mostly because of shared mutable state in Java failing the principle of least surprises. If we forget to synchronize, then unpredictable and potentially catastrophic results await us. But, to err is human; to forget is our nature. Rather than punish us, the tools we rely on should compensate for our deficiencies and help reach the targets our creative minds seek. For predictable behavior and results, we need to look beyond the JDK.

In this chapter, we'll learn how to play it safe with shared mutability using the Software Transactional Memory (STM) model popularized by Clojure. Where possible, we can switch to or mix in Clojure on projects. But we're not forced to use Clojure, because there are ways to use STM directly in Java, thanks to nice tools like Multiverse and Akka. In this chapter, we'll learn STM, a little about what it looks like in Clojure, and then how to program transactional memory in Java and Scala. This model of programming is quite suitable when we have frequent reads and very infrequent write collisions—it's simple to use yet gives predictable results.

6.1 Synchronization Damns Concurrency

Synchronization has some fundamental flaws.

If we use it improperly or forget it totally, the changes made by a thread may not be visible to other threads. We often learn the hard way where we need to synchronize in order to ensure visibility and avoid race conditions.

Unfortunately, when we synchronize, we force contending threads to wait. Concurrency is affected by the granularity of synchronization, so placing this in the hands of programmers increases the opportunity to make it less efficient or outright wrong.

Synchronization can lead to a number of liveness problems. It's easy to deadlock an application if it holds locks while waiting for others. It's also easy to run into livelock issues where threads continuously fail to gain a particular lock.

We may try to improve concurrency by making the locks fine-grained or granular. Although this is a good idea in general, the biggest risk is failing to synchronize at the right level. What's worse, we get no indication of failure to synchronize properly. Furthermore, we've only moved the point where the thread waits: the thread still is requesting an exclusive access and is expecting other threads to wait.

That's simply life in the big city for most Java programmers using the JDK concurrency facilities. We've been led down the path of the imperative style of programming with mutable state for so long that it's very hard to see alternatives to synchronization, but there are.

6.2 The Deficiency of the Object Model

As Java programmers, we're well versed in object-oriented programming (OOP). But the language has greatly influenced the way we model OO apps. OOP didn't quite turn out to be what Alan Kay had in mind when he coined the term. His vision was primarily message passing, and he wanted to get rid of data (he viewed systems to be built using messages that are passed between biological cell-like objects that performed operations but did not hold any state)—see "The Meaning of Object-Oriented Programming" in Appendix 2, *Web Resources*, on page 255. Somewhere along the way, OO languages started down the path of data hiding through Abstract Data Types (ADTs), binding data with procedure or combining state and behavior. This largely led us toward encapsulating and mutating state. In the process, we ended up merging the identity with state—the merging of the instance with its data.

This merging of identity and state snuck up on many Java programmers in a way that its consequences may not be obvious. When we traverse a pointer or reference to an instance, we land at the chunk of memory that holds its state. It feels natural to manipulate the data at that location. The location represents the instance and what it contains. The combined identity and state worked out to be quite simple and easy to comprehend. However, this had some serious ramifications from the concurrency point of view.

We'll run into concurrency issues if, for example, we're running a report to print various details about a bank account—the number, current balance, transactions, minimum balance, and so on. The reference on hand is the gateway to the state that could change at any time. So, we're forced to lock other threads while we view the account. And the result is low concurrency. The problem didn't start with the locking but with the merging of the account identity with its state.

We were told that OO programming models the real word. Sadly, the real world does not quite behave as the current OO paradigm tries to model. In the real world, the state does not change; the identity does. We'll discuss next how that's true.

6.3 Separation of Identity and State

Quick, what's the price of Google stock? We may argue that the value of the stock changes by the minute when the market is open, but that's in some way just playing with words. To take a simple example, the closing price of Google stock on December 10, 2010, was $592.21, and that'll never change—it's immutable and written in history. We're looking at a snapshot of its value at a said time. Sure, the price of Google stock today is different from the one on that day. If we check back a few minutes later (assuming the market is open), we're looking at a different value, but the older values don't change. We can change the way we view objects, and that changes the way we use them. Separate identity from its immutable state value. We'll see how this change enables lock-free programming, improves concurrency, and reduces contention to the bare minimum.

This separation of identity from state is pure brilliance—a key step that Rich Hickey took in implementing Clojure's STM model; see "Values and Change: Clojure's approach to Identity and State" in Appendix 2, *Web Resources*, on page 255. Imagine our Google stock object has two parts; the first part represents the stock's identity, which in turn has a pointer to the second part, immutable state of the latest value of the stock, as shown in Figure 9, *Separation of mutable identity from immutable state value*, on page 92.

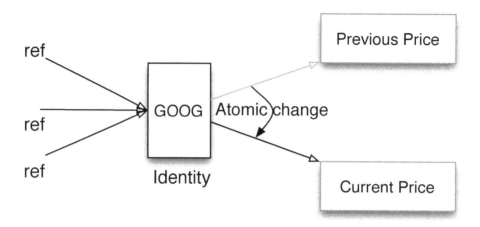

Figure 9—Separation of mutable identity from immutable state value

When we receive a new price, we add to the historic price index, without changing anything that exists. Since the old values are immutable, we share existing data. So, we have no duplication and can enjoy faster operations as well if we use persistent data structures for this, as we discussed in Section 3.6, *Persistent/Immutable Data Structures*, on page 39. Once the new data is in place, we make a quick change of the identity to point to the new value.

The separation of identity from state is pure bliss for concurrency. We don't have to block any requests for stock price. Since the state does not change, we can readily hand over the pointer to the requesting thread. Any request arriving after we change the identity will see the update. Nonblocking reads means higher scalable concurrency. We simply need to ensure that the threads get a consistent view of their world. The best part of it all is that we don't have to; STM does it for us. I'm sure you're eager to learn more about STM now.

6.4 Software Transactional Memory

The separation of identity from state helps STM solve the two major concerns with synchronization: crossing the memory barrier and preventing race conditions. We'll first look at STM in the context of Clojure and then use it in Java.

Clojure removes the menacing details of memory synchronization (see *Programming Clojure* [Hal09] and *The Joy of Clojure* [FH11]) by placing access to memory within *transactions*. Clojure keenly watches over and coordinates the activities of threads. If there are no conflicts—for example, threads working with different accounts—then no locks are involved, and there are no delays, resulting in maximum concurrency. When two threads try to access the same data, the transaction manager steps in to resolve the conflict, and again, no explicit locking is involved in our code. Let's explore how this works.

By design, values are immutable, and identities are mutable only within transactions in Clojure. There's simply no way to change the state, and no programming facility for that, in Clojure. If any attempt is made to change the identity of an object outside any transactions, it will fail with a stern IllegalStateException. On the other hand, when bound by transactions, changes are instantaneous when there are no conflicts. If conflicts arise, Clojure will automatically roll back transactions and retry. It's our responsibility to ensure that the code within the transactions is idempotent—in functional programming we try to avoid side effects, so this goes well with the programming model in Clojure.

It's time to see an example of Clojure STM. We use refs to create mutable identities in Clojure. A ref provides coordinated synchronous change[1] to the identity of the immutable state it represents. Let's create a ref and try to change it.

usingTransactionalMemory/clojure/mutate.clj
```
(def balance (ref 0))

(println "Balance is" @balance)

(ref-set balance 100)

(println "Balance is now" @balance)
```

We defined a variable named balance and marked it as mutable using ref. Now balance represents a mutable identity with an immutable value of 0. Then we print the current value of this variable. Next we attempt to modify balance using the command ref-set. If this succeeded, we should see the new balance printed by the last statement. Let's see how this turns out; I'm

---

1. Clojure provides a few other models for concurrency such as Agents, Atoms, and Vars that we will not cover here; please refer to Clojure documentation or books for more details.

simply running this script using clj mutable.clj. Refer to Clojure documentation on how to install and run it on your system.

```
Balance is 0
Exception in thread "main"
  java.lang.IllegalStateException: No transaction running (mutate.clj:0)
...
```

The first two statements worked well: we were able to print the initial balance of 0. Our effort to change the value, however, failed with an IllegalStateException. We made the Clojure gods angry by mutating the variable outside of transactions. Contrast this clear failure to the nefarious behavior of Java when we modify a shared mutable variable without synchronization. This is quite an improvement since we'd much rather have our code behave right or fail loudly than quietly produce unpredictable results. I'd invite you to celebrate, but I see you're eager to fix that blunt error from Clojure STM, so let's move on.

Creating a transaction is easy in Clojure. We simply wrap the block of code in a dosync call. Structurally this feels like the synchronized block in Java, but there are quite a few differences:

- We get a clear warning if we forget to place dosync around mutating code.

- Rather than create an exclusive lock, dosync lets code compete fairly with other threads by wrapping in a transaction.

- Since we don't perform any explicit locks, we don't have to worry about lock order and can enjoy a deadlock-free concurrency.

- Rather than forcing design-time forethoughts of "who locks what and in which order," STM provides a simple runtime transactional composition of locks.

- Having no explicit locks means no programmer placed conservative mutually exclusive blocks of code. The result is maximum concurrency dictated directly and dynamically by the application behavior and data access.

When a transaction is in progress, if there was no conflict with other threads/transactions, the transaction can complete, and its changes can be written to the memory. However, as soon as Clojure finds that some other transaction has progressed far ahead in a way to jeopardize this transaction, it quietly rolls back the changes and repeats the transaction. Let's fix the code so we can successfully change the balance variable.

```
usingTransactionalMemory/clojure/mutatesuccess.clj
(def balance (ref 0))

(println "Balance is" @balance)

(dosync
  (ref-set balance 100))

(println "Balance is now" @balance)
```

The only change in the code was to wrap the call to ref-set into a call to dosync. We certainly are not restricted to one line of code within dosync; we can wrap an entire block of code or several expressions within a transaction. Let's run the code to see the change.

```
Balance is 0
Balance is now 100
```

The state value of 0 for the balance is immutable, but the identity variable balance is mutable. Within the transaction we first created a new value of 100 (we need to get used to the notion of immutable value), but the old value of 0 is still there, and balance is pointing to it at this moment. Once we created the new value, we ask Clojure to quickly modify the pointer in balance to the new value. If there are no other references to the old value, the garbage collector will take care of it appropriately.

Clojure provides three options to modify a mutable identity, all only from within a transaction:

- ref-set sets the value of the identity and returns the value.

- alter sets the in-transaction value of the identity to a value resulting from applying a specified function and returns the value. This is the most preferred form to modify a mutable identity.

- commute separates the in-transaction change from the commit point. It sets the in-transaction-value of the identity to a value resulting from applying a specified function and returns the value. Then, during the commit point, the value of the identity is set to the result from applying the specified function using the most recent committed value of the identity.

commute is useful when we're happy with last-one-in-wins behavior and provides greater concurrency than alter. However, in most situations, alter is more suitable than commute.

In addition to refs, Clojure also provides atoms. These provide synchronous change to data; however, unlike refs, the changes are uncoordinated and can't be grouped with other changes in a transaction. Atoms don't participate in transactions (we can think of each change to atom as belonging to a separate transaction). For isolated, discrete changes, use atoms; for more grouped or coordinated changes, use refs.

6.5   Transactions in STM

You've undoubtedly used transactions in databases and are familiar with their Atomicity, Consistency, Isolation, and Durability (ACID) properties. Clojure's STM provides the first three of these properties, but it doesn't provide durability, because the data is entirely in memory and not in a database or file system.

Atomicity: STM transactions are atomic. Either all the changes we make in a transaction are visible outside the transaction or none of them are visible. All changes to refs in a transaction are kept or none at all.

Consistency: Either the transactions entirely run to completion and we see its net change or they fail, leaving things unaffected. From the outside of these transactions, we see one change consistently following another. For example, at the end of two separate and concurrent deposit and withdraw transactions, the balance is left in a consistent state with the cumulative effect of both actions.

Isolation: Transactions don't see partial changes of other transactions, and changes are seen only upon successful completion.

These properties focus on the integrity and visibility of data. However, the isolation does not mean a lack of coordination. To the contrary, STM closely monitors the progress of all transactions and tries to help each one of them run to completion (barring any application-based exceptions).

Clojure STM uses Multiversion Concurrency Control (MVCC) much like databases do. STM concurrency control is similar to optimistic locking in databases. When we start a transaction, STM notes the timestamps and copies the refs our transaction will use. Since the state is immutable, this copying of refs is quick and inexpensive. When we make a "change" to any immutable state, we're really not modifying the values. Instead, we're creating new copies of these values. The copies are kept local to the transaction, and thanks to persistent data structures (Section 3.6, *Persistent/Immutable Data Structures*, on page 39), this step is quick as well. If at any point STM determines that the refs we've changed have been modified by another transaction, it aborts and retries our transaction. When a transaction successfully completes, the changes are written to memory and the timestamps are updated (see Figure 9, *Separation of mutable identity from immutable state value*, on page 92).

6.6 Concurrency Using STM

Transactions are nice, but what happens if two transactions try to change the same identity? Sorry, I didn't mean to keep you on the edge of your seat this long. We'll take a look at a couple of examples of that in this section.

A word of caution, though, before we walk through the examples. In production code, make sure that transactions are idempotent and don't have any side effects, because they may be retried a number of times. That means no printing to the console, no logging, no sending out emails, and no making any irreversible operations within transactions. If we do any of these, we're responsible for reversing the operations or dealing with the consequences. In general, it's better to gather up these side-effect actions and perform them after the transaction succeeds.

Contrary to my advice, we'll see print statements within transactions in the examples. This is purely for illustrative purpose. Don't try this at the office!

We already know how to change the balance within a transaction. Let's now let multiple transactions compete for the balance:

usingTransactionalMemory/clojure/concurrentChangeToBalance.clj
```
(defn deposit [balance amount]
  (dosync
    (println "Ready to deposit..." amount)
    (let [current-balance @balance]
      (println "simulating delay in deposit...")
      (. Thread sleep 2000)
      (alter balance + amount)
      (println "done with deposit of" amount))))

(defn withdraw [balance amount]
  (dosync
    (println "Ready to withdraw..." amount)
    (let [current-balance @balance]
      (println "simulating delay in withdraw...")
      (. Thread sleep 2000)
      (alter balance - amount)
      (println "done with withdraw of" amount))))

(def balance1 (ref 100))

(println "Balance1 is" @balance1)
```

```
(future (deposit balance1 20))
(future (withdraw balance1 10))

(. Thread sleep 10000)

(println "Balance1 now is" @balance1)
```

We created two transactions in this example, one for deposit and the other for withdrawal. In the function deposit() we first get a local copy of the given balance. We then simulate a delay to set the transactions on a collision course. After the delay, we increase the balance. The withdraw() is very similar, except that we decrease the balance. It's time to exercise these two methods. Let's first initialize the variable balance1 to 100 and let the previous two methods run in two separate threads using the future() function. Go ahead and run the code and observe the output:

```
Balance1 is 100
Ready to deposit... 20
simulating delay in deposit...
Ready to withdraw... 10
simulating delay in withdraw...
done with deposit of 20
Ready to withdraw... 10
simulating delay in withdraw...
done with withdraw of 10
Balance1 now is 110
```

Both the functions obtained their own local copy of the balance. Right after the simulated delay, the deposit() transaction completed, but the withdraw() transaction was not that lucky. The balance was changed behind its back, and so the change it attempts to make is no longer valid. Clojure STM quietly aborted the transaction and retried. If we did not have these print statements, we'd be oblivious of these activities. All that should matter is that the net effect of balance is consistent and reflects both the deposit and the withdrawal.

We intentionally set the two transactions on a collision course in this example by prefetching the balance and delaying the execution. If we remove the let statement from both the transactions, we'll notice that both the transactions complete in a consistent manner without the need for either of them to repeat, showing us that STM provides maximum concurrency while preserving consistency.

We now know how to change a simple variable, but what if we have a collection of values? Lists are immutable in Clojure. However, we can obtain a mutable reference whose identity can change, making it appear as though we changed the list. The list has not changed; we simply changed the view of the list. Let's explore this with an example. My family's wish list originally contains only one item, an iPad. I'd like to add a new MacBook Pro (MBP), and one of my kids wants to add a new bike. So, we set out in two different threads to add these items to the list. Here's some code for that:

```
usingTransactionalMemory/clojure/concurrentListChange.clj
(defn add-item [wishlist item]
  (dosync (alter wishlist conj item)))

(def family-wishlist (ref '("iPad")))
(def original-wishlist @family-wishlist)

(println "Original wish list is" original-wishlist)

(future (addItem family-wishlist "MBP"))
(future (addItem family-wishlist "Bike"))

(. Thread sleep 1000)

(println "Original wish list is" original-wishlist)
(println "Updated wish list is" @family-wishlist)
```

In the add-item() function, we add the given item to the list. The alter function alters the in-transaction ref by applying the provided function, in this case the conj() function. The function conj() returns a new collection with the given element conjoined or added to the collection. We then call the add-item() method from two different threads. Run the code to see the net effect of the two transactions:

```
Original wish list is (iPad)
Original wish list is (iPad)
Updated wish list is (Bike MBP iPad)
```

The original list is immutable, so it remains the same at the end of the code. As we added elements to this list, we were getting new copies of the list. However, since a list is a persistent data structure, we benefited both in memory and in performance from sharing the items (elements) under the hood, as shown in Figure 10, *"Adding" elements to immutable wish list*, on page 100.

Both the state of the list and the reference originalWishList are immutable. familyWishList, however, is a mutable reference. Each of the add item requests run in their own transaction. The first one to succeed changed the mutable reference to the new list (shown as (2) in the figure). However, since the list itself is immutable, the new list is able to share the element "iPad" from the

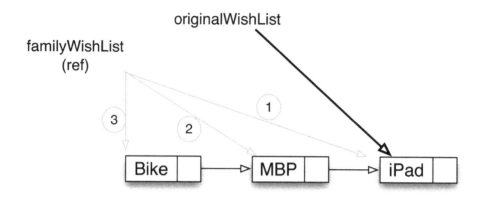

Figure 10—"Adding" elements to immutable wish list

original list. When the second add item succeeds, it in turn shares internally the other two items previously added (shown as (3) in the figure).

Handling Write Skew Anomaly

We saw how STM handles write conflicts between transactions. Sometimes the conflicts are not so direct. Imagine we have a checking account and a savings account in a bank that has placed minimum total balance requirements of $1,000 between the two accounts. Now suppose the balance in these accounts is $500 and $600, respectively. We can withdraw up to $100 from either one of these accounts but not both. If a withdraw of $100 is attempted on each of these accounts sequentially, the first attempt will succeed but not the second. The so-called write skew anomaly will not prevent these two transactions if done concurrently—both transactions see the total balance is more than $1,000 and proceed to modify two different values with no write conflicts. The net result, a balance of $900, is less than the permitted limit. Let's create this anomaly in code, then figure out how to fix it.

usingTransactionalMemory/clojure/writeSkew.clj
```
(def checking-balance (ref 500))
(def savings-balance (ref 600))

(defn withdraw-account [from-balance constraining-balance amount]
  (dosync
    (let [total-balance (+ @from-balance @constraining-balance)]
      (. Thread sleep 1000)
      (if (>= (- total-balance amount) 1000)
        (alter from-balance - amount)
        (println "Sorry, can't withdraw due to constraint violation")))))
```

```
(println "checking-balance is" @checking-balance)
(println "savings-balance is" @savings-balance)
(println "Total balance is" (+ @checking-balance @savings-balance))

(future (withdraw-account checking-balance savings-balance 100))
(future (withdraw-account savings-balance checking-balance 100))

(. Thread sleep 2000)

(println "checking-balance is" @checking-balance)
(println "savings-balance is" @savings-balance)
(println "Total balance is" (+ @checking-balance @savings-balance))
```

We start with the given balances for the two accounts. In the withdraw-account()
function, we first read the balance of the two accounts and compute the
total balance. Then after the induced delay, which puts the transactions on
a collision course, we update the balance of one of the accounts represented
by from-balance only if the total balance is not less than the required minimum.
In the rest of the code, we concurrently run two transactions, where the
first withdraws $100 from the checking balance, while the second withdraws
$100 from savings. Since the two transactions run in isolation and aren't
modifying anything in common, they're quite oblivious of the violation and
fall into the write skew, as we can see from the output:

```
checking-balance is 500
savings-balance is 600
Total balance is 1100
checking-balance is 400
savings-balance is 500
Total balance is 900
```

With Clojure, we can easily avoid write skew with the ensure() method. We
can tell a transaction to keep an eye on a variable that is only read and not
modified. STM will then ensure that the writes are committed only if the
values we've read have not changed outside the transaction; it retries the
transaction otherwise.

Let's modify the withdraw-account() method:

```
Line 1  (defn withdraw-account [from-balance constraining-balance amount]
     2    (dosync
     3      (let [total-balance (+ @from-balance (ensure constraining-balance))]
     4        (. Thread sleep 1000)
     5        (if (>= (- total-balance amount) 1000)
     6          (alter from-balance - amount)
     7          (println "Sorry, can't withdraw due to constraint violation")))))
```

On line 3, we called ensure() on the value constraining-balance, which we read but don't modify in the transaction. At this point, STM places a read lock on that value, preventing other transactions from gaining a write lock. When the transaction nears completion, STM releases all read locks before it performs the commit. This prevents any possibility of deadlock while increasing concurrency.

Even though the two transactions run concurrently as before, with this modified withdraw-account() method calling ensure(), the constraint of total balance is preserved, as we see in the output:

```
checking-balance is 500
savings-balance is 600
Total balance is 1100
checking-balance is 500
savings-balance is 500
Total balance is 1000
Sorry, can't withdraw due to constraint violation
```

The explicit lock-free execution model of STM is quite powerful. When there are no conflicts, there's no blocking at all. When there are conflicts, one winner proceeds without a hitch, while the contenders are repeated. Clojure uses a max number of tries and also ensures two threads do not repeat at the same pace and end up losing out repeatedly. STM is a great model when we have frequent reads and very infrequent write collisions. For example, this model will fit nicely for typical web applications—we generally have several concurrent users performing updates of their own data but have little collision of shared state. Any infrequent write collisions can be resolved effortlessly by STM.

Clojure STM is the aspirin of the programming concurrency world—it can remove so much pain. If we forget to create a transaction, we're sternly rebuked. For simply placing dosync at the right place, we're rewarded with high concurrency and consistency between threads. Such low ceremony, concise, highly expressive, and very predictable behavior all make Clojure STM an option worth serious consideration.

6.7 Concurrency Using Akka/Multiverse STM

We saw how to use STM from within Clojure. I guess by now you're curious how to use STM in Java code. We have a few options for that:

- We can use Clojure STM from within Java. It's fairly simple—wrap the transactional code within an implementation of the Callable interface.

We'll see this in Chapter 7, *STM in Clojure, Groovy, Java, JRuby, and Scala*, on page 141.

- Those among us who're fans of annotations may prefer Multiverse's STM API.

- In addition to using STM, if we plan to use actors, then we'd want to reach for the Akka library.

Multiverse, created by Peter Veentjer, is a Java-based STM implementation. From pure Java code, we can use annotations to indicate transaction boundaries. We can mark individual methods transactional using @TransactionalMethod. Or mark a class with @TransactionalObject to make all its methods transactional. For integration with other JVM languages, Multiverse provides a rich set of APIs to control when transactions start and end.

Akka, created by Jonas Bonér, is a Scala-based solution that can be used from many different JVM languages including Java. Akka provides both actor-based concurrency and STM, as well as an option to mix them both. Akka uses Multiverse for the STM implementation and providing the ACI (subset of ACID) properties.

Akka provides excellent performance, and since it supports both STM and an actor-based model (discussed in Chapter 8, *Favoring Isolated Mutability*, on page 163), we'll use it to illustrate the Java STM examples in this chapter.

Transactions in Akka/Multiverse

Akka uses Multiverse's Clojure-style STM for Java code. The main difference from Clojure, other than Java-introduced verbosity, is that Akka doesn't force us to create a transaction before we can modify a mutable identity. If we don't provide a transaction, Akka/Multiverse wraps the access automatically in a transaction. So, when we're in a transaction, Akka refs behave like Clojure refs, and when we're not in a transaction, they behave like Clojure atoms. In other words, start a transaction to coordinate synchronous change; we get uncoordinated synchronous change otherwise. In any case, Akka ensures that changes to refs are still atomic, isolated, and consistent, while providing varying degree of granularity of coordination.

In Akka, we can configure transactions programmatically at the transaction level or at the application/JVM level using configuration files. We can define a transaction as readonly, and Akka will not permit any changes to any Akka references in the bounds of that transaction. We can gain performance by setting nonmutating transactions as readonly. We can control the maximum number of times Akka will retry transactions in the event of conflicts. There are a number of other parameters we can configure—consult the Akka documentation for details.

Akka extends the nested transaction (see Section 6.9, *Creating Nested Transactions*, on page 111) support of Multiverse, so from within transactions, we can conveniently call methods that start transactions. By default these inner or nested transactions are rolled into an outer transaction.

Using Akka Refs and Transactions

Unlike Clojure, where refs were defined at the language level, Akka can't rely on any existing language support. Instead, Akka provides, as part of the akka.stm package, a managed transactional reference Ref<T> and specialized classes for primitive types such as IntRef, LongRef, and so on. The Ref<T> (and the specialized references) represents the managed mutable identity to an immutable value of type T. Types like Integer, Long, Double, String, and other immutable types fit the bill well to serve as value objects. If we use one of our own classes, we must make sure it's immutable, that is, that it contains only final fields.

We can create a managed transactional reference, which is an instance of Ref<T>, by providing an initial value or by omitting the value, defaulting to null. To obtain the current value from the reference, use the get() method. To change the mutable identity to point to a new value, use the swap() method. These calls are performed within the transaction we provide or in their own individual transactions if none is provided.

When multiple threads try to change the same managed reference, Akka ensures that changes by one are written to memory and the others are retried. The transactional facility takes care of crossing the memory barriers. That is, Akka, through Multiverse, guarantees that the changes to a managed ref committed by a transaction happen before, and are visible to, any reads of the same ref later in other transactions.

6.8 Creating Transactions

We create transactions to coordinate changes to multiple managed references. The transaction will ensure these changes are atomic; that is, all the managed references are committed or all of them are discarded. Outside the transactions, we'll never see any partial changes. We also create transactions to coordinate a read followed by a write to a single ref.

Akka was built on Scala, and we can enjoy its concise API if we're using Scala. For programmers who can't make that switch, Akka also provides a convenient API to use its features from the Java language. Alternately, we may directly use Multiverse STM from Java. We'll see how to create transactions using Akka in Java and Scala in this section.

First we need an example to apply transactions. The EnergySource class we refactored in Chapter 5, *Taming Shared Mutability*, on page 73 used explicit lock and unlock (the final version was in Section 5.7, *Ensure Atomicity*, on page 82). Let's trade those explicit locks/unlocks for Akka's transactional API.

Creating Transactions in Java

For transactional support, extend the Atomic class and place code into the atomically() method of this class to wrap it into a transaction. To run transactional code, call the execute() method of the Atomic instance, like this:

```
return new Atomic<Object>() {
  public Object atomically() {
    //code to run in a transaction...
    return resultObject;
  }
}.execute();
```

The thread that calls the execute() method runs the code within the atomically() method. However, the call is wrapped in a transaction if the caller is not already in a transaction.

Let's implement EnergySource using Akka transactions. As the first step, let's wrap the immutable state in mutable Akka managed references.

```
usingTransactionalMemory/java/stm/EnergySource.java
public class EnergySource {
  private final long MAXLEVEL = 100;
  final Ref<Long> level = new Ref<Long>(MAXLEVEL);
  final Ref<Long> usageCount = new Ref<Long>(0L);
  final Ref<Boolean> keepRunning = new Ref<Boolean>(true);
  private static final ScheduledExecutorService replenishTimer =
    Executors.newScheduledThreadPool(10);
```

level and usageCount are declared as Akka Refs, and each of these holds an immutable Long value. We can't change the value of a Long in Java, but we can change the managed reference (the identity) safely to point to a new value.

In the previous version of EnergySource, the ScheduledExecutorService was used to periodically run the replenish() method each second until it was canceled. Recollect that this required the stopEnergySource() method to be synchronized. In this version, rather than running the method periodically, we schedule it only once at the beginning. Upon each call, we decide, based on the value of the flag keepRunning, if the method should be scheduled again for future execution a second later. This change eliminates the coupling between the stopEnergySource() method and the scheduler/timer. Instead, this method now depends on the flag, which can be easily managed using the STM transaction.

We carry over the code that creates an instance of EnergySource from the previous version and modify it to use the managed reference for the keepRunning flag. In this version, there's no need to synchronize the stopEnergySource() method because it relies on transactions. It's adequate that the swap() method runs in its own transaction, so we don't have to create an explicit transaction.

usingTransactionalMemory/java/stm/EnergySource.java
```
private EnergySource() {}

private void init() {
  replenishTimer.schedule(new Runnable() {
    public void run() {
      replenish();
      if (keepRunning.get()) replenishTimer.schedule(
        this, 1, TimeUnit.SECONDS);
    }
  }, 1, TimeUnit.SECONDS);
}

public static EnergySource create() {
  final EnergySource energySource = new EnergySource();
  energySource.init();
  return energySource;
}

public void stopEnergySource() { keepRunning.swap(false); }
```

The methods that return the current energy level and the usage count will use the managed references, but that requires merely calling the get() method.

usingTransactionalMemory/java/stm/EnergySource.java
```
public long getUnitsAvailable() { return level.get(); }

public long getUsageCount() { return usageCount.get(); }
```

Within the getUnitsAvailable() and getUsageCount() methods, the calls to get() run in their own transactions, since we didn't wrap them explicitly in a transaction.

The useEnergy() method will need an explicit transaction, since we will change both the energy level and the usage count here; we need to ensure that the changes are consistent with the values being read and that the changes to these two fields are atomic. We'll use the Atomic interface and its atomically() method to wrap our code in a transaction.

```
usingTransactionalMemory/java/stm/EnergySource.java
public boolean useEnergy(final long units) {
  return  new Atomic<Boolean>() {
    public Boolean atomically() {
      long currentLevel = level.get();
      if(units > 0 && currentLevel >= units) {
        level.swap(currentLevel - units);
        usageCount.swap(usageCount.get() + 1);
        return true;
      } else {
        return false;
      }
    }
  }.execute();
}
```

In the useEnergy() method we decrement from the current level. We want to ensure that both the get and the set are within the same transaction. So, we wrap the operations in the atomically() method. We finally call execute() to run the sequence of operations in one transaction.

We have one more method to take care of, replenish(), which takes care of refilling the source. We have the same transactional need in this method as well, so we'll use Atomic in it too.

```
usingTransactionalMemory/java/stm/EnergySource.java
  private void replenish() {
    new Atomic() {
      public Object atomically() {
        long currentLevel = level.get();
        if (currentLevel < MAXLEVEL) level.swap(currentLevel + 1);
        return null;
      }
    }.execute();
  }
}
```

Let's exercise the EnergySource using a sample runner code. This code concurrently uses energy, in units of one, from different threads.

```
usingTransactionalMemory/java/stm/UseEnergySource.java
public class UseEnergySource {
  private static final EnergySource energySource = EnergySource.create();

  public static void main(final String[] args)
    throws InterruptedException, ExecutionException {
    System.out.println("Energy level at start: " +
      energySource.getUnitsAvailable());

    List<Callable<Object>> tasks = new ArrayList<Callable<Object>>();
```

```java
    for(int i = 0; i < 10; i++) {
      tasks.add(new Callable<Object>() {
        public Object call() {
          for(int j = 0; j < 7; j++) energySource.useEnergy(1);
          return null;
        }
      });
    }

    final ExecutorService service = Executors.newFixedThreadPool(10);
    service.invokeAll(tasks);

    System.out.println("Energy level at end: " +
      energySource.getUnitsAvailable());
    System.out.println("Usage: " + energySource.getUsageCount());

    energySource.stopEnergySource();
    service.shutdown();
  }
}
```

To compile and run the code, we need to include the Akka-related JARs, as shown next.

```
export AKKA_JARS="$AKKA_HOME/lib/scala-library.jar:\
$AKKA_HOME/lib/akka/akka-stm-1.1.3.jar:\
$AKKA_HOME/lib/akka/akka-actor-1.1.3.jar:\
$AKKA_HOME/lib/akka/multiverse-alpha-0.6.2.jar:\
$AKKA_HOME/config:\
."
```

Define the classpath based on your operating system and location where Akka is installed on your system. Compile the code using the javac compiler and run it using the java command, as shown here:

```
javac -classpath $AKKA_JARS -d . EnergySource.java UseEnergySource.java
java -classpath $AKKA_JARS com.agiledeveloper.pcj.UseEnergySource
```

Go ahead, compile and run the code. The energy source had 100 units to begin with, and we drained 70 units from various threads we created. The net result should be 30 units of energy left. Depending on the timing of re-plenish, the value may appear different, like 31 instead of 30.

```
Energy level at start: 100
Energy level at end: 30
Usage: 70
```

By default Akka prints extra log messages on the standard output. We can silence those messages by simply creating a file named logback.xml in the

$AKKA_HOME/config directory with just the element <configuration /> in it. Since this directory is in the classpath, the logger knows to silence the messages. Instead of silencing the log, we could also configure it with useful options. For details, see instructions at http://logback.qos.ch/manual/configuration.html.

As we see here, Akka quietly managed the transactions behind the scenes. Spend some time playing with that code and experiment with the transactions and threads.

Creating Transactions in Scala

We saw how to create transactions in Java (and I assume you've read that part so we don't have to repeat the details here). We'll need less code to write the same thing in Scala, partly because of the concise nature of Scala but also because of the elegant Akka API that makes use of closures/function values.

It takes a lot less effort to create transactions in Scala compared to Java. All we need is a call to the atomic() method of Stm, like so:

```
atomic {
  //code to run in a transaction....
  /* return */ resultObject
}
```

The closure/function value we pass to atomic() is run in the current thread but within a transaction.

Here's the Scala version of EnergySource using Akka transactions:

usingTransactionalMemory/scala/stm/EnergySource.scala
```
class EnergySource private() {
  private val MAXLEVEL = 100L
  val level = Ref(MAXLEVEL)
  val usageCount = Ref(0L)
  val keepRunning = Ref(true)

  private def init() = {
    EnergySource.replenishTimer.schedule(new Runnable() {
      def run() = {
        replenish
        if (keepRunning.get) EnergySource.replenishTimer.schedule(
          this, 1, TimeUnit.SECONDS)
      }
    }, 1, TimeUnit.SECONDS)
  }

  def stopEnergySource() = keepRunning.swap(false)
```

```scala
  def getUnitsAvailable() = level.get

  def getUsageCount() = usageCount.get

  def useEnergy(units : Long) = {
    atomic {
      val currentLevel = level.get
      if(units > 0 && currentLevel >= units) {
        level.swap(currentLevel - units)
        usageCount.swap(usageCount.get + 1)
        true
      } else false
    }
  }

  private def replenish() =
    atomic { if(level.get < MAXLEVEL) level.swap(level.get + 1) }
}

object EnergySource {
  val replenishTimer = Executors.newScheduledThreadPool(10)

  def create() = {
    val energySource = new EnergySource
    energySource.init
    energySource
  }
}
```

Scala, being a fully object-oriented language, considers static methods in classes as an aberration. So, the factory method create() is moved to the companion object. The rest of the code is very similar to the Java version, but it's concise when compared. We avoided the ceremony of the Atomic class and the execute() method call with the elegant atomic() method call.

The code to exercise the Scala version of EnergySource is shown next. We could have used the JDK ExecutorService to manage threads like in the Java version. Or, we could use Scala actors[2] to spawn threads for each concurrent task. Each task sends a response back to the caller when done. The caller simply uses this response to block, awaiting task completion before moving on.

usingTransactionalMemory/scala/stm/UseEnergySource.scala
```scala
object UseEnergySource {
  val energySource = EnergySource.create()

  def main(args : Array[String]) {
```

---

2. Scala's actor is used here for convenience. Later we'll see how to use the more powerful Akka actors.

```scala
    println("Energy level at start: " + energySource.getUnitsAvailable())

    val caller = self
    for(i <- 1 to 10) actor {
      for(j <- 1 to 7) energySource.useEnergy(1)
      caller ! true
    }

    for(i <- 1 to 10) { receiveWithin(1000) { case message => } }

    println("Energy level at end: " + energySource.getUnitsAvailable())
    println("Usage: " + energySource.getUsageCount())

    energySource.stopEnergySource()
  }
}
```

Compile and run the code using the Akka-related JARs, as shown next, where AKKA_JARS is the same as defined in the Java example:

```
scalac -classpath $AKKA_JARS *.scala
java -classpath $AKKA_JARS com.agiledeveloper.pcj.UseEnergySource
```

The output should be no different from what we saw with the Java version; again, depending on the timing of replenish, a slightly different value like 31 instead of 30 may appear.

```
Energy level at start: 100
Energy level at end: 30
Usage: 70
```

6.9 Creating Nested Transactions

The methods we call may create their own transactions, and their changes will get independent commits. That's not adequate if we want to coordinate the transactions in these methods into one atomic operation. We can achieve such coordination with nested transactions.

With nested transactions, all the transactions created by methods we call get rolled into the calling method's transaction by default. Using Akka/Multiverse provides ways to configure other options like new isolated transactions, among others. As a result, with nested transactions, all the changes get committed only when the outermost transaction commits. It's our responsibility to ensure that methods complete within the configurable timeout period for the overall nested transactions to succeed.

The AccountService and its transfer() method from *The Lock Interface*, on page 67 will benefit from nested transactions. The previous version of the transfer()

method had to sort the accounts in natural order and manage locks explic-itly. STM removes all that burden. Let's first use nested transactions in that example in Java and then see how that would look like in Scala.

Nested Transactions in Java

Let's first get the Account class into the realm of transactions. The account balance should be a managed reference, so let's start with defining that field and a getter for it.

usingTransactionalMemory/java/nested/Account.java
```
public class Account {
  final private Ref<Integer> balance = new Ref<Integer>();

  public Account(int initialBalance) { balance.swap(initialBalance); }

  public int getBalance() { return balance.get(); }
```

In the constructor, we set the initial balance to the given amount by calling the swap() method on the ref. This operation will run in its own transaction, since we didn't provide one (and let's assume the caller didn't provide one either). Similarly, the getBalance() will access the balance in its own transaction.

The entire deposit() method has to run in one transaction, because it involves both reading and changing the balance. So, let's wrap these two operations into a separate transaction.

usingTransactionalMemory/java/nested/Account.java
```
public void deposit(final int amount) {
  new Atomic<Boolean>() {
    public Boolean atomically() {
      System.out.println("Deposit " + amount);
      if (amount > 0) {
        balance.swap(balance.get() + amount);
        return true;
      }

      throw new AccountOperationFailedException();
    }
  }.execute();
}
```

Likewise, the operations in withdraw() should be wrapped into a separate transaction.

usingTransactionalMemory/java/nested/Account.java
```
  public void withdraw(final int amount) {
    new Atomic<Boolean>() {
      public Boolean atomically() {
        int currentBalance = balance.get();
```

```
      if (amount > 0 && currentBalance >= amount) {
        balance.swap(currentBalance - amount);
        return true;
      }

      throw new AccountOperationFailedException();
    }
  }.execute();
  }
}
```

Transactions are forced to fail upon exception, so we use this to indicate the failure when a sufficient balance is not available or when the deposit/withdraw amount is invalid. Pretty simple, eh? There's no need to worry about synchronization, locking, deadlocking, and so on.

It's time to visit the AccountService class that'll perform the transfer. Let's take a look at the transfer method first:

usingTransactionalMemory/java/nested/AccountService.java
```
public class AccountService {
  public void transfer(
    final Account from, final Account to, final int amount) {
    new Atomic<Boolean>() {
      public Boolean atomically() {
        System.out.println("Attempting transfer...");
        to.deposit(amount);
        System.out.println("Simulating a delay in transfer...");
        try { Thread.sleep(5000); } catch(Exception ex) {}
        System.out.println("Uncommitted balance after deposit $" +
          to.getBalance());
        from.withdraw(amount);
        return true;
      }
    }.execute();
  }
```

In this example, we'll set the transactions on a collision course to illustrate their behavior while we study nested transactions. The operations in the transfer() method are bound within a transaction. As part of the transfer, we first deposit money into the target account. Then, after the delay induced to cause transaction collision, we withdraw money from the source account. We want the deposit into the target account to succeed if and only if the withdraw from the source succeeds—that's the job for our transaction.

We can see whether the transfer succeeded by printing the balance. A convenience method to invoke the transfer(), handle the exception, and finally print the balances will be nice, so let's write one:

usingTransactionalMemory/java/nested/AccountService.java

```java
public static void transferAndPrintBalance(
  final Account from, final Account to, final int amount) {
  boolean result = true;
  try {
    new AccountService().transfer(from, to, amount);
  } catch(AccountOperationFailedException ex) {
    result = false;
  }

  System.out.println("Result of transfer is " + (result ? "Pass" : "Fail"));
  System.out.println("From account has $" + from.getBalance());
  System.out.println("To account has $" + to.getBalance());
}
```

The last method we need is the main() to get the transfer rolling:

usingTransactionalMemory/java/nested/AccountService.java

```java
public static void main(final String[] args) throws Exception {
  final Account account1 = new Account(2000);
  final Account account2 = new Account(100);

  final ExecutorService service = Executors.newSingleThreadExecutor();
  service.submit(new Runnable() {
    public void run() {
      try { Thread.sleep(1000); } catch(Exception ex) {}
      account2.deposit(20);
    }
  });
  service.shutdown();

  transferAndPrintBalance(account1, account2, 500);

  System.out.println("Making large transfer...");
  transferAndPrintBalance(account1, account2, 5000);
  }
}
```

In the main() method, we created two accounts and started the deposit of $20 in a separate thread. In the meantime, we ask money to be transferred between the accounts. This should set the two transactions on a collision course, because they both affect a common instance. One of them will succeed, and the other will be retried. Finally, in the end, we attempt a transfer amount in excess of the available balance. This will illustrate that the two transactions in deposit and withdraw are not independent, but nested and atomic within the transfer's transaction. The effect of deposit should be reversed because of the failure of withdraw. Let's watch the behavior of these transactions in the output:

```
Attempting transfer...
Deposit 500
Attempting transfer...
Deposit 500
Simulating a delay in transfer...
Deposit 20
Uncommitted balance after deposit $600
Attempting transfer...
Deposit 500
Simulating a delay in transfer...
Uncommitted balance after deposit $620
Result of transfer is Pass
From account has $1500
To account has $620
Making large transfer...
Attempting transfer...
Deposit 5000
Simulating a delay in transfer...
Uncommitted balance after deposit $5620
Result of transfer is Fail
From account has $1500
To account has $620
```

It's a bit odd that the transfer transaction got retried at the start. Such unexpected retries are because of the default optimization (speculative configuration) of Multiverse for read-only transactions on a single object. There are ways to configure this behavior, but that has performance consequences. Refer to the Akka/Multiverse documentation to learn about the ramifications of changing it.

The deposit of $20 succeeded first. While this happened, the transfer transaction was in the middle of its simulated delay. As soon as the transaction realizes that an object it manages has changed behind its back, it quietly rolls back and starts another attempt. The retries will continue until it succeeds or the timeout is exceeded. This time around, the transfer transaction succeeded. The net result of both the transactions is reflected in the balance displayed—the first account lost $500 in the transfer, while the second account gained a total of $520 from the concurrent deposit and transfer activities.

Our next and final attempt was to transfer $5,000. The deposit was completed, but the change within that transaction was withheld to check the fate of the withdraw. The withdraw, however, failed with an exception because of insufficient balance. This caused the pending deposit transaction to roll back, leaving the balance unaffected by the final transfer attempt.

The print message and delays are certainly not good practices, but I used them here so we can see the transaction sequences and retries—avoid these kinds of printing or logging in real code. Remember, transactions should have no side effects. Delegate any code with side effects to post-commit handlers, which we will discuss later.

I promised that the transactions would lift some of the burden from our shoulders, so let's find out just how much. Take a look at the transfer() method from *The Lock Interface*, on page 67, shown here for convenience:

```
scalabilityAndTreadSafety/locking/AccountService.java
public boolean transfer(
  final Account from, final Account to, final int amount)
  throws LockException, InterruptedException {
  final Account[] accounts = new Account[] {from, to};
  Arrays.sort(accounts);
  if(accounts[0].monitor.tryLock(1, TimeUnit.SECONDS)) {
    try {
      if (accounts[1].monitor.tryLock(1, TimeUnit.SECONDS)) {
        try {
          if(from.withdraw(amount)) {
            to.deposit(amount);
            return true;
          } else {
            return false;
          }
        } finally {
          accounts[1].monitor.unlock();
        }
      }
    } finally {
      accounts[0].monitor.unlock();
    }
  }
  throw new LockException("Unable to acquire locks on the accounts");
}
```

Contrast that code with the latest version, but first get rid of the delay and print statements:

```
public void transfer(
  final Account from, final Account to, final int amount) {
  new Atomic<Boolean>() {
    public Boolean atomically() {
      to.deposit(amount);
      from.withdraw(amount);
      return true;
    }
  }.execute();
}
```

There was so much dancing around with ordering and locking in the old version that it's easy to mess up. The code we don't write has the fewest bugs, hands down. In the new version, we reduced both the code and the complexity. This reminds me of C.A.R. Hoare's words: "There are two ways of constructing a software design. One way is to make it so simple that there are obviously no deficiencies. And the other way is to make it so complicated that there are no obvious deficiencies." Less code, lesser complexity and more time to devote to the application logic.

Nested Transactions in Scala

The Java version of the transfer method using nested transactions is already concise. Sure, nested transactions removed the synchronization cruft, but there's still some Java syntax that can use cleaning. Scala's expressiveness and elegance will play a role in that, as we'll see next:

Here's the Scala version of the Account class:

```
usingTransactionalMemory/scala/nested/Account.scala
class Account(val initialBalance : Int) {
  val balance = Ref(initialBalance)

  def getBalance() = balance.get()

  def deposit(amount : Int) = {
    atomic {
      println("Deposit " + amount)
      if(amount > 0)
        balance.swap(balance.get() + amount)
      else
        throw new AccountOperationFailedException()
    }
  }

  def withdraw(amount : Int) = {
    atomic {
      val currentBalance = balance.get()
      if(amount > 0 && currentBalance >= amount)
        balance.swap(currentBalance - amount)
      else
        throw new AccountOperationFailedException()
    }
  }
}
```

The Scala version of Account is a direct translation from the Java version with Scala and Akka conciseness. We see the same advantage in the Scala version of AccountService:

usingTransactionalMemory/scala/nested/AccountService.scala
```scala
object AccountService {
  def transfer(from : Account, to : Account, amount : Int) = {
    atomic {
      println("Attempting transfer...")
      to.deposit(amount)
      println("Simulating a delay in transfer...")
      Thread.sleep(5000)
      println("Uncommitted balance after deposit $" + to.getBalance())
      from.withdraw(amount)
    }
  }

  def transferAndPrintBalance(
    from : Account, to : Account, amount : Int) = {
    var result = "Pass"
    try {
      AccountService.transfer(from, to, amount)
    } catch {
      case ex => result = "Fail"
    }

    println("Result of transfer is " + result)
    println("From account has $" + from.getBalance())
    println("To account has $" + to.getBalance())
  }

  def main(args : Array[String]) = {
    val account1 = new Account(2000)
    val account2 = new Account(100)

    actor {
      Thread.sleep(1000)
      account2.deposit(20)
    }

    transferAndPrintBalance(account1, account2, 500)

    println("Making large transfer...")
    transferAndPrintBalance(account1, account2, 5000)
  }
}
```

This version sets the transactions on a collision course just like the Java version did. Not surprisingly, the output is the same as the Java version's:

```
Attempting transfer...
Deposit 500
Attempting transfer...
Deposit 500
Simulating a delay in transfer...
```

```
Deposit 20
Uncommitted balance after deposit $600
Attempting transfer...
Deposit 500
Simulating a delay in transfer...
Uncommitted balance after deposit $620
Result of transfer is Pass
From account has $1500
To account has $620
Making large transfer...
Attempting transfer...
Deposit 5000
Simulating a delay in transfer...
Uncommitted balance after deposit $5620
Result of transfer is Fail
From account has $1500
To account has $620
```

We've already compared the synchronized version of transfer with the Java version using nested transaction (which is repeated next):

```
public void transfer(
  final Account from, final Account to, final int amount) {
  new Atomic<Boolean>() {
    public Boolean atomically() {
      to.deposit(amount);
      from.withdraw(amount);
      return true;
    }
  }.execute();
}
```

Now compare it with the Scala version:

```
def transfer(from : Account, to : Account, amount : Int) = {
  atomic {
    to.deposit(amount)
    from.withdraw(amount)
  }
}
```

It's nothing but the most essential code. It reminds me of the quotation by Alan Perlis: "A programming language is low level when its programs require attention to the irrelevant."

We know how to create transactions in Akka and how to compose nested transactions. That's only a start; Akka allows us to configure transactions, as we'll see next.

6.10 Configuring Akka Transactions

Akka assumes a number of default settings, but it allows us to change these either programmatically or through the configuration file akka.conf. See the Akka documentation for details on how to specify or change the location of the configuration file.

We can programmatically change the settings on a per-transaction basis using a TransactionFactory. Let's change some settings programmatically from Java and then from Scala.

Configuring Transactions in Java

We extended Atomic to implement transactions in Java. We can provide an optional constructor parameter of type TransactionFactory to change the transaction properties. For example, we can set a transaction as readonly to gain performance and prevent changes to any references by configuring a transaction. Let's create a class called CoffeePot that holds a number of cups of coffee and try to manipulate it from within a readonly transaction:

usingTransactionalMemory/java/configure/CoffeePot.java
```
public class CoffeePot {
  private static final Ref<Integer> cups = new Ref<Integer>(24);

  public static int readWriteCups(final boolean write) {
    final TransactionFactory factory =
      new TransactionFactoryBuilder().setReadonly(true).build();

    return new Atomic<Integer>(factory) {
      public Integer atomically() {
        if(write) cups.swap(20);
        return cups.get();
      }
    }.execute();
  }
```

To programmatically set the transaction configuration, we need a Transaction-Factory. The TransactionFactoryBuilder provides convenience methods to create the factory. We created an instance of TransactionFactoryBuilder to configure the TransactionFactory with the readonly option using the setReadonly() method. The TransactionFactoryBuilder implements the Cascade[3] design pattern, so we can chain more methods for other properties we want to set before calling the build() method. Send this factory instance as a parameter to the constructor

---

3. Some of the patterns discussed in *Smalltalk Best Practice Patterns* [Bec96] by Kent Beck are being rediscovered, especially with the rise of new languages on the JVM.

of Atomic, and we're guaranteed that no action within the transaction can change any managed references.

Our transaction is readonly, but let's see what happens if we try to modify a reference. So, we'll call the readWriteCups() once to only read the reference and then a second time to change it.

usingTransactionalMemory/java/configure/CoffeePot.java

```java
public static void main(final String[] args) {
    System.out.println("Read only");
    readWriteCups(false);

    System.out.println("Attempt to write");
    try {
        readWriteCups(true);
    } catch(Exception ex) {
        System.out.println("Failed " + ex);
    }
}
}
```

The transaction won't be happy about the change request; on the attempt to change, it will throw the org.multiverse.api.exceptions.ReadonlyException exception, and the transaction will roll back.

```
Read only
Attempt to write
Failed org.multiverse.api.exceptions.ReadonlyException:
Can't open for write transactional object 'akka.stm.Ref@1272670619'
because transaction 'DefaultTransaction' is readonly'
```

The runtime exception was raised from the call to swap(). This method modifies the value held by its ref only if the new value is different from the current value; otherwise, it ignores the change request. So, in the example, instead of 20, if we set the value to 24, the current value of the cups ref, we won't get any exception.

Configuring Transactions in Scala

In Scala, we use the atomic() method instead of the Atomic class for creating transactions. This method takes an optional parameter of type TransactionFactory. Creating the instance of the factory is much easier in Scala as well, because we can use the factory method on the companion object.

usingTransactionalMemory/scala/configure/CoffeePot.scala

```scala
object CoffeePot {
    val cups = Ref(24)

    def readWriteCups(write : Boolean) = {
```

```scala
    val factory = TransactionFactory(readonly = true)

    atomic(factory) {
        if(write) cups.swap(20)
        cups.get()
    }
  }

  def main(args : Array[String]) : Unit = {
    println("Read only")
    readWriteCups(false)

    println("Attempt to write")
    try {
      readWriteCups(true)
    } catch {
      case ex => println("Failed " + ex)
    }
  }
}
```

Other than Scala and Akka conciseness, there's not much difference between the Scala and the Java version here, and the code should behave just like the Java version:

```
Read only
Attempt to write
Failed org.multiverse.api.exceptions.ReadonlyException:
Can't open for write transactional object 'akka.stm.Ref@1761506447'
because transaction 'DefaultTransaction' is readonly'
```

6.11 Blocking Transactions—Sensible Wait

A transaction may depend on a variable that's expected to change, and the failure of the transaction may be temporary. As a response to that failure, we may return an error code and ask the transaction to retry after a delay. However, there's no point repeating the request until another task has changed the dependent data. Akka gives us a simple facility, retry(), which will roll back and block the transaction until one of the reference objects the transaction depends on changes or the configurable block timeout is exceeded. I like to call this a "sensible wait" because that sounds better than "blocking." Let's put blocking, I mean sensible wait, to use in an example in Java first and then in Scala.

Blocking Transactions in Java

Programmers in general are addicted to caffeine, so anyone volunteering to get some coffee knows not to return with empty cups. Rather than a busy wait until the coffee pot is refilled, he can place himself in a notify-when-change mode with Akka's help. Let's write a fillCup() method with sensible wait using retry():

usingTransactionalMemory/java/blocking/CoffeePot.java
```java
public class CoffeePot {
  private static final long start = System.nanoTime();
  private static final Ref<Integer> cups = new Ref<Integer>(24);

  private static void fillCup(final int numberOfCups) {
    final TransactionFactory factory =
      new TransactionFactoryBuilder()
      .setBlockingAllowed(true)
      .setTimeout(new DurationInt(6).seconds())
      .build();

    new Atomic<Object>(factory) {
      public Object atomically() {
        if(cups.get() < numberOfCups) {
          System.out.println("retry........ at " +
            (System.nanoTime() - start)/1.0e9);
          retry();
        }
        cups.swap(cups.get() - numberOfCups);
        System.out.println("filled up...." + numberOfCups);
        System.out.println("........ at " +
          (System.nanoTime() - start)/1.0e9);
        return null;
      }
    }.execute();
  }
```

In the fillCup() method, we configured the transaction with blockingAllowed = true and set a timeout of six seconds for the transaction to complete. When the fillCup() method finds there's not enough coffee, rather than returning an error code, it invokes StmUtils's retry() method. This blocks the current transaction until the participating reference cups is changed. Once any participating reference changes, the atomically code that contained the retry is retried, starting another transaction.

Let's call the fillCup() method to see the effect of retry():

usingTransactionalMemory/java/blocking/CoffeePot.java
```java
  public static void main(final String[] args) {
    final Timer timer = new Timer(true);
    timer.schedule(new TimerTask() {
      public void run() {
        System.out.println("Refilling.... at " +
          (System.nanoTime() - start)/1.0e9);
```

```
        cups.swap(24);
      }
    }, 5000);

    fillCup(20);
    fillCup(10);
    try {
      fillCup(22);
    } catch(Exception ex) {
      System.out.println("Failed: " + ex.getMessage());
    }
  }
}
```

In main(), we start a timer that will refill the coffeepot in about five seconds. The guy who jumped in first got twenty cups of coffee right away. When our volunteer goes for the ten cups, he's blocked for the refill to happen. This wait is more efficient than a busy programmatic reattempt operation. Once the refill transaction completes, his request is automatically tried again and this time succeeds. If the refill does not happen in the timeout we configured, the transaction will fail as in the last request in the try block. We can observe this behavior and the benefit of retry() in the output:

```
filled up....20
........ at 0.423589
retry........ at 0.425385
retry........ at 0.427569
Refilling.... at 5.130381
filled up....10
........ at 5.131149
retry........ at 5.131357
retry........ at 5.131521
Failed: Transaction DefaultTransaction has timed with a
total timeout of 6000000000 ns
```

The fill-up request for ten cups was made in 0.40 seconds from the start of the run. Since the refill is not going to happen until after five seconds from the start, this request is blocked because of the call to retry(). Right after the refill transaction completed, the fill-up transaction was restarted and this time ran to completion a little after five seconds from the start. The later request to fill up timed out since no refill happened after this request.

It's not often that we'd use retry(). If the application logic demands performing some operation when the dependent data changes, we can benefit from this feature that monitors change to the data.

Blocking Transactions in Scala

In the Java version, we used the convenience object StmUtils that provided a fluent Java interface. In Scala, we can directly use the StmUnit trait. We can also use the factory method to create the TransactionFactory:

usingTransactionalMemory/scala/blocking/CoffeePot.scala

```scala
object CoffeePot {
  val start = System.nanoTime()
  val cups = Ref(24)

  def fillCup(numberOfCups : Int) = {
    val factory = TransactionFactory(blockingAllowed = true,
      timeout = 6 seconds)

    atomic(factory) {
      if(cups.get() < numberOfCups) {
        println("retry........ at " + (System.nanoTime() - start)/1.0e9)
        retry()
      }
      cups.swap(cups.get() - numberOfCups)
      println("filled up...." + numberOfCups)
      println("........ at " + (System.nanoTime() - start)/1.0e9)
    }
  }

  def main(args : Array[String]) : Unit = {
    val timer = new Timer(true)
    timer.schedule(new TimerTask() {
      def run() {
        println("Refilling.... at " + (System.nanoTime() - start)/1.0e9)
        cups.swap(24)
      }
    }, 5000)

    fillCup(20)
    fillCup(10)
    try {
      fillCup(22)
    } catch {
      case ex => println("Failed: " + ex.getMessage())
    }
  }
}
```

When creating TransactionFactory, to configure the timeout rather than directly using the DurationInt, we use the implicit conversion from int using the intToDurationInt() method. This allowed us to simply invoke 6 seconds, a little syntactic sugar provided by Scala implicit conversions. The rest of the code is a simple translation from Java to Scala, and the output is shown next:

```
filled up....20
........ at 0.325964
retry........ at 0.327425
retry........ at 0.329587
Refilling.... at 5.105191
filled up....10
........ at 5.106074
retry........ at 5.106296
retry........ at 5.106466
Failed: Transaction DefaultTransaction has timed with a
total timeout of 6000000000 ns
```

6.12 Commit and Rollback Events

Java's try-catch-finally facility allows us to handle exceptions and selectively run some code only when there's an exception. Similarly, we can decide to run a piece of code only if a transaction committed and another piece of code only if a transaction rolled back. These are provided as deferred() and compensating() methods, respectively, on StmUtils. The deferred() method is a great place to perform all the side effects that we were holding off to ensure the transaction completes.

Commit and Rollback Events in Java

We place the code that we want to run when a transaction succeeds in the code block (Runnable) that's passed to the deferred() method of StmUtils. Likewise, we'll place the code we want to run when the transaction fails in the code block passed to the compensating() method. Since these methods have to run in the context of a transaction, we'll have to invoke them within the body of the atomically() method.

```
usingTransactionalMemory/java/events/Counter.java
public class Counter {
  private final Ref<Integer> value = new Ref<Integer>(1);

  public void decrement() {
    new Atomic<Integer>() {
      public Integer atomically() {

        deferred(new Runnable() {
          public void run() {
            System.out.println(
              "Transaction completed...send email, log, etc.");
          }
        });
```

```
      compensating(new Runnable() {
        public void run() {
          System.out.println("Transaction aborted...hold the phone");
        }
      });

      if(value.get() <= 0)
        throw new RuntimeException("Operation not allowed");

      value.swap(value.get() - 1);
      return value.get();
    }
  }.execute();
  }
}
```

The Counter class has one instance method named decrement(). In this method, we extend from the class Atomic and implement the required atomically() method. In previous examples, we simply wrote the code to be run in a transaction here. In addition to that, we also provide code to run in case of transaction success and transaction rollback. Let's create a sample code to try Counter:

usingTransactionalMemory/java/events/UseCounter.java
```
package com.agiledeveloper.pcj;

public class UseCounter {
  public static void main(final String[] args) {
    Counter counter = new Counter();
    counter.decrement();

    System.out.println("Let's try again...");
    try {
      counter.decrement();
    } catch(Exception ex) {
      System.out.println(ex.getMessage());
    }
  }
}
```

Exercise the UseCounter to see the code blocks associated with transaction success and failure run as appropriate:

```
Transaction aborted...hold the phone
Transaction completed...send email, log, etc.
Let's try again...
Transaction aborted...hold the phone
Operation not allowed
```

When the transaction completed on the first call to decrement(), the code block provided to the deferred() method is invoked. In the second call to decrement(), as soon as we hit the exception, the transaction was rolled back, and the code block provided to the compensating() method was called. We also see the rollback because of an unexpected retry at the top that's due to the speculative configuration we discussed earlier in *Nested Transactions in Java*, on page 112.

The deferred() handler is a great place to complete work activity in order to make actions permanent. So, feel free to print, display messages, send notifications, commit the database transactions, and so on, from here. If we want anything to stick around, this is the place for that. The compensating() handler is a good place for logging failures. If we had messed with any unmanaged objects (those objects not controlled using the Akka Ref), this is the place to revert the actions—however, it's better to avoid the desire for such design because it's messy and error prone.

Commit and Rollback Events in Scala

We can handle commit and rollback events in Scala just like we did in Java, except we can directly pass closures/function values to the deferred() and compensating() methods. Let's translate the Counter class from Java to Scala.

usingTransactionalMemory/scala/events/Counter.scala
```scala
class Counter {
  private val value = Ref(1)

  def decrement() = {
    atomic {

      deferred { println("Transaction completed...send email, log, etc.") }

      compensating { println("Transaction aborted...hold the phone") }

      if(value.get() <= 0)
        throw new RuntimeException("Operation not allowed")

      value.swap(value.get() - 1)
      value.get()
    }
  }
}
```

The code to run when a transaction succeeds is placed in the closure that's passed to the deferred() method. Likewise, the code to run when a transaction rolls back is presented to the compensating() method as a closure. These two are placed within the closure presented to the atomic() method, along with the transactional code. Again, it's quite simple and concise. Let's translate the UseCounter class from Java to Scala:

usingTransactionalMemory/scala/events/UseCounter.scala

```
package com.agiledeveloper.pcj

object UseCounter {
  def main(args : Array[String]) : Unit = {
    val counter = new Counter()
    counter.decrement()

    println("Let's try again...")
    try {
      counter.decrement()
    } catch {
      case ex => println(ex.getMessage())
    }
  }
}
```

The output from the Scala version should be the same as the Java version:

```
Transaction aborted...hold the phone
Transaction completed...send email, log, etc.
Let's try again...
Transaction aborted...hold the phone
Operation not allowed
```

6.13 Collections and Transactions

As we work through the examples, it's easy to forget that the values we're dealing with are, and should be, immutable. Only the identity is mutable, not the state value. Although STM makes life easy, it can be a challenge to ensure good performance while maintaining immutability.

Take the first step to ensure immutability. Make value classes final, and mark all their fields final (vals in Scala). Then transitively ensure that the classes for each field the values use are immutable as well. It should be first nature to make fields and classes final—this is the first step toward avoiding concurrency issues.

Although immutability will make code better and safer, one prominent reason that programmers are reluctant to use it is performance. If nothing changes, we'll have to make copies. We discussed persistent data structures and how they can ease performance concerns in Section 3.6, *Persistent/Immutable Data Structures*, on page 39. We can make use of persistent data structures already provided in third-party libraries or those we can find in Scala. We don't have to switch languages to take advantage of this. We can use those persistent data structures right from Java code.

Not only do we want immutability, but we also want the data structures to participate in transactions—their values are immutable, but identities change within managed transactions. Akka provides two managed data structures—TransactionalVector and TransactionalMap. These work like Java lists and dictionaries but derive from efficient Scala data structures. Let's take a look at how to use TransactionalMap in Java and Scala.

Using Transactional Collections in Java

Using TransactionalMap from Java is quite simple. As an example, let's keep scores for different players, where the updates to these scores will arrive concurrently. Rather than deal with synchronization and locks, we decide to handle the updates within transactions. Here's some example code for that:

usingTransactionalMemory/java/collections/Scores.java
```java
public class Scores {
  final private TransactionalMap<String, Integer> scoreValues =
    new TransactionalMap<String, Integer>();
  final private Ref<Long> updates = new Ref<Long>(0L);

  public void updateScore(final String name, final int score) {
    new Atomic() {
      public Object atomically() {
        scoreValues.put(name, score);
        updates.swap(updates.get() + 1);
        if (score == 13)
          throw new RuntimeException("Reject this score");
        return null;
      }
    }.execute();
  }

  public Iterable<String> getNames() {
    return asJavaIterable(scoreValues.keySet());
  }

  public long getNumberOfUpdates() { return updates.get(); }

  public int getScore(final String name) {
    return scoreValues.get(name).get();
  }
}
```

In the updateScore() method, we set the score value for a player and increment the update count in a transaction. Both the fields scoreValue of type TransactionalMap and updates of type Ref are managed. The TransactionalMap supports methods we'd expect on a Map, but these methods are transactional—any changes we make to them are discarded if the transaction is rolled back. To see this effect in action, we roll back the transaction after making the change if the score value is 13.

In Java we can use the for-each statement, like for(String name : collectionOfNames), if the collection implements the Iterable interface. The TransactionalMap is a Scala collection and does not directly support that interface. No worries—Scala provides a façade called JavaConversions that provides convenience methods to get favorable Java interfaces. We're using its asJavaIterable() method to get the interface we desire in the getNames() method.

The Scores class is ready; we now need a class to exercise its methods:

usingTransactionalMemory/java/collections/UseScores.java

```java
package com.agiledeveloper.pcj;

public class UseScores {
  public static void main(final String[] args) {
    final Scores scores = new Scores();
    scores.updateScore("Joe", 14);
    scores.updateScore("Sally", 15);
    scores.updateScore("Bernie", 12);
    System.out.println("Number of updates: " + scores.getNumberOfUpdates());

    try {
      scores.updateScore("Bill", 13);
    } catch(Exception ex) {
      System.out.println("update failed for score 13");
    }

    System.out.println("Number of updates: " + scores.getNumberOfUpdates());

    for(String name : scores.getNames()) {
      System.out.println(
        String.format("Score for %s is %d", name, scores.getScore(name)));
    }
  }
}
```

We first add scores for three players. Then we add another score value that will result in the transaction rollback. This last score update should have no effect. Finally, we iterate over the scores in the transactional map. Let's observe the output of this code:

```
Number of updates: 3
update failed for score 13
Number of updates: 3
Score for Joe is 14
Score for Bernie is 12
Score for Sally is 15
```

Using Transactional Collections in Scala

We can use the transactional collections from within Scala much like we did in Java. Since in Scala we'd use Scala's internal iterators, we don't have to use the JavaConversions façade. Let's translate the Scores class to Scala:

usingTransactionalMemory/scala/collections/Scores.scala
```scala
class Scores {
  private val scoreValues = new TransactionalMap[String, Int]()
  private val updates = Ref(0L)

  def updateScore(name : String, score : Int) = {
    atomic {
      scoreValues.put(name, score)
      updates.swap(updates.get() + 1)
      if (score == 13) throw new RuntimeException("Reject this score")
    }
  }

  def foreach(codeBlock : ((String, Int)) => Unit) =
    scoreValues.foreach(codeBlock)

  def getNumberOfUpdates() = updates.get()
}
```

The updateScore() method is pretty much equivalent to the Java version. We eliminated the getNames() and getScore methods and instead provided a foreach() internal-iterator to step through the score values. The Scala version of the UseScores should be a direct translation from the Java version:

usingTransactionalMemory/scala/collections/UseScores.scala
```scala
package com.agiledeveloper.pcj

object UseScores {
  def main(args : Array[String]) : Unit = {
    val scores = new Scores()

    scores.updateScore("Joe", 14)
    scores.updateScore("Sally", 15)
    scores.updateScore("Bernie", 12)

    println("Number of updates: " + scores.getNumberOfUpdates())
```

```
  try {
    scores.updateScore("Bill", 13)
  } catch {
    case ex => println("update failed for score 13")
  }

  println("Number of updates: " + scores.getNumberOfUpdates())

  scores.foreach { mapEntry =>
    val (name, score) = mapEntry
    println("Score for " + name + " is " + score)
  }
  }
}
```

The output of this version should be the same as the Java version, as we'd expect:

```
Number of updates: 3
update failed for score 13
Number of updates: 3
Score for Joe is 14
Score for Bernie is 12
Score for Sally is 15
```

6.14 Dealing with the Write Skew Anomaly

In *Handling Write Skew Anomaly*, on page 100, we discussed write skew and how Clojure STM handles it. Akka also has support for dealing with write skew, but we have to configure it. OK, that word may sound scary, but it's really simple. Let's first see the default behavior without any configuration.

Let's revisit the example of multiple accounts with a restricted combined balance that we looked at earlier. Create a Portfolio class that holds a checking account balance and a savings account balance. These two accounts have a constraint of the total balance not running less than $1,000. This class along with the withdraw() method is shown next. In this method, we obtain the two balances first, compute their total, and after a intentional delay (introduced to set transactions on collision course) we subtract the given amount from either the checking balance or the savings balance if the total is not less than $1,000. The withdraw() method does its operations within a transaction configured using default settings.

usingTransactionalMemory/java/writeSkew/Portfolio.java
```
public class Portfolio {
  final private Ref<Integer> checkingBalance = new Ref<Integer>(500);
  final private Ref<Integer> savingsBalance = new Ref<Integer>(600);
```

```
public int getCheckingBalance() { return checkingBalance.get(); }
public int getSavingsBalance() { return savingsBalance.get(); }

public void withdraw(final boolean fromChecking, final int amount) {
  new Atomic<Object>() {
    public Object atomically() {
      final int totalBalance =
        checkingBalance.get() + savingsBalance.get();
      try { Thread.sleep(1000); } catch(InterruptedException ex) {}
      if(totalBalance - amount >= 1000) {
        if(fromChecking)
          checkingBalance.swap(checkingBalance.get() - amount);
        else
          savingsBalance.swap(savingsBalance.get() - amount);
      }
      else
        System.out.println(
          "Sorry, can't withdraw due to constraint violation");
      return null;
    }
  }.execute();
}
}
```

Let's set two transactions in concurrent motion to change the balances:

usingTransactionalMemory/java/writeSkew/UsePortfolio.java
```
public class UsePortfolio {
  public static void main(final String[] args) throws InterruptedException {
    final Portfolio portfolio = new Portfolio();

    int checkingBalance = portfolio.getCheckingBalance();
    int savingBalance = portfolio.getSavingsBalance();
    System.out.println("Checking balance is " + checkingBalance);
    System.out.println("Savings balance is " + savingBalance);
    System.out.println("Total balance is " +
      (checkingBalance + savingBalance));

    final ExecutorService service = Executors.newFixedThreadPool(10);
    service.execute(new Runnable() {
      public void run() { portfolio.withdraw(true, 100); }
    });
    service.execute(new Runnable() {
      public void run() { portfolio.withdraw(false, 100); }
    });

    service.shutdown();

    Thread.sleep(4000);

    checkingBalance = portfolio.getCheckingBalance();
```

```
    savingBalance = portfolio.getSavingsBalance();
    System.out.println("Checking balance is " + checkingBalance);
    System.out.println("Savings balance is " + savingBalance);
    System.out.println("Total balance is " +
      (checkingBalance + savingBalance));
    if(checkingBalance + savingBalance < 1000)
      System.out.println("Oops, broke the constraint!");
  }
}
```

By default, Akka does not avoid write skew, and the two transactions will proceed running the balances into constraint violation, as we see in the output:

```
Checking balance is 500
Savings balance is 600
Total balance is 1100
Checking balance is 400
Savings balance is 500
Total balance is 900
Oops, broke the constraint!
```

It's time to fix this. Let's reach out to TransactionFactory that will help us configure transactions programmatically. Modify line 9 in the Portfolio class to accept an instance of the factory. That is, change this:

```
new Atomic<Object>() {
```

to the following:

```
akka.stm.TransactionFactory factory =
  new akka.stm.TransactionFactoryBuilder()
  .setWriteSkew(false)
  .setTrackReads(true)
  .build();
```

```
new Atomic<Object>(factory) {
```

We created a TransactionFactoryBuilder and set the writeSkew and trackReads properties to false and true, respectively. This tells the transaction to keep track of reads within a transaction and also to set a read lock on the reads until the commit begins, just as Clojure STM handles ensure.

The rest of the code in Portfolio and the code in UsePortfolio remains unchanged. Set the transactions in motion and watch the output.

```
Checking balance is 500
Savings balance is 600
Total balance is 1100
Sorry, can't withdraw due to constraint violation
Checking balance is 400
```

```
Savings balance is 600
Total balance is 1000
```

Because of the nondeterministic nature of concurrent execution, we can't predict which of the two transactions will win. We can see the difference between the output here, with the ending balances of the two accounts being different and the output in *Handling Write Skew Anomaly*, on page 100, where the ending balance was equal. We may notice differences in both examples when we run them several times.

The previous example was in Java; if we're using Scala, we can configure the transaction properties writeSkew and trackReads using the syntax we saw in *Configuring Transactions in Scala*, on page 121.

6.15 Limitations of STM

STM eliminates explicit synchronization. We no longer have to worry if we forgot to synchronize or if we synchronized at the wrong level. There are no issues of failing to cross the memory barrier or race conditions. I can hear the shrewd programmer in you asking "What's the catch?" Yes, STM has limitations—otherwise, this book would've ended right here. It's suitable only when write collisions are infrequent. If our application has a lot of write contention, we should look beyond STM.

Let's discuss this limitation further. STM provides an explicit lock-free programming model. It allows transactions to run concurrently, and they all complete without a glitch where there are no conflicts between them. This provides for greater concurrency and thread safety at the same time. When transactions collide on write access to the same object or data, one of them is allowed to complete, and the others are automatically retried. The retries delay the execution of the colliding writers but provide for greater speed for readers and the winning writer. The performance doesn't take much of a hit when we have infrequent concurrent writers to the same object. As the collisions increase, things get worse, however.

If we have a high rate of write collision to the same data, in the best case our writes are slow. In the worst case, our writes may fail because of too many retries. The examples we saw so far in this chapter showed the benefits of STM. Although STM is easy to use, not all uses will yield good results, as we'll see in the next example.

In *Coordination Using CountDownLatch*, on page 56, we used AtomicLong to synchronize concurrent updates to the total file size when multiple threads explored directories. Furthermore, we would resort to using synchronization if we had more than one variable to change at the same time. It looks like a nice candidate for STM, but the high contentions don't favor it. Let's see whether that's true by modifying the file size program to use STM.

Instead of using AtomicLong, we'll use Akka managed references for the fields in our file size finder.

usingTransactionalMemory/java/filesize/FileSizeWSTM.java
```
public class FileSizeWSTM {

  private ExecutorService service;
  final private Ref<Long> pendingFileVisits = new Ref<Long>(0L);
  final private Ref<Long> totalSize = new Ref<Long>(0L);
  final private CountDownLatch latch = new CountDownLatch(1);
```

pendingFileVisits needs to be incremented or decremented within the safe haven of a transaction. In the case of AtomicLong, we used a simple incrementAndGet() or decrementAndGet(). However, since the managed reference is generic and does not specifically deal with numbers, we have to put in some more effort. It's easier if we isolate that into a separate method.

usingTransactionalMemory/java/filesize/FileSizeWSTM.java
```
private long updatePendingFileVisits(final int value) {
  return new Atomic<Long>() {
    public Long atomically() {
      pendingFileVisits.swap(pendingFileVisits.get() + value);
      return pendingFileVisits.get();
    }
  }.execute();
}
```

The method to explore directories and find file sizes should now be pretty easy to implement. It's a simple conversion from using AtomicLong to using the managed references:

usingTransactionalMemory/java/filesize/FileSizeWSTM.java
```
private void findTotalSizeOfFilesInDir(final File file) {
  try {
    if (!file.isDirectory()) {
      new Atomic() {
        public Object atomically() {
          totalSize.swap(totalSize.get() + file.length());
          return null;
        }
      }.execute();
    } else {
      final File[] children = file.listFiles();

      if (children != null) {
        for(final File child : children) {
```

```
            updatePendingFileVisits(1);
            service.execute(new Runnable() {
              public void run() {
                findTotalSizeOfFilesInDir(child); }
            });
          }
        }
      }

    if(updatePendingFileVisits(-1) == 0) latch.countDown();
  } catch(Exception ex) {
    System.out.println(ex.getMessage());
    System.exit(1);
  }
}
```

Finally, we need code to create the executor service pool and get it running:

```
usingTransactionalMemory/java/filesize/FileSizeWSTM.java
  private long getTotalSizeOfFile(final String fileName)
    throws InterruptedException {
    service = Executors.newFixedThreadPool(100);
    updatePendingFileVisits(1);
    try {
     findTotalSizeOfFilesInDir(new File(fileName));
     latch.await(100, TimeUnit.SECONDS);
     return totalSize.get();
    } finally {
      service.shutdown();
    }
  }

  public static void main(final String[] args) throws InterruptedException {
    final long start = System.nanoTime();
    final long total = new FileSizeWSTM().getTotalSizeOfFile(args[0]);
    final long end = System.nanoTime();
    System.out.println("Total Size: " + total);
    System.out.println("Time taken: " + (end - start)/1.0e9);
  }
}
```

I suspect this code will run into trouble, so at the sign of an exception indicating failure of a transaction, we terminate the application.

If a value changes before the transaction is committed, the transaction will be retried automatically. Several threads compete to modify these two mutable variables, and results may vary between slow-running code to outright failure. Go ahead and run the code to explore different directories. I report the output on my system for the /etc and /usr directories here:

```
Total file size for /etc
Total Size: 2266408
Time taken: 0.537082

Total file size for /usr
Too many retries on transaction 'DefaultTransaction', maxRetries = 1000
Too many retries on transaction 'DefaultTransaction', maxRetries = 1000
Too many retries on transaction 'DefaultTransaction', maxRetries = 1000
...
```

The STM version gave the same file size for the /etc directory as the earlier version that used AtomicLong. However, the STM version was much slower, by about an order of magnitude, because of several retries. Exploring the /usr directory turned out to be much worse—quite a few transactions exceeded the default maximum retries limit. Even though we asked the application to be terminated, since several transactions are running concurrently, we may notice more failures before the first failure gets a chance to terminate the application.

One of the reviewers asked whether using commute instead of alter helps. You'll recall that we discussed the three functions that Clojure provides to modify a managed reference in Section 6.4, *Software Transactional Memory*, on page 92. commute provides higher concurrency than alter since it will not retry transactions; it instead performs the commits separately without holding the calling transaction. However, for the file size program, using commute only marginally helped, and for the large directory hierarchy it did not yield consistent results with good performance. We can also try using atom with the swap! method. The changes to an atom are uncoordinated and synchronized but don't require a transaction. It can be used only when we want to change one variable (such as the total size in the file size example) and will not encounter any transactional retries. However, we'll still encounter delays because of the under-the-covers synchronization of changes to the atom.

The file size program has a very high frequency of write conflicts because a lot of threads try to update the total size. So, STM is not suitable for this problem. STM will serve well and remove the need to synchronize when we have highly frequent reads and infrequent to reasonably frequent write conflicts. If the problem has enormous write collisions, which is rare considering other delays in general applications, don't use STM. Instead, we can use actors to avoid synchronization, as we'll discuss in Chapter 8, *Favoring Isolated Mutability*, on page 163.

6.16 Recap

STM is a very powerful model for concurrency with quite a few benefits:

- Provides maximum concurrency dictated directly by real application behavior; that is, instead of an overly conservative, predefined synchronization, we let STM dynamically handle contention.

- Provides explicit lock-free programming model with good thread safety and high concurrent performance.

- Ensures identities are changed only within transactions.

- The lack of explicit locks means we don't have to worry about lock order and related problems.

- No explicit locks leads to deadlock-free concurrency.

- Mitigates the need for up-front design decisions as to who locks and what; instead, we rely on dynamic implicit lock composition.

- The model is suitable for concurrent reads and infrequent to reasonably frequent write collisions to the same data.

STM provides an effective way to deal with shared mutability if the application data access fits that pattern. If we have huge write collisions, however, we may want to lean toward the actor-based model, which we discuss in Chapter 8, *Favoring Isolated Mutability*, on page 163. But first, let's see how to use STM from different JVM languages in the next chapter.

*A language that doesn't have everything is
actually easier to program in than some that
do.*

> *Dennis Ritchie*

CHAPTER 7

STM in Clojure, Groovy, Java, JRuby, and Scala

The JVM languages integrate fairly well for the most part. There are some rough edges, however, that we'll run into on occasions as we cross the language boundaries. We consciously pick a particular language for its strengths and capabilities, with the hopes it will make us more productive. So, we certainly don't want the little annoyances to ruin the efforts.

If STM is the right choice for an application, the language we're using on the JVM shouldn't stop us from putting it to good use. Whether STM really is the right choice is decided by the data access patterns of the application and not the language we're using to code it. We can use STM from any language on the JVM.

We have a few options. We could use Clojure STM right from that favorite language. Alternately, we could use the Multiverse library directly or through the Akka library.

If we want to use Clojure STM, it couldn't be easier. The two key components used in Clojure STM, ref and dosync, are sugar-coated Clojure APIs for clojure.lang.Ref and LockingTransaction's runInTransaction() method. So, when we define a ref, we're creating an instance of the Ref class, and when we invoke dosync(), we're calling the runInTransaction() method. Now we have direct access to the Clojure STM from Groovy, Java, JRuby, and any other JVM language.

To use Multiverse, we can use its Java API, its Groovy API, or its JRuby integration API. Alternately, we can use it through the Akka library.

In this chapter, we'll see how to use STM in different JVM languages. Focus on the sections related to the languages you're interested in, and feel free to skip the others.

A word of caution before we proceed: transactions are expected to be idempotent and without any side effects. This means we should ensure that all values are immutable and only managed identities are mutable. This is baked into Clojure; however, if we're using other languages, it is our responsibility to guarantee these expectations.

7.1 Clojure STM

Although STM has been around for a while, Clojure brought it to the limelight with its revolutionary separation of identity and state, as well as its efficient persistent data structures. Since state is entirely immutable in Clojure, it makes it very easy to use STM—we don't have to worry about ensuring immutability, because that's already Clojure's modus operandi. Clojure also disallows changes to mutable identity from outside of transactions, which makes it very safe. We can enjoy explicit lock-free programming with good concurrent performance and thread safety in applications with an access pattern appropriate for STM. Refer to the examples earlier in Chapter 6, *Introduction to Software Transactional Memory*, on page 89, and refer to the Clojure documentation and books if Clojure is in the mix of your language choices.

7.2 Groovy Integration

Groovy is a good choice among languages if we're looking for easy metaprogramming and dynamic typing while preserving Java semantics. In this section, we'll use the Clojure STM and the Multiverse STM through Akka in Groovy Apps. To use Multiverse directly, refer to the Multiverse documentation.

Using Clojure STM in Groovy

Using Clojure STM is as simple as using instances of clojure.lang.Ref for managed references and invoking the runInTransaction() method of LockingTransaction to place a piece of code in a transaction. Let's give it a shot using the account transfer example. Create a class called Account to hold a managed reference to its immutable state, represented by the variable currentBalance:

```
polyglotSTM/groovy/clojure/Transfer.groovy
class Account {
  final private Ref currentBalance
```

```
public Account(initialBalance) {
  currentBalance = new Ref(initialBalance)
}

def getBalance() { currentBalance.deref() }
```

In the constructor, we initialize the reference with the starting balance. In the getBalance() method, we call the deref() method. This is equivalent to the dereferencing we saw in Clojure using the @ prefix. Creating the managed reference was quite simple. Now let's see how to update it in a transaction. For us to run a piece of code in a transaction, we have to send it to the run-InTransaction() method. This method accepts as a parameter an instance that implements the java.util.concurrent.Callable interface. Groovy provides a rich syntax to implement interfaces, especially interfaces with only one method. Simply create a closure—a code block—and call the as operator on it. Under the covers Groovy will implement the required method of that interface with the provided code block as the implementation. Let's write the deposit() method of the Account class, which needs to run its operations in a transaction.

polyglotSTM/groovy/clojure/Transfer.groovy
```
def deposit(amount) {
  LockingTransaction.runInTransaction({
      if(amount > 0) {
        currentBalance.set(currentBalance.deref() + amount)
        println "deposit ${amount}... will it stay"
      } else {
        throw new RuntimeException("Operation invalid")
      }
  } as Callable)
}
```

The deposit modifies the current balance in a transaction if the amount is greater than 0. Otherwise, it causes the transaction to fail by throwing an exception. Implementing withdraw() is not much different; we merely have an extra check to perform.

polyglotSTM/groovy/clojure/Transfer.groovy
```
  def withdraw(amount) {
    LockingTransaction.runInTransaction({
      if(amount > 0 && currentBalance.deref() >= amount)
        currentBalance.set(currentBalance.deref() - amount)
      else
        throw new RuntimeException("Operation invalid")
    } as Callable)
  }
}
```

That's all the code in the Account class. Let's write a separate function that will perform the transfer so we can see nested transactions in action. In the transfer() method, first make a deposit and then a withdrawal. This way we can see the effect of a deposit being discarded if the withdrawal fails.

polyglotSTM/groovy/clojure/Transfer.groovy
```
def transfer(from, to, amount) {
  LockingTransaction.runInTransaction({
    to.deposit(amount)
    from.withdraw(amount)
  } as Callable)
}
```

It's time to exercise all that code, so let's write a simple call sequence to transfer some money between the accounts. We'll let the first transfer be for an amount that will succeed. Then we'll make a large transfer that will fail because of insufficient funds. This way, we can see the effects of the transactions.

polyglotSTM/groovy/clojure/Transfer.groovy
```
def transferAndPrint(from, to, amount) {
  try {
    transfer(from, to, amount)
  } catch(Exception ex) {
    println "transfer failed $ex"
  }
  println "Balance of from account is $from.balance"
  println "Balance of to account is  $to.balance"
}
def account1 = new Account(2000)
def account2 = new Account(100)
transferAndPrint(account1, account2, 500)
transferAndPrint(account1, account2, 5000)
```

Run the code and study the output:

```
deposit 500... will it stay
Balance of from account is 1500
Balance of to account is  600
deposit 5000... will it stay
transfer failed java.lang.RuntimeException: Operation invalid
Balance of from account is 1500
Balance of to account is  600
```

The first transfer succeeded, and the balances displayed reflects that. The second transfer completed the deposit first, but the withdrawal failed. The total effect of the failed transaction was to leave the balance of the two accounts unaffected.

Using Akka STM in Groovy

Using the Akka API in Groovy requires just a little bit more effort and some patience.

In Akka the transactional method atomic() is exposed through what's called a *package object*. Scala 2.8 package objects manifest themselves as a pair of classes in bytecode—the package and package$ classes. Groovy is not thrilled to see these lowercase names and names with $ for classes. So, we'll run into trouble if we try to use them directly.

There's a simple workaround, thankfully. Get a class reference to the package object using Class.forName(). The dynamic nature of Groovy will take us through the rest of the way quite easily. Simply invoke the atomic() method on the package reference and pass it a closure that implements Scala's closure represented by scala.Function0. We will also send a reference to the transaction factory. The atomic() method defines the second parameter, the transaction factory, as an implicit optional parameter. However, that's not recognized from Groovy, and so we're required to send it. We can obtain the default factory, to use default configuration settings, from the package object, or we can create our own instance of the factory with the configuration parameters we desire. Let's write the Account class to put all that to use:

polyglotSTM/groovy/akka/Transfer.groovy
```
class Account {
  private final Ref currentBalance
  private final stmPackage = Class.forName('akka.stm.package')
  public Account(initialBalance) { currentBalance = new Ref(initialBalance) }
  def getBalance() { currentBalance.get() }
  def deposit(amount) {
    stmPackage.atomic({
      if(amount > 0) {
        currentBalance.set(currentBalance.get() + amount)
        println "deposit ${amount}... will it stay"
      }
    } as scala.Function0, stmPackage.DefaultTransactionFactory())
  }
  def withdraw(amount) {
    stmPackage.atomic({
      if(amount > 0 && currentBalance.get() >= amount)
        currentBalance.set(currentBalance.get() - amount)
      else
        throw new RuntimeException("Operation invalid")
      } as scala.Function0, stmPackage.DefaultTransactionFactory())
  }
}
```

We pass the Java class name of the Scala package object to the forName() method and get a reference stmPackage to its Class meta-object. We then call the atomic() method of this class simply as stmPackage.atomic() and pass the two parameters: a closure and the stmPackage.DefaultTransactionFactory(). The code within our closure will run in a transaction managed by Akka/Multiverse.

The rest of the code for the transfer() method comes next; we again perform the deposit and then the withdraw from within a transaction.

polyglotSTM/groovy/akka/Transfer.groovy
```groovy
def transfer(from, to, amount) {
  def stmPackage = Class.forName('akka.stm.package')
  stmPackage.atomic({
    to.deposit(amount)
    from.withdraw(amount)
    } as scala.Function0, stmPackage.DefaultTransactionFactory())
}

def transferAndPrint(from, to, amount) {
  try {
    transfer(from, to, amount)
  } catch(Exception ex) {
    println "transfer failed $ex"
  }

  println "Balance of from account is $from.balance"
  println "Balance of to account is  $to.balance"
}

def account1 = new Account(2000)
def account2 = new Account(100)

transferAndPrint(account1, account2, 500)
transferAndPrint(account1, account2, 5000)
```

Run the Groovy code and see the transactions in action:

```
deposit 500... will it stay
deposit 500... will it stay
Balance of from account is 1500
Balance of to account is  600
deposit 5000... will it stay
transfer failed java.lang.RuntimeException: Operation invalid
Balance of from account is 1500
Balance of to account is  600
```

7.3 Java Integration

Although Java is showing its age, it's still one of the most widely used language. In this section, we'll see that selecting a concurrency model does not force us down the path of language selection. We'll reach out to the STM models right from within Java. We'll have to endure some Java-induced verbosity and have to ensure immutability; however, it's a breeze to use the STM API itself, as we'll see.

Using Clojure STM in Java

We can use Clojure STM for Java quite easily because Ref and LockingTransaction are exposed as simple classes. The runInTransaction() method takes as a parameter an instance that implements the Callable interface. So, wrapping code in a transaction is as simple as wrapping it in the Callable interface's call() method.

We'll implement the account transfer example using Clojure STM in Java. First let's create a class Account that will hold a managed reference to its immutable state represented by the variable balance:

```
polyglotSTM/java/clojure/Account.java
public class Account {
  final private Ref balance;

  public Account(final int initialBalance) throws Exception {
    balance = new Ref(initialBalance);
  }

  public int getBalance() { return (Integer) balance.deref(); }
```

We initialize the managed reference with the starting balance. To obtain the current balance, we use the deref() method, which is the Java-side API for the @ prefix we used in Clojure to dereference. The code to be wrapped within the transaction will sit within the Callable that's passed to the runInTransaction(), as we'll see in the deposit() method:

```
polyglotSTM/java/clojure/Account.java
public void deposit(final int amount) throws Exception {
  LockingTransaction.runInTransaction(new Callable<Boolean>() {
    public Boolean call()  {
      if(amount > 0) {
        final int currentBalance = (Integer) balance.deref();
        balance.set(currentBalance + amount);
        System.out.println("deposit " + amount + "... will it stay");
        return true;
      } else throw new RuntimeException("Operation invalid");
    }
  });
}
```

The deposit modifies the current balance in a transaction if the amount is greater than 0. Otherwise, it fails the transaction by throwing an exception.

Implementing withdraw() is not much different; it's just an extra check to perform:

polyglotSTM/java/clojure/Account.java
```java
  public void withdraw(final int amount) throws Exception {
    LockingTransaction.runInTransaction(new Callable<Boolean>() {
      public Boolean call() {
        final int currentBalance = (Integer) balance.deref();
        if(amount > 0 && currentBalance >= amount) {
          balance.set(currentBalance - amount);
          return true;
        } else throw new RuntimeException("Operation invalid");
      }
    });
  }
}
```

That takes care of the Account class. Let's focus on the transfer now; we'll write that in a separate class. To see the effect of a deposit being discarded by the failed withdraw, let's perform the deposit first followed by the withdraw:

polyglotSTM/java/clojure/Transfer.java
```java
public class Transfer {
  public static void transfer(
    final Account from, final Account to, final int amount)
    throws Exception {
    LockingTransaction.runInTransaction(new Callable<Boolean>() {
      public Boolean call() throws Exception {
        to.deposit(amount);
        from.withdraw(amount);
        return true;
      }
    });
  }
```

We'll need a convenience method that will handle the failed transfer and report the status of the accounts after the transfer:

polyglotSTM/java/clojure/Transfer.java
```java
  public static void transferAndPrint(
    final Account from, final Account to, final int amount) {
    try {
      transfer(from, to, amount);
    } catch(Exception ex) {
      System.out.println("transfer failed " + ex);
    }

    System.out.println("Balance of from account is " + from.getBalance());
    System.out.println("Balance of to account is " + to.getBalance());
  }
```

Let's perform a successful transfer first followed by a transfer that will fail because of insufficient funds:

polyglotSTM/java/clojure/Transfer.java
```java
  public static void main(final String[] args) throws Exception {
    final Account account1 = new Account(2000);
    final Account account2 = new Account(100);

    transferAndPrint(account1, account2, 500);
    transferAndPrint(account1, account2, 5000);
  }
}
```

Run the code and study the output:

```
deposit 500... will it stay
Balance of from account is 1500
Balance of to account is 600
deposit 5000... will it stay
transfer failed java.lang.RuntimeException: Operation invalid
Balance of from account is 1500
Balance of to account is 600
```

As we expected, the first transfer succeeded, and the balance displayed reflects that. The second transfer should fail because of insufficient funds. We see that the effect of the deposit that took effect was negated by the failed withdraw when the transaction rolled back. The failed transfer left the balance of the two accounts unaffected.

Using Multiverse/Akka STM in Java

If there's no need for actors (see Chapter 8, *Favoring Isolated Mutability*, on page 163), consider using Multiverse STM directly. With Multiverse, we can use Java-based annotation syntax and APIs. Akka is a good choice if the plan involves the use of actors or mixes them with STM. Even though Akka was built on Scala, they've done a wonderful job of providing a Java API. Chapter 6, *Introduction to Software Transactional Memory*, on page 89 is filled with Akka examples in Java to help you get started.

7.4 JRuby Integration

JRuby brings the power of Ruby along with its elegance, expressiveness, and conciseness to the Java platform. In this section, we'll use Clojure STM and Multiverse STM through Akka in JRuby code. If you'd like to use Multiverse directly, refer to the Multiverse documentation for the JRuby integration API.

Using Clojure STM in JRuby

To use Clojure STM from JRuby, we'll use clojure.lang.Ref for managed references and the runInTransaction() method of LockingTransaction for the transaction. Let's give that a try using the account transfer example. Create a class called Account that will hold a managed reference to its immutable state represented by the JRuby field @balance:

```
polyglotSTM/jruby/clojure/account.rb
require 'java'
java_import 'clojure.lang.Ref'
java_import 'clojure.lang.LockingTransaction'

class Account
  def initialize(initialBalance)
    @balance = Ref.new(initialBalance)
  end

  def balance
    @balance.deref
  end
```

We've initialized the managed reference with an initial balance. Just like in the Java integration, we use the deref() method to get the balance. To run a piece of code within a transaction, we'll have to send it to the runInTransaction() method, which takes a Callable class as the parameter. JRuby is quite fluent in implementing interfaces; simply send a code block, and it takes care of wrapping that into an interface implementation. Let's write the deposit() method of the Account class, which needs to run its operations in a transaction:

```
polyglotSTM/jruby/clojure/account.rb
def deposit(amount)
  LockingTransaction.run_in_transaction do
    if amount > 0
      @balance.set(@balance.deref + amount)
      puts "deposited $#{amount}... will it stay"
    else
      raise "Operation invalid"
    end
  end
end
```

The deposit modifies the balance within the transaction if the amount is appropriate; otherwise, it fails the transaction by throwing an exception. The withdraw() method will be similar:

polyglotSTM/jruby/clojure/account.rb

```ruby
  def withdraw(amount)
    LockingTransaction.run_in_transaction do
      if amount > 0 && @balance.deref >= amount
        @balance.set(@balance.deref - amount)
      else
        raise "Operation invalid"
      end
    end
  end
end
```

The Account class is ready. Now we need a method to nest the transactions and transfer money between accounts; let's write that as a separate function. To see that the effects of the deposit are negated by a failing withdraw, we'll perform the two operations in that order.

polyglotSTM/jruby/clojure/account.rb

```ruby
def transfer(from, to, amount)
  LockingTransaction.run_in_transaction do
    to.deposit(amount)
    from.withdraw(amount)
  end
end
```

Finally, it's time to exercise all that code, so write a simple call sequence to transfer some money between the accounts. Let's write it in a way that the first transfer succeeds and the second one fails because of an insufficient balance. This should show us the effect of transactions.

polyglotSTM/jruby/clojure/account.rb

```ruby
def transfer_and_print(from, to, amount)
  begin
    transfer(from, to, amount)
  rescue => ex
    puts "transfer failed #{ex}"
  end

  puts "Balance of from account is #{from.balance}"
  puts "Balance of to account is #{to.balance}"
end

account1 = Account.new(2000)
account2 = Account.new(100)

transfer_and_print(account1, account2, 500)
transfer_and_print(account1, account2, 5000)
```

Run the code and study the output:

```
deposited $500... will it stay
Balance of from account is 1500
Balance of to account is 600
deposited $5000... will it stay
transfer failed Operation invalid
Balance of from account is 1500
Balance of to account is 600
```

The behavior of the code is consistent with what we'd expect—the first transaction succeeded, and the balance reflects that. The second transfer failed and left the balance unaffected. The deposit that occurred as part of this transaction was discarded upon the transaction's failure.

Using Akka STM in JRuby

Using the Multiverse STM in JRuby requires just a little bit more effort and some patience. The main reason is that Multiverse relies on exceptions to retry transactions, but JRuby wraps exceptions into NativeException—so if we're not careful, Multiverse will not see the exceptions it expects, and the transaction will fail to commit. We will first face this problem in the example, but we will figure out a way to work around the problem.

In Akka the transactional method atomic() is exposed through what's called a *package object*. Scala package objects manifest themselves as a pair of classes in bytecode—the package and package$ classes. When we import the package class in JRuby, we will get a weird error: cannot import class `package' as `package'. To fix this error, let's redefine the package name to something other than package, such as java_import 'akka.stm.package' do |pkgname, classname| "J#{classname}" end. Now when we refer to Jpackage, we're referring to the Akka akka.stm.package package object.

We'll create the account transfer example using JRuby and Akka STM. Let's isolate the method that will use the Akka transaction into a separate module so it's easier to reuse that code:

```
polyglotSTM/jruby/akka/broken/akka_stm.rb
require 'java'
java_import 'akka.stm.Ref'
java_import 'akka.stm.package' do |pkgname, classname| "J#{classname}" end

module AkkaStm
  def atomic(&block)
    Jpackage.atomic Jpackage.DefaultTransactionFactory, &block
  end
end
```

We import Akka's Ref class and the package object akka.stm.package. In our AkkaStm module, we write a method called atomic() that receives a block of code and passes it to the akka.stm.package's atomic() method. Since the API exposed outside of Scala for this method requires the factory as well, we obtain the default transaction factory from the package object itself. Let's use this method to place Account methods in the transaction:

polyglotSTM/jruby/akka/transfer.rb
```ruby
require 'akka_stm'

class Account
  include AkkaStm
  def initialize(initialBalance)
    @balance = Ref.new(initialBalance)
  end
  def balance
    @balance.get
  end
  def deposit(amount)
    atomic do
      if amount > 0
        @balance.set(@balance.get + amount)
        puts "deposited $#{amount}... will it stay"
      end
    end
  end
  def withdraw(amount)
    atomic do
      raise "Operation invalid" if amount < 0 || @balance.get < amount
      @balance.set(@balance.get - amount)
    end
  end
end
```

We create a managed reference for the @balance field and place the operations in the deposit() and withdraw() methods in transactions by using our AkkaStm module's atomic() method. We bring that method into our Account class using incude—JRuby's *mixin* facility. We can write the transfer() method as a stand-alone method, and we can mix the AkkaStm module into it as well to reuse the atomic() method.

polyglotSTM/jruby/akka/transfer.rb
```ruby
def transfer(from, to, amount)
  include AkkaStm
  atomic do
    to.deposit(amount)
    from.withdraw(amount)
  end
end
```

As the final step, let's exercise all this code by invoking a couple of transfers:

polyglotSTM/jruby/akka/transfer.rb

```ruby
def transfer_and_print(from, to, amount)
  begin
    transfer(from, to, amount)
  rescue => ex
    puts "transfer failed #{ex}"
  end

  puts "Balance of from account is #{from.balance}"
  puts "Balance of to account is #{to.balance}"
end

account1 = Account.new(2000)
account2 = Account.new(100)

transfer_and_print(account1, account2, 500)
transfer_and_print(account1, account2, 5000)
```

We can expect the first transfer to succeed since the amount is less than the available funds. We'd want the second transfer to fail because of insufficient funds and leave the balance of the two accounts unaffected. Let's see what's in store when we run the code:

```
transfer failed
  org.multiverse.api.exceptions.SpeculativeConfigurationFailure: null
...
```

It's not quite what we wanted to see. This error did more than fail the first transfer's transaction—it also cost us significant time and hair loss. This is the error we alluded in the beginning of this section. The failure reported a SpeculativeConfigurationFailure exception, which is part of the org.multiverse.api.exceptions package. Let's understand where this came from and why things are failing suddenly in the JRuby version when the other language versions worked flawlessly.

By default Multiverse (and so Akka STM) uses speculative transactions, which we discussed in *Nested Transactions in Java*, on page 112. At first Multiverse assumes the transaction is read-only, and upon seeing the first set operation on a managed ref, it throws the SpeculativeConfigurationFailure exception. In the Multiverse layer, it handles this exception and retries the transaction, this time allowing for change to a managed ref. This is the reason we saw transactions being retried in Chapter 6, *Introduction to Software Transactional Memory*, on page 89. OK, that's Multiverse's business, and it seems to work fine so far in other languages, so let's figure out why things went wrong with JRuby.

If we replace this:

```
puts "transfer failed #{ex}"
```

with the following:

```
puts "transfer failed #{ex.class}"
```

we'll see the exception class name is not SpeculativeConfigurationFailure but Native-Exception. This is JRuby placing the exception in its own wrapper exception. So, from the JRuby code, we called into Akka, which in turn called into our JRuby closure. This closure tried to update the managed reference, and that caused the Multiverse exception like it's designed to do. Our JRuby closure code—unfortunately—internally wrapped that exception into a Na-tiveException. So, instead of seeing the familiar SpeculativeConfigurationFailure, Multiverse sees this strange unexpected NativeException and simply fails the transaction and propagates the exception up the chain without retrying the transaction.

So, what's the fix? Not a pleasant one: we have to handle it explicitly. We need to check whether the exception belongs to Multiverse and, if so, unwrap it up the chain. It's an ugly workaround, but it's not too much code. Let's modify AkkaStm's atomic() method to compensate for the JRuby behavior:

```
polyglotSTM/jruby/akka/akka_stm.rb
require 'java'
java_import 'akka.stm.Ref'
java_import 'akka.stm.package' do |pkgname, classname| "J#{classname}" end
module AkkaStm
  def atomic(&block)
    begin
      Jpackage.atomic Jpackage.DefaultTransactionFactory, &block
    rescue NativeException => ex
      raise ex.cause if
        ex.cause.java_class.package.name.include? "org.multiverse"
      raise ex
    end
  end
end
```

We wrap the call to akka.stm.package.atomic around a begin-rescue block, and if the exception thrown at us is a NativeException and if the embedded real cause is a Multiverse exception, then we throw the unwrapped exception so Multi-verse can handle it and take the appropriate action.

Now that we have fixed it, let's see whether the two transactions behave as expected, the first one succeeding and the second one failing, leaving the balance unaffected:

```
deposited $500... will it stay
deposited $500... will it stay
Balance of from account is 1500
Balance of to account is 600
deposited $5000... will it stay
transfer failed Operation invalid
Balance of from account is 1500
Balance of to account is 600
```

After the fix, the JRuby version behaves like the versions in other languages.

7.5 Choices in Scala

Scala is a statically typed language on the JVM, which bridges object-oriented style and functional style of programming. We have quite a few options to make use of STM from this highly expressive language. It's likely that we'd lean toward the Akka solution because the Scala API it provides will be the most fluent. However, if we're on a multilanguage project that's already using Clojure STM, nothing stops us from using that from Scala. Let's explore using Clojure STM here.

Using Clojure STM in Scala

Using Clojure STM in Scala is going to follow along pretty much the lines of Java. We can use the Ref class and the runInTransaction() method of the LockingTransaction class. We create an instance that implements Callable to wrap the method that should run in a transaction. Let's implement the account transfer example using Scala and Clojure STM. It's pretty much a direct translation of the code from Java to Scala.

polyglotSTM/scala/clojure/Transfer.scala
```scala
class Account(val initialBalance : Int) {
  val balance = new Ref(initialBalance)

  def getBalance() = balance.deref
```

In the primary constructor, which is part of the class definition in Scala, we initialized the reference with the initial balance value. In the getBalance() method, we obtain the balance using a call to the deref() method. To update the managed reference in a transaction, we simply need to wrap it into a Callable and pass it to the runInTransaction() method. Let's write the deposit method whose operations need to run in a transaction:

polyglotSTM/scala/clojure/Transfer.scala
```scala
def deposit(amount : Int) = {
  LockingTransaction runInTransaction new Callable[Boolean] {
    def call() = {
      if(amount > 0) {
```

```
      val currentBalance = balance.deref.asInstanceOf[Int]
      balance.set(currentBalance + amount)
      println("deposit " + amount + "... will it stay")
      true
    } else throw new RuntimeException("Operation invalid")
    }
  }
}
```

The withdraw is going to follow along similar steps:

polyglotSTM/scala/clojure/Transfer.scala
```
  def withdraw(amount : Int) = {
    LockingTransaction runInTransaction new Callable[Boolean] {
      def call() = {
        val currentBalance = balance.deref.asInstanceOf[Int]
        if(amount > 0 && currentBalance >= amount) {
          balance.set(currentBalance - amount)
          true
        } else throw new RuntimeException("Operation invalid")
      }
    }
  }
}
```

We've completed the Account class. We can write the transfer() method as a stand-alone method, since we don't need a class for that in Scala if we run it as a script. If we plan to compile the code, then we have to wrap it into an object and write the main() method:

polyglotSTM/scala/clojure/Transfer.scala
```
def transfer(from : Account, to : Account, amount : Int) = {
  LockingTransaction runInTransaction new Callable[Boolean] {
    def call() = {
      to.deposit(amount)
      from.withdraw(amount)
      true
    }
  }
}
```

In the transfer() method, we first make the deposit and then the withdrawal. As in the previous examples, we want to study the effect of transactions:

polyglotSTM/scala/clojure/Transfer.scala
```
def transferAndPrint(from : Account, to : Account, amount : Int) = {
  try {
    transfer(from, to, amount)
  } catch {
    case ex => println("transfer failed " + ex)
  }
```

```
    println("Balance of from account is " + from.getBalance())
    println("Balance of to account is " + to.getBalance())
}

val account1 = new Account(2000)
val account2 = new Account(100)

transferAndPrint(account1, account2, 500)
transferAndPrint(account1, account2, 5000)
```

Let's run the code and study the output:

```
deposit 500... will it stay
Balance of from account is 1500
Balance of to account is 600
deposit 5000... will it stay
transfer failed java.lang.RuntimeException: Operation invalid
Balance of from account is 1500
Balance of to account is 600
```

That's exactly what we'd expect—a successful first transaction that changes the balance appropriately, followed by a failed transaction that leaves the balance unaffected.

Using Akka/Multiverse STM in Scala

Akka is certainly a good choice, because it was written in Scala and the APIs it exposes will feel natural to Scala programmers. Refer to the Scala examples in Chapter 6, *Introduction to Software Transactional Memory*, on page 89 to get started on using STM with Akka. Scala, being a hybrid functional programming language, allows us to create both mutable (var) variables and immutable (val) values. As good practice, it's better to promote immutability: use vals more than vars. Do a quick grep/search to see whether we have vars and examine them closely. Ensure that the state is immutable and only the identity Refs are mutable.

7.6 Recap

In this chapter, we learned the following:

- Concurrency choice is orthogonal to language choice; we can program concurrency with STM from any of the JVM languages.

- There are a few rough edges with integration we'll run into, but the workarounds are fairly easy.

- We have to ensure that values are immutable and transactions are idempotent.

For applications with frequent reads and reasonable write collisions, we can make use of STM from any JVM language. But when huge write collisions creep in, STM may not be suitable. In that case, to avoid synchronization and shared mutability nightmares, we can benefit from the actor-based model we discuss in the next chapter.

Part IV

Actor-Based Concurrency

There is always a better way.
    Thomas Alva Edison

CHAPTER 8

Favoring Isolated Mutability

"If it hurts, stop doing it" is a doctor's good advice. In concurrent programming, shared mutability is "it."

With the JDK threading API, it's easy to create threads, but it soon becomes a struggle to prevent them from colliding and messing up. The STM eases that pain quite a bit; however, in languages like Java, we must still be very careful to avoid unmanaged mutable variables and side effects. Surprisingly, the struggles disappear when shared mutability disappears.

Letting multiple threads converge and collide on data is an approach we've tried in vain. Fortunately, there's a better way—event-based message passing. In this approach, we treat tasks as lightweight processes, internal to the application/JVM. Instead of letting them grab the data, we pass immutable messages to them. Once these asynchronous tasks complete, they pass back or pass on their immutable results to other coordinating task(s). We design applications with coordinating actors[1] that asynchronously exchange immutable messages.

This approach has been around for a few decades but is relatively new in the JVM arena. The actor-based model is quite successful and popular in Erlang (see *Programming Erlang: Software for a Concurrent World* [Arm07] and *Concurrent Programming in Erlang* [VWWA96]). Erlang's actor-based model was adopted and brought into the fold of the JVM when Scala was introduced in 2003 (see *Programming in Scala* [OSV08] and *Programming Scala* [Sub09]).

---

1. Someone asked me what these *actors* have to do with actors in use cases—nothing. These actors *act* upon messages they receive, perform their dedicated tasks, and pass response messages for other actors...to act upon in turn.

In Java, we get to choose from more than half a dozen libraries[2] that provide actor-based concurrency: ActorFoundary, Actorom, Actors Guild, Akka, FunctionalJava, Kilim, Jetlang, and so on. Some of these libraries use aspect-oriented bytecode weaving. Each of them is at a different level of maturity and adoption.

In this chapter, we'll learn how to program actor-based concurrency. For the most part, we'll use Akka as a vehicle to drive home the concepts. Akka is a high-performing Scala-based solution that exposes fairly good Java API. We can use it for both actor-based concurrency and for STM (see Chapter 6, *Introduction to Software Transactional Memory*, on page 89).

8.1 Isolating Mutability Using Actors

Java turned OOP into mutability-driven development,[3] while functional programming emphasizes immutability; both extremes are problematic. If everything is mutable, we have to tackle visibility and race conditions. In a realistic application, everything can't be immutable. Even pure functional languages provide restricted areas of code that allow side effects and ways to sequence them. Whichever programming model we favor, it's clear we must avoid shared mutability.

Shared mutability—the root of concurrency problems—is where multiple threads can modify a variable. Isolated mutability—a nice compromise that removes most concurrency concerns—is where only one thread (or actor) can access a mutable variable, ever.

In OOP, we encapsulate so only the instance methods can manipulate the state of an object. However, different threads may call these methods, and that leads to concurrency concerns. In the actor-based programming model, we allow only one actor to manipulate the state of an object. While the application is multithreaded, the actors themselves are single-threaded, and so there are no visibility and race condition concerns. Actors request operations to be performed, but they don't reach over the mutable state managed by other actors.

We take a different design approach when programming with actors compared to programming merely with objects. We divide the problem into asynchronous computational tasks and assign them to different actors. Each actor's focus is on performing its designated task. We confine any mutable state to within at most one actor, period (see Figure 11, *Actors*

---

2. Imagine how boring it would be if we had just one good solution to pick.
3. Java had other partners in this crime, so it doesn't deserve all the blame.

isolate mutable state and communicate by passing immutable messages., on page 166). We also ensure that the messages we pass between actors are totally immutable.

In this design approach, we let each actor work on part of the problem. They receive the necessary data as immutable objects. Once they complete their assigned task, they send the results, as immutable objects, to the calling actor or another designated post-processing actor. We can think of this as taking OOP to the next level where select objects—mutable and active—run in their own threads. The only way we're allowed to manipulate these objects is by sending messages to them and not by directly calling methods.

8.2 Actor Qualities

An actor is a free-running activity that can receive messages, process requests, and send responses. Actors are designed to support asynchrony and efficient messaging.

Each actor has a built-in message queue much like the message queue behind a cell phone. Both Sally and Sean may leave a message at the same time on Bob's cell phone. The cell phone provider saves both their messages for Bob to retrieve at his convenience. Similarly, the actor library allows multiple actors to send messages concurrently. The senders are nonblocking by default; they send off a message and proceed to take care of their business. The library lets the designated actor sequentially pick its messages to process. Once an actor processes a message or delegates to another actor for concurrent processing, it's ready to receive the next message.

The life cycle of an actor is shown in Figure 12, *Life cycle of an actor*, on page 167. Upon creation, an actor may be started or stopped. Once started, it prepares to receive messages. In the active states, the actor is either processing a message or waiting for a new message to arrive. Once it's stopped, it no longer receives any messages. How much time an actor spends waiting vs. processing a message depends on the dynamic nature of the application they're part of.

If actors play a major role in our design, we'd expect many of them to float around during the execution of the application. However, threads are limited resources, and so tying actors to their threads will be very limiting. To avoid that, actor libraries in general decouple actors from threads. Threads are to actors as cafeteria seats are to office employees. Bob doesn't have a designated seat at his company cafeteria (he needs to find another job if he does), and each time he goes for a meal, he gets seated in one of the available

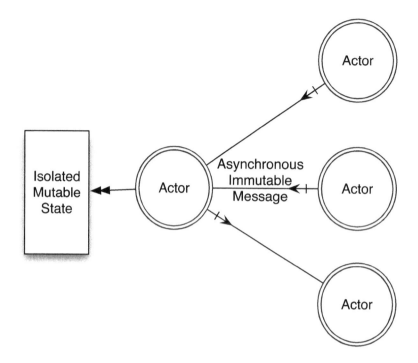

Figure 11—Actors isolate mutable state and communicate by passing immutable messages.

seats. When an actor has a message to process or a task to run, it's provided an available thread to run. Good actors don't hold threads when they're not running a task. This allows for a greater number of actors to be active in different states and provides for efficient use of limited available threads. Although multiple actors may be active at any time, only one thread is active in an actor at any instance. This provides concurrency among actors while eliminating contention within each actor.

8.3 Creating Actors

We have quite a few choices of actor libraries to pick from, as I mentioned earlier. In this book, we use Akka, a Scala-based library[4] with pretty good performance and scalability and with support for both actors and STM. We can use it from multiple languages on the JVM. In this chapter, we'll stick

---

4. In addition to Akka, there are at least two more Scala-based libraries—Scala actors library and the Lift actors.

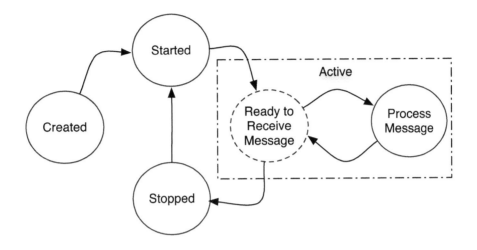

Figure 12—Life cycle of an actor

to Java and Scala. In the next chapter, we'll take a look at using Akka actors with other languages.

Akka was written in Scala, so it's quite simple and more natural to create and use actors from Scala. Scala conciseness and idioms shine in the Akka API. At the same time, they've done quite a wonderful job of exposing a traditional Java API so we can easily create and use actors in Java code. We'll first take a look at using it in Java and then see how that experience simplifies and changes when we use it in Scala.

Creating Actors in Java

Akka's abstract class akka.actor.UntypedActor represents an actor. Simply extend this and implement the required onReceive() method—this method is called whenever a message arrives for the actor. Let's give it a shot. We'll create an actor...how about a HollywoodActor that'll respond to requests to play different roles?

favoringIsolatedMutability/java/create/HollywoodActor.java
```java
public class HollywoodActor extends UntypedActor {
  public void onReceive(final Object role) {
    System.out.println("Playing " + role +
      " from Thread " + Thread.currentThread().getName());
  }
}
```

The onReceive() method takes an Object as a parameter. In this example, we're simply printing it out along with the details of the thread that's processing the message. We'll learn how to deal with different types of messages later.

Our actor is all set and waiting for us to say "action." We need to create an instance of the actor and send messages with their role, so let's get to that:

favoringIsolatedMutability/java/create/UseHollywoodActor.java
```
public class UseHollywoodActor {
  public static void main(final String[] args) throws InterruptedException {
    final ActorRef johnnyDepp = Actors.actorOf(HollywoodActor.class).start();
    johnnyDepp.sendOneWay("Jack Sparrow");
    Thread.sleep(100);
    johnnyDepp.sendOneWay("Edward Scissorhands");
    Thread.sleep(100);
    johnnyDepp.sendOneWay("Willy Wonka");
    Actors.registry().shutdownAll();
  }
}
```

In Java we'd generally create objects using new, but Akka actors are not simple objects—they're active objects. So, we create them using a special method actorOf(). Alternately, we could create an instance using new and wrap it around a call to actorOf() to get an actor reference, but let's get to that later. As soon as we create the actor, we start it by calling the start() method. When we start an actor, Akka puts it into a registry; the actor is accessible through the registry until the actor is stopped. In the example, now johnnyDepp, of type ActorRef, is a reference to our actor instance.

Next we send a few messages to the actor with roles to play using the sendOneWay() method. Once a message is sent, we really don't have to wait. However, in this case, the delay will help us learn one more detail, which is how actors switch threads, as we'll see soon. In the end, we ask to close down all running actors. Instead of calling the shutdownAll() method, we may call the stop() method on individual actors or send them a kill message as well.

All right, to run the example, let's compile the code using javac and remember to specify the classpath to Akka library files. We can simply run the program as we would run regular Java programs. Again, we must remember to provide the necessary JARs in the classpath. Here's the command I used on my system:

```
javac -d . -classpath $AKKA_JARS HollywoodActor.java UseHollywoodActor.java
java -classpath $AKKA_JARS com.agiledeveloper.pcj.UseHollywoodActor
```

where AKKA_JARS is defined as follows:

```
export AKKA_JARS="$AKKA_HOME/lib/scala-library.jar:\
$AKKA_HOME/lib/akka/akka-stm-1.1.3.jar:\
$AKKA_HOME/lib/akka/akka-actor-1.1.3.jar:\
$AKKA_HOME/lib/akka/multiverse-alpha-0.6.2.jar:\
$AKKA_HOME/lib/akka/akka-typed-actor-1.1.3.jar:\
$AKKA_HOME/lib/akka/aspectwerkz-2.2.3.jar:\
$AKKA_HOME/config:\
."
```

We need to define the AKKA_JARS environment variable appropriately for our operating system to match the location where we have Scala and Akka installed. We may use the scala-library.jar file that comes with Akka, or we may use it from the local Scala installation.

By default Akka prints extra log messages on the standard output; we saw how to configure that in *Creating Transactions in Java*, on page 105.

Let's compile and run the code to watch our actor responding to messages:

```
Playing Jack Sparrow from Thread akka:event-driven:dispatcher:global-1
Playing Edward Scissorhands from Thread akka:event-driven:dispatcher:global-2
Playing Willy Wonka from Thread akka:event-driven:dispatcher:global-3
```

The actor responds to the messages one at a time. The output also lets us peek at the thread that's running the actor, and it's not the same thread each time. It's possible that the same thread handles multiple messages, or it could be different like in this sample output—but in any case only one message will be handled at any time. The key point is that the actors are single-threaded but don't hold their threads hostage. They gracefully release their threads when they wait for a message; the delay we added helped introduce this wait and illustrate this point.

The actor we created did not take any parameters at construction time. If we desire, we can send parameters during actor creation. For example, to initialize the actor with the Hollywood actor's name:

favoringIsolatedMutability/java/params/HollywoodActor.java
```java
public class HollywoodActor extends UntypedActor {
  private final String name;
  public HollywoodActor(final String theName) { name = theName; }

  public void onReceive(final Object role) {
    if(role instanceof String)
      System.out.println(String.format("%s playing %s", name, role));
    else
      System.out.println(name + " plays no " + role);
  }
}
```

The new version of the class HollywoodActor takes a value name of type String as the constructor parameter. While we're at it, let's take care of handling the unrecognized incoming message format. In this example, we simply print a message saying the Hollywood actor does not play that unrecognized message. We can take other actions such as returning an error code, logging, calling the user's mom to report, and so on. Let's see how we can pass the actual argument for this constructor parameter:

favoringIsolatedMutability/java/params/UseHollywoodActor.java

```java
public class UseHollywoodActor {
  public static void main(final String[] args) throws InterruptedException {

    final ActorRef tomHanks = Actors.actorOf(new UntypedActorFactory() {
      public UntypedActor create() { return new HollywoodActor("Hanks"); }
    }).start();

    tomHanks.sendOneWay("James Lovell");
    tomHanks.sendOneWay(new StringBuilder("Politics"));
    tomHanks.sendOneWay("Forrest Gump");
    Thread.sleep(1000);
    tomHanks.stop();
  }
}
```

We communicate with actors by sending messages and not by invoking methods directly. Akka wants to make it hard to get a direct reference to actors and wants us to get only a reference to ActorRef. This allows Akka to ensure that we don't add methods to actors and interact with them directly, because that would take us back to the evil land of shared mutability that we're trying so hard to avoid. This controlled creation of actors also allows Akka to garbage collect the actors appropriately. So, if we try to create an instance of an actor class directly, we'll get the runtime exception akka.actor.ActorInitializationException with the message "You can not create an instance of an actor explicitly using 'new'."

Akka allows us to create an instance in a controlled fashion, within a create() method. So, let's implement this method in an anonymous class that implements the UntypedActorFactory interface and within this method create our actor instance, sending the appropriate construction-time parameters. The subsequent call to actorOf() turns the regular object that extends from UntypedActor into an Akka actor. We can then pass messages to this actor like before.

Our HollywoodActor only accepts messages of type String, but in the example, we're sending an instance of StringBuilder with the value Politics. The runtime type checking we performed in the onReceive() takes care of this. Finally, we stop the actor by calling the stop() method. The delay introduced gives time for the actor to respond to messages before we shut it down. Let's take it for a ride to see the output:

```
Hanks playing James Lovell
Hanks plays no Politics
Hanks playing Forrest Gump
```

Creating Actors in Scala

To create an Akka actor in Scala, instead of the UntypedActor we extended in the Java version, we'll extend from the Actor trait and implement the required receive() method. Let's implement in Scala the HollywoodActor actor class that we wrote earlier in Java:

favoringIsolatedMutability/scala/create/HollywoodActor.scala
```
class HollywoodActor extends Actor {
  def receive = {
    case role =>
    println("Playing " + role +
      " from Thread " + Thread.currentThread().getName())
  }
}
```

The receive() method implements a PartialFunction and takes the form of Scala pattern matching, but let's not let those details distract us now. This method is called when a message arrives; if it helps, think of the receive() as a glorified switch statement for now. The implementation is much the same as in the Java version.

Now that we've seen how to define an actor, let's turn our attention to using this actor:

favoringIsolatedMutability/scala/create/UseHollywoodActor.scala
```
object UseHollywoodActor {
  def main(args : Array[String]) :Unit = {
    val johnnyDepp = Actor.actorOf[HollywoodActor].start()

    johnnyDepp ! "Jack Sparrow"
    Thread.sleep(100)
    johnnyDepp ! "Edward Scissorhands"
    Thread.sleep(100)
    johnnyDepp ! "Willy Wonka"

    Actors.registry.shutdownAll
  }
}
```

There are a few flavors of the actorOf() method, and here we are using the version that takes as a parameter an actor class manifest, presented as [HollywoodActor]. As soon as we create the actor, we start it by calling the start() method. In the example, now johnnyDepp, of type ActorRef, is a reference to our actor instance; however, since Scala has type inference, we didn't have to specify the type.

Next we send a few messages to the actor with the roles to play. Oh wait, there's one other detail; we use a special method ! to send the message. When you see actor ! message, read it right to left, like sending the message to the actor. Scala's conciseness again is at play here. Instead of calling actor.!(message), we can simply drop the dot and parentheses and write actor ! message. If we prefer, we can use the Java-style methods with Scala conciseness, as in actor sendOneWay message. The rest of the code in the example is similar to the Java example.

Let's compile the code using the scalac compiler, but first we must remember to specify the classpath to Akka library files. We can simply run the program as we would run regular Java programs. Again, we must remember to provide the necessary JARs in the classpath. Here's the command I used on my system; we need to substitute the paths as appropriate for the system based on where Scala and Akka are installed:

```
scalac -classpath $AKKA_JARS HollywoodActor.scala UseHollywoodActor.scala
java -classpath $AKKA_JARS com.agiledeveloper.pcj.UseHollywoodActor
```

If we see log messages on the standard output and want to silence them, see the details presented for that after the Java actor example. Once we compile and run the code, the output we'll see will be similar to the one the Java version produced:

```
Playing Jack Sparrow from Thread akka:event-driven:dispatcher:global-1
Playing Edward Scissorhands from Thread akka:event-driven:dispatcher:global-2
Playing Willy Wonka from Thread akka:event-driven:dispatcher:global-3
```

If we want to pass parameters, such as the Hollywood actor's name, to the actor, it's a lot simpler in Scala than in the Java version. Let's first change the class HollywoodActor to accept a constructor parameter:

favoringIsolatedMutability/scala/params/HollywoodActor.scala
```
class HollywoodActor(val name : String) extends Actor {
  def receive = {
    case role : String => println(String.format("%s playing %s", name, role))
    case msg => println(name + " plays no " + msg)
  }
}
```

The new version of the class HollywoodActor takes a value name of type String as the constructor parameter. While we're at it, let's take care of handling the unrecognized incoming message format. Rather than using instanceof, the case statements take care of matching the message with various patterns—the type of the message, in this example.

Creating an actor that accepts a constructor parameter took some effort in Java, but it fizzles down to something quite simple in Scala:

favoringIsolatedMutability/scala/params/UseHollywoodActor.scala
```scala
object UseHollywoodActor {
  def main(args : Array[String]) : Unit = {

    val tomHanks = Actor.actorOf(new HollywoodActor("Hanks")).start()

    tomHanks ! "James Lovell"
    tomHanks ! new StringBuilder("Politics")
    tomHanks ! "Forrest Gump"
    Thread.sleep(1000)
    tomHanks.stop()
  }
}
```

We instantiated the actor using the new keyword and then passed the instance to the actorOf() method (here again Akka prevents us from creating instances of actors arbitrarily outside of calls to the actorOf() method). This turns the regular object that extends from Actor into an Akka actor. We then pass messages like we did before. The rest of the code is similar to the Java version. Let's run the code and ensure the output is similar to the Java version's output:

```
Hanks playing James Lovell
Hanks plays no Politics
Hanks playing Forrest Gump
```

8.4 Sending and Receiving Messages

We can send just about any type of message to an actor—String, Integer, Long, Double, List, Map, tuples, Scala case classes...all of which are immutable. I have a special liking for tuples, not because it's amusing when we mispronounce them as "two-ples" but because they're lightweight, immutable, and one of the easiest instances to create. For example, to create a tuple of two numbers in Scala, we simply write (number1, number2). Scala's case classes are ideal to serve as message types—they're immutable, work well with pattern matching, and are quite easy to make copy of. In Java we could pass an unmodifiable Collection as messages to send more than one object in a message. When we pass a message to an actor, by default we're passing the message's reference if both the sender and the receiver are within the same JVM.[5] It's our responsibility to ensure that the messages we pass are immutable, especially if we decide to send instances of our own classes. We may also ask Akka to serialize a message so a copy of the message is delivered instead of a reference.

The simplest way to communicate with an actor is "fire and forget." That is, send a message and move on. This is also the preferred way from the performance point of view. The send is nonblocking, and the calling actor/thread proceeds with its work. We use the sendOneWay() method, or the ! method in Scala, to send a one-way message.

Akka also provides two-way communication where we can send a message and expect a response from the actor. The calling thread, in this case, will block until it receives a response or exceeds a timeout. Let's take a look at how to send and receive messages first in Java and then in Scala.

Send/Receive in Java

We use the sendRequestReply() method to send a message and wait for a response. If a response does not arrive within a (configurable) timeout, we receive an ActorTimeoutException. Let's take a look at an example of two-way messaging:

favoringIsolatedMutability/java/2way/FortuneTeller.java
```java
public class FortuneTeller extends UntypedActor {
  public void onReceive(final Object name) {
      getContext().replyUnsafe(String.format("%s you'll rock", name));
  }

  public static void main(final String[] args) {
    final ActorRef fortuneTeller =
      Actors.actorOf(FortuneTeller.class).start();
    try {
      final Object response = fortuneTeller.sendRequestReply("Joe");
      System.out.println(response);
    } catch(ActorTimeoutException ex) {
      System.out.println("Never got a response before timeout");
    } finally {
      fortuneTeller.stop();
    }
  }
}
```

---

5. Akka also supports remote actors, allowing us to send messages between discrete processes running on different machines.

We have a FortuneTeller actor that wants to respond to the message it receives. It responds to the message sender by calling the replyUnsafe() method on the call context obtained through getContext(). The replyUnsafe() method sends off, without blocking, a response to the caller, but there's no calling actor in the code. In the main() method, we invoked the sendRequestReply() method. This method internally creates a Future class and waits on that until it gets a result, an exception, or a timeout. Let's check Joe's fortune by running the code:

```
Joe you'll rock
```

There's one thing that is a bit unfortunate with this FortuneTeller: it relies on the sender waiting for a response to be available. We called the sendRequestReply() method, so there was an internal Future that was used to wait for a response. If we had called sendOneWay() instead, the replyUnsafe() method would fail. To avoid this from happening, we need to check whether a blocking sender is available before we call the replyUnsafe() method. We can do this by obtaining the sender reference from the context. Alternately, we can use the replySafe() method, which will return a true if the sender reference was present and a false if no sender reference is available. So, here's the modified FortuneTeller that'll handle the case when no sender is waiting for a response:

favoringIsolatedMutability/java/2waysafe/FortuneTeller.java
```java
public class FortuneTeller extends UntypedActor {
  public void onReceive(final Object name) {
    if(getContext().replySafe(String.format("%s you'll rock", name)))
      System.out.println("Message sent for " + name);
    else
      System.out.println("Sender not found for " + name);
  }

  public static void main(final String[] args) {
    final ActorRef fortuneTeller =
      Actors.actorOf(FortuneTeller.class).start();

    try {
      fortuneTeller.sendOneWay("Bill");
      final Object response = fortuneTeller.sendRequestReply("Joe");
      System.out.println(response);
    } catch(ActorTimeoutException ex) {
      System.out.println("Never got a response before timeout");
    } finally {
      fortuneTeller.stop();
    }
  }
}
```

The new version of FortuneTeller will not fail if a sender is not known; it gracefully handles the misfortune.

```
Sender not found for Bill
Message sent for Joe
Joe you'll rock
```

The call to sendRequestReply() blocks while waiting for a response, but the call to sendOneWay() is nonblocking and yields no response. If we want to receive a response but don't want to wait for it, we can use the more elaborate method sendRequestReplyFuture(), which will return a Future object. We can go about doing work until we want the response, at which time we can either block or query the future object to see whether a response is available. Similarly, on the side of the actor, we can get the senderFuture from the context reference and communicate through that right away or later when we have a response ready. We'll take a look at using these later in an example.

Exercise caution when using the sendRequestReply() and sendRequestReplyFuture() methods because calls to these methods block and can have a negative impact on performance and scalability.

Send/Receive in Scala

We have to be ready for some differences from the Java API if we want to send/receive messages to actors from Scala:

- We can directly use the self property to get access to the actor. Using this property, we can call the reply() method, which is the unsafe equivalent on the Scala side, or we can use the replySafe() method.

- We could call the sendRequestReply() method, or we could call a more elegant !! method—they say beauty is in the eyes of the beholder. Similarly, !!! can be used in place of the sendRequestReplyFuture() method.

- Instead of returning an Object, the sendRequestReply() method returns a Scala Option. If the response arrived, this would be an instance of Some[T], which holds the result, and None in the case of a timeout. So, unlike the Java version, there's no exception in the case of a timeout.

Let's implement the FortuneTeller in Scala using the unsafe reply() method first:

favoringIsolatedMutability/scala/2way/FortuneTeller.scala
```scala
class FortuneTeller extends Actor {
  def receive = {
    case name : String =>
      self.reply(String.format("%s you'll rock", name))
  }
}
```

```scala
object FortuneTeller {
  def main(args : Array[String]) : Unit = {
    val fortuneTeller = Actor.actorOf[FortuneTeller].start()

    val response = fortuneTeller !! "Joe"
    response match {
      case Some(responseMessage) => println(responseMessage)
      case None => println("Never got a response before timeout")
    }

    fortuneTeller.stop()
  }
}
```

In the actor code we can see the two differences; one is related to self instead of getContext(), and the other is reply() instead of replyUnsafe(). On the caller side, we apply pattern matching on the response we received from the call to !!, which is the sendRequestReply() method. The first case is exercised if an actual response arrived, and the second case with None is used in case of a timeout. The output of this code is the same as the Java version, as we'd expect:

```
Joe you'll rock
```

Other than the changes we discussed, using the safe version of reply() is not much different from the Java version. We can use the reply_?() or replySafe().

favoringIsolatedMutability/scala/2waysafe/FortuneTeller.scala
```scala
class FortuneTeller extends Actor {
  def receive = {
    case name : String =>
      if(self.reply_?(String.format("%s you'll rock", name)))
        println("Message sent for " + name)
      else
        println("Sender not found for " + name)
  }
}
object FortuneTeller {
  def main(args : Array[String]) : Unit = {
    val fortuneTeller = Actor.actorOf[FortuneTeller].start()
    fortuneTeller ! "Bill"
    val response = fortuneTeller !! "Joe"
    response match {
      case Some(responseMessage) => println(responseMessage)
      case None => println("Never got a response before timeout")
    }
    fortuneTeller.stop()
  }
}
```

The new version of FortuneTeller will not fail if a sender is not known:

```
Sender not found for Bill
Message sent for Joe
Joe you'll rock
```

It is quite convenient that Akka passes the sender references under the covers when it sends a message. This eliminates the need to pass the sender explicitly as part of the message and removes so much noise and effort in the code.

If the use of method names like !, !!, !!!, and reply_?() bothers our eyes, we can use alternate names like sendOneWay(), sendRequestReply(), sendRequestReplyFuture(), and replySafe(), respectively.

8.5 Working with Multiple Actors

We now know how to create an actor and send messages to it. Let's get a feel for putting multiple actors to work. In Chapter 2, *Division of Labor*, on page 15, we created a concurrent program to count primes in a range. In the example in *Concurrent Computation of Prime Numbers*, on page 27, we used ExecutorService, Callable, and Future and filled up a little over a page with code. Let's see how that example shapes up with Akka actors first in Java and then in Scala.

Multiple Actors in Java

Given a number like 10 million, we divided the computation of primes into different ranges and distributed these ranges over several threads. Here we're going to use actors. Let's start with the actor's onReceive() method:

favoringIsolatedMutability/java/primes/Primes.java
```java
public class Primes extends UntypedActor {
  public void onReceive(final Object boundsList) {
    final List<Integer> bounds = (List<Integer>) boundsList;
    final int count =
      PrimeFinder.countPrimesInRange(bounds.get(0), bounds.get(1));
    getContext().replySafe(count);
  }
}
```

To compute the number of primes in a range, we need the lower and upper bounds of the range. Our actor receives this bundled as a List in the message parameter to onReceive(). We invoke the countPrimesInRange() method of the yet to be written PrimeFinder and send back the result to the caller using the replySafe() method.

Given a number, we need to divide it into the given number of parts and delegate the finding of primes in each of these parts to different actors. Let's do that in a countPrimes() static method:

favoringIsolatedMutability/java/primes/Primes.java
```
public static int countPrimes(
  final int number, final int numberOfParts) {
  final int chunksPerPartition = number / numberOfParts;
  final List<Future<?>> results = new ArrayList<Future<?>>();
  for(int index = 0; index < numberOfParts; index++) {
    final int lower = index * chunksPerPartition + 1;
    final int upper = (index == numberOfParts - 1) ? number :
        lower + chunksPerPartition - 1;
    final List<Integer> bounds = Collections.unmodifiableList(
      Arrays.asList(lower, upper));
    final ActorRef primeFinder = Actors.actorOf(Primes.class).start();
    results.add(primeFinder.sendRequestReplyFuture(bounds));
  }

  int count = 0;
  for(Future<?> result : results)
    count += (Integer)(result.await().result().get());

  Actors.registry().shutdownAll();
  return count;
}
```

Once we determined the bounds for each part, we wrapped that into an unmodifiable collection—remember, messages have to be immutable. We then call sendRequestReplyFuture() so we can send requests to all the partitions without being blocked. We save away Future (here it's akka.dispatch.Future and not the JDK's java.util.concurrent.Future) returned by this method so we can query later for the number of primes resulting from each part. We call await() on Future and invoke the result() method on the Future instance returned by await(). This gives us an instance of Scala Option—think of this as a fancy union that holds the value if available. We get the Integer value from that object finally by calling the get() method.

OK, let's drive the code using the command-line parameters for the number and parts:

favoringIsolatedMutability/java/primes/Primes.java
```
  public static void main(final String[] args) {
    if (args.length < 2)
      System.out.println("Usage: number numberOfParts");
    else {
      final long start = System.nanoTime();
      final int count = countPrimes(
        Integer.parseInt(args[0]), Integer.parseInt(args[1]));
```

```
    final long end = System.nanoTime();
    System.out.println("Number of primes is " + count);
    System.out.println("Time taken " + (end - start)/1.0e9);
  }
 }
}
```

The main() method exercises the code and times it. Our last step is to write the PrimeFinder that will do the actual work of computing the primes in a range:

favoringIsolatedMutability/java/primes/PrimeFinder.java
```
public class PrimeFinder {
  public static boolean isPrime(final int number) {
    if (number <= 1) return false;
    final int limit = (int) Math.sqrt(number);
    for(int i = 2; i <= limit; i++) if(number % i == 0) return false;
    return true;
  }
  public static int countPrimesInRange(final int lower, final int upper) {
    int count = 0;
    for(int index = lower; index <= upper; index++)
      if(isPrime(index)) count += 1;
    return count;
  }
}
```

Let's go ahead and exercise the example code with a large number like 10 million and 100 parts:

```
Number of primes is 664579
Time taken 3.890996
```

Let's compare the code and output in this section with the code and output in *Concurrent Computation of Prime Numbers*, on page 27. In both versions we set the number of partitions to 100. There is no pool size to set in the Akka version of primes counting. This is a computation-intensive problem, and setting the pool size for the ExecutorService version above the number of cores made little difference. So, they're fairly close in performance, and there is slightly less ceremony in the Akka version than in ExecutorService. This difference becomes more prominent when we need more coordination between the threads/actors, as we progress further in this chapter.

Multiple Actors in Scala

If we use Scala to implement the primes example, we get to enjoy the Scala conciseness for implementing the actor and interacting with it. Let's look at the Scala version of Primes:

favoringIsolatedMutability/scala/primes/Primes.scala

```scala
class Primes extends Actor {
  def receive = {
    case (lower : Int, upper : Int) =>
      val count = PrimeFinder.countPrimesInRange(lower, upper)
      self.replySafe(new Integer(count))
  }
}

object Primes {
  def countPrimes(number : Int, numberOfParts : Int) = {
    val chunksPerPartition : Int = number / numberOfParts

    val results = new Array[Future[Integer]](numberOfParts)
    var index = 0

    while(index < numberOfParts) {
      val lower = index * chunksPerPartition + 1
      val upper = if (index == numberOfParts - 1)
        number else lower + chunksPerPartition - 1
      val bounds = (lower, upper)
      val primeFinder = Actor.actorOf[Primes].start()
      results(index) = (primeFinder !!! bounds).asInstanceOf[Future[Integer]]
      index += 1
    }

    var count = 0
    index = 0
    while(index < numberOfParts) {
      count += results(index).await.result.get.intValue()
      index += 1
    }
    Actors.registry.shutdownAll
    count
  }

  def main(args : Array[String]) : Unit = {
    if (args.length < 2)
      println("Usage: number numberOfParts")
    else {
      val start = System.nanoTime
      val count = countPrimes(args(0).toInt, args(1).toInt)
      val end = System.nanoTime
      println("Number of primes is " + count)
      println("Time taken " + (end - start)/1.0e9)
    }
  }
}
```

There are a few differences between the Java version and this one. The message format is a simple tuple instead of an unmodifiable list. The case within the receive() was able to easily match for this. The for loop in Java has turned into a while loop here. Scala does have quite an elegant for loop; however, it will incur object to primitive conversion overhead. To get a decent performance comparison, I've avoided that elegance here.

Similarly, in the PrimeFinder, we'll use a while loop instead of a Scala for loop:

favoringIsolatedMutability/scala/primes/PrimeFinder.scala

```scala
object PrimeFinder {
  def isPrime(number : Int) : Boolean = {
    if (number <= 1) return false

    var limit = scala.math.sqrt(number).toInt
    var i = 2
    while(i <= limit) {
      if(number % i == 0) return false
      i += 1
    }
    return true
  }

  def countPrimesInRange(lower : Int, upper : Int) : Int = {
    var count = 0
    var index = lower
    while(index <= upper) {
      if(isPrime(index)) count += 1
      index += 1
    }
    count
  }
}
```

The performance of this version of the primes example for a large number like 10 million and 100 parts is comparable to the earlier one we saw:

```
Number of primes is 664579
Time taken 3.88375
```

8.6 Coordinating Actors

The real benefit and fun is when actors coordinate with each other to solve problems. To make use of concurrency, we'd divide a problem into parts. Different actors may take on different parts, and we need to coordinate the communication between them. That's what we'll learn here by using the file size program as an example.

In Section 4.2, *Coordinating Threads*, on page 49, we wrote a program to find the total size of all files under a given directory. In that we launched 100 threads, each of which explored different subdirectories. We then totaled the sizes that were computed asynchronously. We saw different approaches to doing that, with AtomicLongs and queues. We can sum up those approaches as hard work to deal with shared mutability.

We can save quite a bit of effort and trouble by using isolated mutability with actors to solve that problem. We can do that without compromising performance compared to the shared mutability solutions in that chapter. As an added bonus to synchronization free coding, we'll have a lot simpler code as well, as we'll see soon.

As the first step, let's create a design for the problem with multiple coordinating actors—we can use two types of actors as in Figure 13, *Design of the total file size problem using actors*, on page 184. We'll isolate mutable state within the SizeCollector actor. It'll receive a handful of messages to keep track of directories that need to be visited, to keep a total of the file size, and to feed requesting FileProcessor actors with directories to explore. The main code will set these actors in motion. We'll have 100 FileProcessor actors to navigate the files under the given directory.

We'll first implement this design in Java using Akka actors and then in Scala.

Coordinating Actors in Java

Let's first define the messages the SizeCollector class will receive:

favoringIsolatedMutability/java/filesize/ConcurrentFileSizeWAkka.java
```
class RequestAFile {}

class FileSize {
  public final long size;
  public FileSize(final long fileSize) { size = fileSize; }
}

class FileToProcess {
  public final String fileName;
  public FileToProcess(final String name) { fileName = name; }
}
```

The messages are represented by immutable classes. Each FileProcessor will use messages of type RequestAFile to place itself on a list with SizeCollector. FileSize is a message from FileProcessors that will carry the size of files in directories

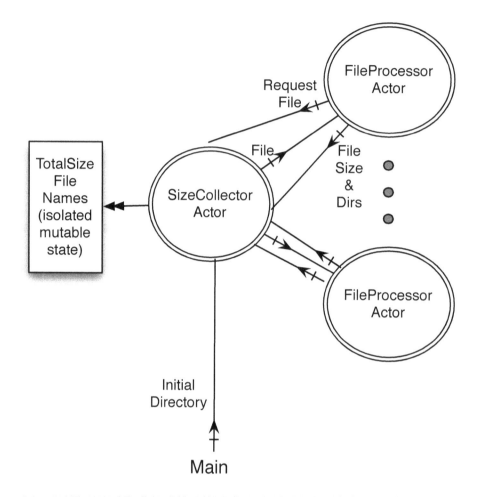

Figure 13—Design of the total file size problem using actors

they explore. Finally, FileToProcess is a message that carries the name of the file that needs to be explored.

FileProcessors are the workers with the job to explore a given directory and send back the total size of files and names of subdirectories they find. Once they finish that task, they send the RequestAFile class to let SizeCollector know they're ready to take on the task of exploring another directory. They also need to register with SizeCollector in the first place to receive the first directory to explore. A great place for this is the preStart() method, which is called when an actor is started. Let's implement FileProcessor; we must remember to receive a reference to the SizeCollector as the constructor parameter:

favoringIsolatedMutability/java/filesize/ConcurrentFileSizeWAkka.java

```java
class FileProcessor extends UntypedActor {
  private final ActorRef sizeCollector;

  public FileProcessor(final ActorRef theSizeCollector) {
    sizeCollector = theSizeCollector;
  }

  @Override public void preStart() { registerToGetFile(); }

  public void registerToGetFile() {
    sizeCollector.sendOneWay(new RequestAFile(), getContext());
  }

  public void onReceive(final Object message) {
    FileToProcess fileToProcess = (FileToProcess) message;
    final File file = new java.io.File(fileToProcess.fileName);
    long size = 0L;
    if(file.isFile()) {
      size = file.length();
    } else {
      File[] children = file.listFiles();
      if (children != null)
        for(File child : children)
          if (child.isFile())
            size += child.length();
          else
            sizeCollector.sendOneWay(new FileToProcess(child.getPath()));
    }

    sizeCollector.sendOneWay(new FileSize(size));
    registerToGetFile();
  }
}
```

In the registerToGetFile() method, we send a RequestAFile message to SizeCollector. We send along a self-reference to the FileProcessor actor instance, which is obtained using the getContext() method. SizeCollector will add this reference to a list of available idle FileProcessors that will explore directories.

The SizeCollector class will ask a FileProcessor to explore a directory, the code for which we'll see soon, by sending a message. FileProcessor's onReceive() method will respond to that message. In the onReceive() method, we discover subdirectories of the given directory and send them to SizeCollector using the sendOneWay() method. For the files in the given directory, we total their sizes and in the end of the task send that to SizeCollector. As the task's final step, we register the FileProcessor class with SizeCollector to get another directory to explore.

FileProcessor is all set and ready to explore directories. SizeCollector is the mastermind that manages the isolated mutable state and keeps FileProcessors busy with directories to explore until the final result is computed. It handles the three types of messages we discussed. Let's first look at the code and then discuss the actions for each of these messages:

favoringIsolatedMutability/java/filesize/ConcurrentFileSizeWAkka.java

```java
class SizeCollector extends UntypedActor {
  private final List<String> toProcessFileNames = new ArrayList<String>();
  private final List<ActorRef> idleFileProcessors =
    new ArrayList<ActorRef>();
  private long pendingNumberOfFilesToVisit = 0L;
  private long totalSize = 0L;
  private long start = System.nanoTime();

  public void sendAFileToProcess() {
    if(!toProcessFileNames.isEmpty() && !idleFileProcessors.isEmpty())
      idleFileProcessors.remove(0).sendOneWay(
        new FileToProcess(toProcessFileNames.remove(0)));
  }

  public void onReceive(final Object message) {
    if (message instanceof RequestAFile) {
      idleFileProcessors.add(getContext().getSender().get());
      sendAFileToProcess();
    }

    if (message instanceof FileToProcess) {
      toProcessFileNames.add(((FileToProcess)(message)).fileName);
      pendingNumberOfFilesToVisit += 1;
      sendAFileToProcess();
    }

    if (message instanceof FileSize) {
      totalSize += ((FileSize)(message)).size;
      pendingNumberOfFilesToVisit -= 1;

      if(pendingNumberOfFilesToVisit == 0) {
        long end = System.nanoTime();
        System.out.println("Total size is " + totalSize);
        System.out.println("Time taken is " + (end - start)/1.0e9);
        Actors.registry().shutdownAll();
      }
    }
  }
}
```

SizeCollector keeps two lists, one for the directories to visit and the other of idling FileProcessors. The three long variables are used to keep track of how many directories are being explored at any time, the evolving total file size, and a note of the start time to compute the time take to get the total size.

The sendAFileToProcess() method is used to dispatch directories to idling FileProcessors to explore.

SizeCollector expects to receive three types of messages in the onReceive() message handler. Each of these messages has distinct purpose.

As FileProcessors become idle, they send the RequestAFile message, and the SizeCollector saves the actors' references in the idling processors list.

FileToProcess is a message that SizeCollector both sends and receives. It will send a message of this type, in the sendAFileToProcess() method, to an idle FileProcessor. As the FileProcessors discover subdirectories, they use messages of this type to send the directories to the SizeCollector so it can further schedule other FileProcessors to explore.

The final message handled by the SizeCollector is FileSize, which is sent by the FileProcessors, and it carries the size of files in a directory explored.

Each time a directory name is received, SizeCollector increments an isolated mutable counter called pendingNumberOfFilesToVisit. It decrements this counter each time a FileSize message is received with the size for a directory. If it finds this count to be zero, it prints the total size and the time taken and shuts down all the actors, essentially shutting down the program.

Let's implement the last piece of the design, the main code:

favoringIsolatedMutability/java/filesize/ConcurrentFileSizeWAkka.java

```java
public class ConcurrentFileSizeWAkka {
  public static void main(final String[] args) {
    final ActorRef sizeCollector =
      Actors.actorOf(SizeCollector.class).start();

    sizeCollector.sendOneWay(new FileToProcess(args[0]));

    for(int i = 0; i < 100; i++)
      Actors.actorOf(new UntypedActorFactory() {
        public UntypedActor create() {
          return new FileProcessor(sizeCollector);
        }
      }).start();
  }
}
```

The main code first creates an instance of SizeCollector and tells it, using a FileToProcess message, the directory to find the size for. The main code then creates 100 FileProcessor actors. The SizeCollector takes care of coordinating with the FileProcessors and completing the task of finding the file size.

Let's get these actors rolling and ask them to explore the /usr directory:

```
Total size is 3793911517
Time taken is 8.599308
```

Compare the output of this code that uses isolated mutability with the versions of code that used shared mutability in Section 4.2, *Coordinating Threads*, on page 49. All the versions produced the same file size for the /usr directory and had comparable performance. The biggest difference in the actor-based version is that there's no synchronization involved in the code, no latches, no queues, and no AtomicLongs to mess with. The result—comparable performance with greater simplicity and no worries.

Coordinating Actors in Scala

We got the file size program working in Java using Akka actors. We can implement that design in Scala and benefit from its conciseness. The first difference from the Java version is in the messages. Scala has case classes that provide highly expressive syntax to create immutable classes. These serve really well for message types. So, let's implement the message types using case classes:

favoringIsolatedMutability/scala/filesize/ConcurrentFileSizeWAkka.scala
```scala
case object RequestAFile
case class FileSize(size : Long)
case class FileToProcess(fileName : String)
```

The FileProcessor class is a direct translation from the Java version to Scala; there is nothing new other than things we've discussed so far:

favoringIsolatedMutability/scala/filesize/ConcurrentFileSizeWAkka.scala
```scala
class FileProcessor(val sizeCollector : ActorRef) extends Actor {
  override def preStart = registerToGetFile

  def registerToGetFile = { sizeCollector ! RequestAFile }

  def receive = {
    case FileToProcess(fileName) =>
      val file = new java.io.File(fileName)

      var size = 0L
      if(file.isFile()) {
        size = file.length()
      } else {
        val children = file.listFiles()
        if (children != null)
```

```
        for(child <- children)
          if (child.isFile())
            size += child.length()
          else
            sizeCollector ! FileToProcess(child.getPath())
    }

    sizeCollector ! FileSize(size)
    registerToGetFile
  }
}
```

Let's translate the SizeCollector actor. Since we're using case classes for message types, the Scala pattern matching served here nicely. It helped to easily extract values such as filename and file size from the appropriate messages:

favoringIsolatedMutability/scala/filesize/ConcurrentFileSizeWAkka.scala
```
class SizeCollector extends Actor {
  var toProcessFileNames = List.empty[String]
  var fileProcessors = List.empty[ActorRef]
  var pendingNumberOfFilesToVisit = 0L
  var totalSize = 0L
  val start = System.nanoTime()

  def sendAFileToProcess() : Unit = {
    if(!toProcessFileNames.isEmpty && !fileProcessors.isEmpty) {
      fileProcessors.head ! FileToProcess(toProcessFileNames.head)
      fileProcessors = fileProcessors.tail
      toProcessFileNames = toProcessFileNames.tail
    }
  }
  def receive = {
    case RequestAFile =>
      fileProcessors = self.getSender().get :: fileProcessors
      sendAFileToProcess()
    case FileToProcess(fileName) =>
      toProcessFileNames = fileName :: toProcessFileNames
      pendingNumberOfFilesToVisit += 1
      sendAFileToProcess()
    case FileSize(size) =>
      totalSize += size
      pendingNumberOfFilesToVisit -= 1
      if(pendingNumberOfFilesToVisit == 0) {
        val end = System.nanoTime()
        println("Total size is " + totalSize)
        println("Time taken is " + (end - start)/1.0e9)
        Actors.registry.shutdownAll
      }
  }
}
```

Finally, we need to translate the main code from Java to Scala; once again, it's a direct translation.

favoringIsolatedMutability/scala/filesize/ConcurrentFileSizeWAkka.scala

```
object ConcurrentFileSizeWAkka {
  def main(args : Array[String]) : Unit = {
    val sizeCollector = Actor.actorOf[SizeCollector].start()

    sizeCollector ! FileToProcess(args(0))

    for(i <- 1 to 100)
      Actor.actorOf(new FileProcessor(sizeCollector)).start()
  }
}
```

Let's try the Scala version of the file size program, like we did for the /usr directory, and observe whether the performance is comparable and the size is the same as in the Java version:

```
Total size is 3793911517
Time taken is 8.321386
```

8.7 Using Typed Actors

The actors we saw so far accepted messages. We passed different types of messages, a String, tuples, case classes/custom messages, and so on. Yet, passing these messages felt quite different from the regular method calls we're used to in everyday programming. Typed actors help bridge that gap by allowing us to make regular method calls and translating them to messages under the covers. Think of a typed actor as an active object, which runs in its own single lightweight event-driven thread, with an intercepting proxy to turn normal-looking method calls into asynchronous nonblocking messages.

Since typed actors convert regular method calls into messages under the covers, we can enjoy the benefits of static typing to the fullest extent. We don't have to second-guess the types of messages an actor receives, and we can rely on the IDE support such as code completion.

To implement an actor, we simply wrote a class that extended UntypedActor or Actor trait/abstract classes. To implement a typed actor, we'll create an interface-implementation pair (in Scala we don't write interfaces; instead, we use traits with no implementation).

To instantiate an actor, we used the actorOf() method of the Actor class. To instantiate a typed actor, we'll use TypedActor's newInstance() method.

The reference we receive from the TypedActor is the intercepting proxy that converts methods to asynchronous messages. void methods transform to the sendOneWay() or ! methods, while methods that return results are transformed into sendRequestReply() or !! methods. Methods that return Future are transformed into sendRequestReplyFuture() or !!! methods.

The EnergySource class we refactored in Chapter 5, *Taming Shared Mutability*, on page 73 with the modern Java concurrency API and in *Using Akka Refs and Transactions*, on page 104 using STM is a good candidate to be a typed actor. It has mutable state that we can isolate using an actor. Each instance of EnergySource will run only in a single thread, so there's no issue of race conditions. When multiple threads call on an instance of EnergySource, the calls will jump threads and run sequentially on the instance. Remember, actors graciously don't hold threads hostage, so they share threads across instances and provide better throughput—typed actors do the same.

EnergySource did quite a few things; it allowed us to query for energy level and the usage count and to utilize energy, and it even replenished energy automatically in the background. We certainly want the actor-based version to do all that, but let's not rush in. We'll build it incrementally so we can focus on one thing at a time. Let's build the Java version first and then the Scala version.

Using Typed Actors in Java

Typed actors need a pair of interface and implementation. So, let's start with the interface for EnergySource:

favoringIsolatedMutability/java/typed1/EnergySource.java
```java
public interface EnergySource {
  long getUnitsAvailable();
  long getUsageCount();
  void useEnergy(final long units);
}
```

The pairing implementation for this interface is the EnergySourceImpl. The only difference between this and a regular Java class is that we extend the TypedActor class to turn it into an active object:

favoringIsolatedMutability/java/typed1/EnergySourceImpl.java
```java
public class EnergySourceImpl extends TypedActor implements EnergySource {
  private final long MAXLEVEL = 100L;
  private long level = MAXLEVEL;
  private long usageCount = 0L;

  public long getUnitsAvailable() { return level; }
```

```
  public long getUsageCount() { return usageCount; }

  public void useEnergy(final long units) {
    if (units > 0 && level - units >= 0) {
      System.out.println(
        "Thread in useEnergy: " + Thread.currentThread().getName());
      level -= units;
      usageCount++;
    }
  }
}
```

TypedActor ensures these methods are all mutually exclusive; that is, only one of these methods will run at any given instance. So, there is no need to synchronize or lock access to any of the fields in our class. To get a feel for the threads that execute the actor, let's sprinkle a few print statements in this sample code. Finally, we're ready to use the typed actor, so let's write the code for UseEnergySource.

favoringIsolatedMutability/java/typed1/UseEnergySource.java
```
public class UseEnergySource {
  public static void main(final String[] args)
    throws InterruptedException {
    System.out.println("Thread in main: " +
      Thread.currentThread().getName());

    final EnergySource energySource =
      TypedActor.newInstance(EnergySource.class, EnergySourceImpl.class);

    System.out.println("Energy units " + energySource.getUnitsAvailable());

    System.out.println("Firing two requests for use energy");
    energySource.useEnergy(10);
    energySource.useEnergy(10);
    System.out.println("Fired two requests for use energy");
    Thread.sleep(100);
    System.out.println("Firing one more requests for use energy");
    energySource.useEnergy(10);

    Thread.sleep(1000);
    System.out.println("Energy units " + energySource.getUnitsAvailable());
    System.out.println("Usage " + energySource.getUsageCount());

    TypedActor.stop(energySource);
  }
}
```

We create an instance of the typed actor using the TypedActor's newInstance() method. Then we first call the getUnitsAvailable() method, and since this method returns a value, our calling thread will block for a response from the typed actor. Calls to useEnergy() are nonblocking since that's a void method returning no response. We make two consecutive calls to this method by placing them one after the other. These calls will return immediately. After a slight delay, we'll make one more call to useEnergy() to study the behavior of actors and threads. Finally, we ask for the usage count and energy level again, after a delay, to allow the asynchronous messages to finish. In the end, we ask the actor to be shut down. Let's take a look at the output from this code:

```
Thread in main: main
Energy units 100
Firing two requests for use energy
Fired two requests for use energy
Thread in useEnergy: akka:event-driven:dispatcher:global-2
Thread in useEnergy: akka:event-driven:dispatcher:global-2
Firing one more requests for use energy
Thread in useEnergy: akka:event-driven:dispatcher:global-3
Energy units 70
Usage 3
```

The typed actor EnergySourceImpl executed only one method at a time. The first two useEnergy() requests we fired did not block the main thread. However, these two tasks were run on the actor's thread, in sequence. The code gracefully switched execution threads between the calls in main and the methods on the actor. While the main() ran in the main thread, the methods of the actor ran sequentially but in different threads managed by Akka. We also notice that the actor did not hold its thread hostage; the last request to useEnergy() ran in a different Akka managed thread.

The mutable state of the energy source is isolated within the EnergySourceImpl actor—I say it's isolated not because it's encapsulated within this class but because typed actors control access to the mutable state to only one actor with at most one thread running at any time.

Using Typed Actors in Scala

We saw how typed actors need a pair of interface and implementation. In Scala we don't create interface; instead, we create traits with no implementation. Let's define EnergySource as a trait:

favoringIsolatedMutability/scala/typed1/EnergySource.scala
```scala
trait EnergySource {
  def getUnitsAvailable() : Long
  def getUsageCount() : Long
  def useEnergy(units : Long) : Unit
}
```

The implementation of EnergySourceImpl is a pretty direct translation of the class EnergySourceImpl from the Java version. We extend the TypedActor class and mix in the EnergySource trait:

favoringIsolatedMutability/scala/typed1/EnergySourceImpl.scala

```scala
class EnergySourceImpl extends TypedActor with EnergySource {
  val MAXLEVEL = 100L
  var level = MAXLEVEL
  var usageCount = 0L

  def getUnitsAvailable() = level

  def getUsageCount() = usageCount

  def useEnergy(units : Long) = {
    if (units > 0 && level - units >= 0) {
      println("Thread in useEnergy: " + Thread.currentThread().getName())
      level -= units
      usageCount += 1
    }
  }
}
```

Let's port over the UseEnergySource class from Java:

favoringIsolatedMutability/scala/typed1/UseEnergySource.scala

```scala
object UseEnergySource {
  def main(args : Array[String]) : Unit = {
    println("Thread in main: " + Thread.currentThread().getName())

    val energySource = TypedActor.newInstance(
      classOf[EnergySource], classOf[EnergySourceImpl])

    println("Energy units " + energySource.getUnitsAvailable)

    println("Firing two requests for use energy")
    energySource.useEnergy(10)
    energySource.useEnergy(10)
    println("Fired two requests for use energy")
    Thread.sleep(100)
    println("Firing one more requests for use energy")
    energySource.useEnergy(10)

    Thread.sleep(1000);
    println("Energy units " + energySource.getUnitsAvailable)
    println("Usage " + energySource.getUsageCount)

    TypedActor.stop(energySource)
  }
}
```

Let's run the Scala version and observe the output:

```
Thread in main: main
Energy units 100
Firing two requests for use energy
Fired two requests for use energy
Thread in useEnergy: akka:event-driven:dispatcher:global-2
Thread in useEnergy: akka:event-driven:dispatcher:global-2
Firing one more requests for use energy
Thread in useEnergy: akka:event-driven:dispatcher:global-3
Energy units 70
Usage 3
```

The Scala version enjoyed a bit of conciseness in addition to the benefit of active objects.

8.8 Typed Actors and Murmurs

The typed actor version of the EnergySource allowed us to invoke methods but ran them as asynchronous messages in sequence under the covers, providing us with thread safety without the need for synchronization. That was easy to create, but our EnergySource is half-baked at this point, missing a key feature—the energy level needs to be replenished automatically.

In the versions we implemented in the previous chapters, the replenish action did not require any user intervention; it was done automatically in the background. As soon as we started the energy source, a timer took care of appropriately increasing the energy level one unit per second.

Implementing that feature in the typed actor version is going to take some effort—we need to ensure the single-threaded nature of our typed actor is not violated by the replenish operation. Let's explore some options before we jump into the code.

We could add the replenish() method to the EnergySource interface. The user of the energy source could call this method every second. Unfortunately, this places an unnecessary burden on the user of the energy source; they could forget, and also it would no longer match in functionality with the other versions of EnergySource. Strike that option.

We could create a timer within the typed actor, and this timer could periodically replenish the energy level. TypedActors provide a special method called preStart() that's called as soon as the actor is created and a method called postStop() that's called right after an actor is stopped or shut down. These two methods will serve well; we can start the timer in the preStart() method and cancel it in the postStop() method. It seems like a good plan, but that opens up another problem.

The glitch is that the timers run in their own threads, and we don't want to touch the mutable state of our actor from those threads. Remember, we want the state to be isolated mutable, not shared mutable. What we need is a way to cause internal method calls—I call these *murmurs*—to be executed properly by the actor. These murmurs will not be visible to the outside user of our typed actor but run as asynchronous messages, like those externally invoked messages that are sequenced and interleaved with other messages. Let's figure out how to get that coded.

Remember, typed actors are really actors with added convenience. They do receive messages just like actors do. The base class TypedActor's receive() method receives the messages from the proxies and dispatches the appropriate method on our class. We can override this method to implement a special message for the murmurs, the internal operations. That way, users of the actor invoke methods published through the interface, and our class internally can use this (unpublished) message. We could even take an extra step to ensure the sender of this message is our own actor, if we desire.

It's going to take some effort to get this done in Java, but it's a lot easier in Scala. Let's first take a look at the Java implementation, and then we'll look at the Scala version.

Implementing Murmurs in Java

While the external users of our EnergySourceImpl communicate through the EnergySource interface, internally we'll set the actor to send itself a Replenish request message every second using a timer. The replenish() method we'll write is private and can't be called directly from outside the class, but we'll refrain from calling it directly from the timer also. The timer will only send a message to the actor. Let's take a look at that part of the code:

favoringIsolatedMutability/java/typed2/EnergySourceImpl.java

```java
@SuppressWarnings("unchecked")
public class EnergySourceImpl extends TypedActor implements EnergySource {
  private final long MAXLEVEL = 100L;
  private long level = MAXLEVEL;
  private long usageCount = 0L;
  class Replenish {}
  @Override public void preStart() {
    Scheduler.schedule(
      optionSelf().get(), new Replenish(), 1, 1, TimeUnit.SECONDS);
  }
```

```
@Override public void postStop() { Scheduler.shutdown(); }

private void replenish() {
  System.out.println("Thread in replenish: " +
    Thread.currentThread().getName());
  if (level < MAXLEVEL) level += 1;
}
```

In the preStart() method, which is automatically called right after the actor is started, we kick off a timer. We're using the Akka-provided Scheduler, which is an actor-based timer. This timer provides a few overloaded schedule() methods to fire off tasks once or repeatedly. We can use this to execute arbitrary functions or, as in this example, fire a message on an actor.

We've set up the timer to fire a Replenish message every second on the actor after an initial delay of one second. We obtain a handle to the actor's ActorRef reference by calling the optionSelf() method on the instance. When the actor is stopped, we should stop the timer; therefore, we have the postStop() method. In the private replenish() method, which we haven't tied to the Replenish message yet, we increment the level value.

The proxy used by the users of typed actors converts method calls to messages. The TypedActor base class's receive() method converts those messages to method calls on the implementation. If we examine the receive() method's signature, it returns a scala.PartialFunction.[6] Think of a partial function, for our discussion here, as a glorified switch statement. It dispatches different pieces of code based on the type of the message received. So, the base class maps the messages to our methods, and we want to take up an added responsibility of mapping an additional, but private, message. In other words, we want to combine our message handling with the efforts of the base class's receive() method. The orElse() method of PartialFunction allows us to easily do that, so we'll use that:

favoringIsolatedMutability/java/typed2/EnergySourceImpl.java
```
@Override public PartialFunction receive() {
  return processMessage().orElse(super.receive());
}
```

We override the receive() method and, in it, combine the partial function returned by a, yet to be implemented, processMessage() method with the partial function returned by the base's receive(). Now can we turn our attention to implementing the processMessage() method. This method should receive a

---

6. Technically the type is scala.PartialFunction<Any, Unit>, where scala.Any can be read as Object in Java. Unfortunately, Java's type erasure will result in some warnings in this code.

Replenish message and call the private replenish() method. Since this is part of the message-handling sequence, we've taken care of thread synchronization using the actor-based communication. Load up your cup if it's low on coffee; you're gonna need that extra shot of caffeine to implement this method.

PartialFunction is a trait in Scala, and traits with implementations manifest in Java as a pair of interface and an abstract class. So, to implement a trait in Java, we'll implement that interface and delegate calls, as appropriate, to the corresponding abstract class.

The key method we'll implement is the apply() method where we handle the Replenish message. We'll also provide the implementation for the isDefinedAt() method, which tells whether our PartialFunction supports a particular message format or type. The rest of the methods of this interface can be delegated. We can avoid implementing some methods of the interface by extending the AbstractFunction1, which shares the common interface Function1 with PartialFunction.

favoringIsolatedMutability/java/typed2/EnergySourceImpl.java
```
private PartialFunction processMessage() {

  class MyDispatch extends AbstractFunction1 implements PartialFunction {
    public boolean isDefinedAt(Object message) {
      return message instanceof Replenish;
    }

    public Object apply(Object message) {
      if (message instanceof Replenish) replenish();
      return null;
    }

    public Function1 lift() {
      return PartialFunction$class.lift(this);
    }

    public PartialFunction andThen(Function1 function) {
      return PartialFunction$class.andThen(this, function);
    }

    public PartialFunction orElse(PartialFunction function) {
      return PartialFunction$class.orElse(this, function);
    }
  };

  return new MyDispatch();
}
```

In the apply() method we checked whether the message is of type Replenish and invoked the private replenish(). isDefinedAt() indicated that we support only this one message type, leaving the rest of the messages at the discretion of the base class's receive(). OK, the last step is not to forget the methods that have not changed from the previous typed actor version, so let's get them over:

favoringIsolatedMutability/java/typed2/EnergySourceImpl.java

```java
public long getUnitsAvailable() { return level; }
public long getUsageCount() { return usageCount; }
public void useEnergy(final long units) {
  if (units > 0 && level - units >= 0) {
    System.out.println(
      "Thread in useEnergy: " + Thread.currentThread().getName());
    level -= units;
    usageCount++;
  }
}
}
```

There's no change to the EnergySource interface, and UseEnergySource continues to use the actor as before. So, let's compile the new version of the EnergySourceImpl and run it with the UseEnergySource we wrote in the previous section. In the previous section, at the end of the run, we were left with seventy units of energy. Since we have the automatic replenish now working, the units should be higher by one or two points.

```
Thread in main: main
Energy units 100
Firing two requests for use energy
Fired two requests for use energy
Thread in useEnergy: akka:event-driven:dispatcher:global-2
Thread in useEnergy: akka:event-driven:dispatcher:global-2
Firing one more requests for use energy
Thread in useEnergy: akka:event-driven:dispatcher:global-3
Thread in replenish: akka:event-driven:dispatcher:global-4
Energy units 71
Usage 3
```

The print statements we sprinkled to print the thread information shows that the use energy requests and the replenish request ran in Akka's actor's thread, thus once again relieving us of the synchronization concerns. If we add sleep calls to delay any of these tasks, we'll see the execution of subsequent calls to the actor are delayed since the actor is single-threaded.

Implementing Murmurs in Scala

The essence of the approach was to combine our own partial function implementation with the partial function returned by the base class's receive() method. It was quite an effort in Java to do that but is a lot easier in Scala. Let's look at the part that deals with handling the murmur, the internal message.

favoringIsolatedMutability/scala/typed2/EnergySourceImpl.scala
```
class EnergySourceImpl extends TypedActor with EnergySource {
  val MAXLEVEL = 100L
  var level = MAXLEVEL
  var usageCount = 0L
  case class Replenish()
  override def preStart() =
    Scheduler.schedule(self, Replenish, 1, 1, TimeUnit.SECONDS)
  override def postStop() = Scheduler.shutdown
  override def receive = processMessage orElse super.receive

  def processMessage : Receive = {
    case Replenish =>
      println("Thread in replenish: " + Thread.currentThread.getName)
      if (level < MAXLEVEL) level += 1
  }
```

The preStart() and postStop() methods are a simple translation from the Java version. The message class Replenish() became a case class here. The receive() is pretty much the same except for Scala conciseness. The biggest change is in the processMessage() method. It fizzled into simple pattern matching for the Replenish message—no messing with inheritance and delegation like on the Java side. Since this is so simple, we might as well implement the logic for Replenish() right here instead of creating a private function. We can define the return type of the processMessage() method as PartialFunction[Any, Unit] or, as we did in the example, Receive, which is an alias for that.

Let's bring in the rest of the code for EnergySourceImpl from the previous Scala version:

favoringIsolatedMutability/scala/typed2/EnergySourceImpl.scala
```
  def getUnitsAvailable() = level
  def getUsageCount() = usageCount
  def useEnergy(units : Long) = {
    if (units > 0 && level - units >= 0) {
      println("Thread in useEnergy: " + Thread.currentThread.getName)
      level -= units
      usageCount += 1
    }
  }
}
```

We can use EnergySource and UseEnergySource from the previous Scala version. So, let's compile the new version of EnergySourceImpl and run it to compare the output:

```
Thread in main: main
Energy units 100
Firing two requests for use energy
```

```
Fired two requests for use energy
Thread in useEnergy: akka:event-driven:dispatcher:global-2
Thread in useEnergy: akka:event-driven:dispatcher:global-2
Firing one more requests for use energy
Thread in useEnergy: akka:event-driven:dispatcher:global-3
Thread in replenish: akka:event-driven:dispatcher:global-4
Energy units 71
Usage 3
```

It was much easier to implement this in Scala compared to Java. Even though the two pieces of code produced the same logical result, it took less effort in the Scala version compared to the Java version.

8.9 Mixing Actors and STM

Actors nicely allow us to isolate mutable state. They work great if a problem can be divided into concurrent tasks that can run independently and communicate with each other asynchronously using messages. Actors, however, don't provide a way to manage consensus across tasks. We may want the actions of two or more actors to all succeed or fail collectively; that is, either all of them succeed or all of them fail. Actors alone can't do that for us, but we can achieve that by bringing STM into the mix. In this section, I assume you've read Chapter 6, *Introduction to Software Transactional Memory*, on page 89 and the discussions on actors and typed actors in this chapter.

The AccountService class that helped us transfer between two Accounts in *The Lock Interface*, on page 67 and Section 6.9, *Creating Nested Transactions*, on page 111 will serve as a good example to understand this interplay of actors and STM. The operations of deposit and withdraw are isolated to individual accounts. So, Account can be implemented using a simple actor or a typed actor. However, the operation of transfer has to coordinate a pair of deposit and withdraw across two accounts. In other words, the operation of deposit, handled by one actor, should succeed if and only if the corresponding withdraw operation, handled by another actor as part of the overarching transfer, also succeeds. Let's mix actors and STM to implement the account transfer sample.

Akka provides a few options to mix actors and STM. We can create a separate transaction coordination object and manage the sequencing of the various actors into the transaction ourselves (see the Akka documentation for that level of control). Alternately, we can rely on one of two convenient ways to manage transactions among actors. We'll take a look at these two ways: how to use their *transactors* and how to *coordinate* typed actors.

8.10 Using Transactors

Akka transactors or transactional actors bring execution of multiple actors into the folds of a transaction. Transactors make atomic the changes to managed STM Ref objects from multiple coordinating actors. The changes to these objects are retained only if the encompassing transaction commits; otherwise, the changes are discarded.

Transactors provide three options to process messages:

- The default option is to process a message in its own transaction.

- We can implement a normally() method that can process select messages stand-alone, that is, not as part of any transaction.

- We can ask for messages to be processed Coordinated, that is, as part of an overarching transaction.

Transactors provide us with the flexibility to link in other actors into our coordinated transactions. In addition, transactors provide optional pre- and post-transaction methods. We can use these methods to prepare for a transaction and perform any post-commit processing.

Let's create a transactor first in Java and then in Scala.

Transactors in Java

To use transactors in Java, we'll extend the UntypedTransactor class and implement the required atomically() method. In addition, if we want to include other actors in the transaction, we implement the coordinate() method. Let's use transactors to reimplement the account transfer example. Let's first start with the message classes we'll need.

We'll use a Deposit message to perform the deposit operations on accounts. This message is represented by an immutable class, which will carry the deposit amount as part of the message.

favoringIsolatedMutability/java/transactors/Deposit.java
```
public class Deposit {
  public final int amount;
  public Deposit(final int theAmount) { amount = theAmount; }
}
```

Next, we have the Withdraw message that is similar in structure to the Deposit message:

```
favoringIsolatedMutability/java/transactors/Withdraw.java
public class Withdraw {
  public final int amount;
  public Withdraw(final int theAmount) { amount = theAmount; }
}
```

No data needs to be carried for the message to get the balance, so an empty class is good enough for that:

```
favoringIsolatedMutability/java/transactors/FetchBalance.java
public class FetchBalance {}
```

The response to such a message would be the actual balance embedded in the Balance message:

```
favoringIsolatedMutability/java/transactors/Balance.java
public class Balance {
  public final int amount;
  public Balance(final int theBalance) { amount = theBalance; }
}
```

The final message definition we need is for Transfer, which will contain details of the accounts and the amount of transfer:

```
favoringIsolatedMutability/java/transactors/Transfer.java
public class Transfer {
  public final ActorRef from;
  public final ActorRef to;
  public final int amount;
  public Transfer(final ActorRef fromAccount,
    final ActorRef toAccount, final int theAmount) {
    from = fromAccount;
    to = toAccount;
    amount = theAmount;
  }
}
```

The AccountService transactor will use the Transfer message, and the Account transactor will use the other messages we've defined. Let's take a look at the Account transactor now:

```
favoringIsolatedMutability/java/transactors/Account.java
public class Account extends UntypedTransactor {
  private final Ref<Integer> balance = new Ref<Integer>(0);

  public void atomically(final Object message) {
    if(message instanceof Deposit) {
      int amount = ((Deposit)(message)).amount;
      if (amount > 0) {
        balance.swap(balance.get() + amount);
        System.out.println("Received Deposit request " + amount);
```

```
      }
    }

    if(message instanceof Withdraw) {
      int amount = ((Withdraw)(message)).amount;
      System.out.println("Received Withdraw request " + amount);
      if (amount > 0 && balance.get() >= amount)
        balance.swap(balance.get() - amount);
      else {
        System.out.println("...insufficient funds...");
        throw new RuntimeException("Insufficient fund");
      }
    }

    if(message instanceof FetchBalance) {
      getContext().replySafe(new Balance(balance.get()));
    }
  }
}
```

The Account class extends UntypedTransactor and implements the atomically()
method. This method will run under the context of a transaction provided
to it—this may be the transaction of the caller or a separate transaction if
none is provided. If the message received is the Deposit message, we increase
the balance that's stored in the STM-managed Ref object. If the message is
Withdraw, then we decrease the balance only if sufficient money is available.
Otherwise, we throw an exception. The exception, if thrown, will trigger a
rollback of the encompassing transaction. Finally, if the message is FetchBal-
ance, we respond to the sender with the current value of balance. Since this
entire method is running within one transaction, we don't have to worry
about multiple accesses to the Ref object(s) within the transactor. The changes
we make to the Ref objects will be retained only if the encompassing transaction is committed—remember, we're responsible for maintaining immutable
state.

The job of coordinating the operation of deposit on one transactor (account)
and the withdraw on another transactor (account) belongs to the AccountService
transactor, which we will write next:

favoringIsolatedMutability/java/transactors/AccountService.java
```
public class AccountService extends UntypedTransactor {

  @Override public Set<SendTo> coordinate(final Object message) {
    if(message instanceof Transfer) {
      Set<SendTo> coordinations = new java.util.HashSet<SendTo>();
      Transfer transfer = (Transfer) message;
      coordinations.add(sendTo(transfer.to, new Deposit(transfer.amount)));
```

```
    coordinations.add(sendTo(transfer.from,
      new Withdraw(transfer.amount)));
    return java.util.Collections.unmodifiableSet(coordinations);
  }

  return nobody();
}

  public void atomically(final Object message) {}
}
```

Coordinating the deposit and withdraw is the only responsibility of the AccountService, so in the coordinate() method we direct the appropriate messages
to be sent to the two accounts. We do that by grouping actors and messages
for each actor into a set. When we return this set from the coordinate() method,
the AccountService transactor's base implementation will send the appropriate
message to each transactor in the set. Once the messages are sent, it will
call its own atomically() implementation. Since we have nothing more to do
here, we leave this method blank.

Let's exercise these transactors using some sample code:

favoringIsolatedMutability/java/transactors/UseAccountService.java
```
public class UseAccountService {
  public static void printBalance(
    final String accountName, final ActorRef account) {

    Balance balance =
      (Balance)(account.sendRequestReply(new FetchBalance()));
    System.out.println(accountName + " balance is " + balance.amount);
  }

  public static void main(final String[] args)
    throws InterruptedException {
    final ActorRef account1 = Actors.actorOf(Account.class).start();
    final ActorRef account2 = Actors.actorOf(Account.class).start();
    final ActorRef accountService =
      Actors.actorOf(AccountService.class).start();

    account1.sendOneWay(new Deposit(1000));
    account2.sendOneWay(new Deposit(1000));

    Thread.sleep(1000);

    printBalance("Account1", account1);
    printBalance("Account2", account2);

    System.out.println("Let's transfer $20... should succeed");
    accountService.sendOneWay(new Transfer(account1, account2, 20));
```

```
    Thread.sleep(1000);

    printBalance("Account1", account1);
    printBalance("Account2", account2);

    System.out.println("Let's transfer $2000... should not succeed");
    accountService.sendOneWay(new Transfer(account1, account2, 2000));

    Thread.sleep(6000);

    printBalance("Account1", account1);
    printBalance("Account2", account2);

    Actors.registry().shutdownAll();
  }
}
```

There's no difference between how we interact with an actor and a transactor. If we send a regular message (like new Deposit(1000)), it is automatically wrapped into a transaction. We can also create our own coordinated transaction by creating an instance of akka.transactor.Coordinated and wrapping a message into it (like, for example, new Coordinated(new Deposit(1000))). Since we're dealing with only one-way messages in this example, we give sufficient time for the message to be handled before making the next query. This will give time for the coordinating transaction to succeed or fail, and we can see the effect of the transaction in the subsequent call.

Since the coordinating transaction can commit only if all the messages to the participating transactors complete without exception, the coordinating request waits at most for the timeout period (configurable) for the transaction to complete. The output from the code is shown next:

```
Received Deposit request 1000
Received Deposit request 1000
Account1 balance is 1000
Account2 balance is 1000
Let's transfer $20... should succeed
Received Deposit request 20
Received Withdraw request 20
Account1 balance is 980
Account2 balance is 1020
Let's transfer $2000... should not succeed
Received Withdraw request 2000
...insufficient funds...
Received Deposit request 2000
Account1 balance is 980
Account2 balance is 1020
```

The first two deposits and the first transfer completed without a glitch. The last transfer, however, was for an amount larger than the balance available in the from account. The deposit part of the transfer was carried out, as we can see from the printed message in the output (the deposits and withdraws run concurrently, so the order of the print may vary each time we run the code). However, the withdraw did not complete, and so the entire transfer was rolled back. The change made in the deposit was discarded, and the second attempted transfer did not affect the balance of the two accounts.

Transactors in Scala

To use transactors in Scala, we'll extend the Transactor class and implement the required atomically() method. In addition, if we want to include other actors in our transaction, we implement the coordinate() method. Let's translate the example from Java to Scala. We will start with the message classes—these can be written concisely in Scala as case classes.

favoringIsolatedMutability/scala/transactors/Messages.scala
```
case class Deposit(val amount : Int)

case class Withdraw(val amount : Int)

case class FetchBalance()

case class Balance(val amount : Int)

case  class Transfer(val from : ActorRef, val to : ActorRef, val amount : Int)
```

Next let's translate the Account transactor to Scala. We can use pattern matching to handle the three messages.

favoringIsolatedMutability/scala/transactors/Account.scala
```
class Account extends Transactor {
  val balance = Ref(0)

  def atomically = {
    case Deposit(amount) =>
      if (amount > 0) {
        balance.swap(balance.get() + amount)
        println("Received Deposit request " + amount)
      }

    case Withdraw(amount) =>
      println("Received Withdraw request " + amount)
      if (amount > 0 && balance.get() >= amount)
        balance.swap(balance.get() - amount)
      else {
        println("...insufficient funds...")
```

```
        throw new RuntimeException("Insufficient fund")
      }

    case FetchBalance =>
      self.replySafe(Balance(balance.get()))
  }
}
```

Next, we translate the AccountService transactor. Again, here we will leave the atomically() method blank, and in the coordinate() method we'll mention which objects coordinate to participate in the transaction. The syntax for that is a lot more concise here on the Scala side than in the Java code:

favoringIsolatedMutability/scala/transactors/AccountService.scala
```
class AccountService extends Transactor {

  override def coordinate = {
    case Transfer(from, to, amount) =>
      sendTo(to -> Deposit(amount), from -> Withdraw(amount))
  }

  def atomically = { case message => }
}
```

Let's exercise these transactors using some sample code:

favoringIsolatedMutability/scala/transactors/UseAccountService.scala
```
object UseAccountService {

  def printBalance(accountName : String, account : ActorRef) = {
    (account !! FetchBalance) match {
      case Some(Balance(amount)) =>
        println(accountName + " balance is " + amount)
      case None =>
        println("Error getting balance for " + accountName)
    }
  }

  def main(args : Array[String]) = {
    val account1 = Actor.actorOf[Account].start()
    val account2 = Actor.actorOf[Account].start()
    val accountService = Actor.actorOf[AccountService].start()

    account1 ! Deposit(1000)
    account2 ! Deposit(1000)

    Thread.sleep(1000)

    printBalance("Account1", account1)
    printBalance("Account2", account2)
```

```
    println("Let's transfer $20... should succeed")
    accountService ! Transfer(account1, account2, 20)

    Thread.sleep(1000)

    printBalance("Account1", account1)
    printBalance("Account2", account2)

    println("Let's transfer $2000... should not succeed")
    accountService ! Transfer(account1, account2, 2000)

    Thread.sleep(6000)

    printBalance("Account1", account1)
    printBalance("Account2", account2)

    Actors.registry.shutdownAll
  }
}
```

That was a direct translation from Java; again, we see the areas where Scala conciseness plays a nice role. This version behaves just like the Java version when we observe the output.

```
Received Deposit request 1000
Received Deposit request 1000
Account1 balance is 1000
Account2 balance is 1000
Let's transfer $20... should succeed
Received Deposit request 20
Received Withdraw request 20
Account1 balance is 980
Account2 balance is 1020
Let's transfer $2000... should not succeed
Received Deposit request 2000
Received Withdraw request 2000
...insufficient funds...
Account1 balance is 980
Account2 balance is 1020
```

Using Transactors

We saw how to implement transactors in Java and Scala. Transactors combine the benefits of actors and STM and allow us to provide consensus between otherwise independently running actors. Just like in the use of STMs, transactors are useful when the write collisions are highly infrequent. Ideally, if multiple actors have to participate in a quorum or voting of some sort, transactors can be quite convenient.

8.11 Coordinating Typed Actors

Typed actors, as we saw in Section 8.7, *Using Typed Actors*, on page 190, are a glamour child of object-oriented programming and actor-based programming. They bring together the all-too-familiar, convenient method calls and the benefits of actors. So, in an OO-application, instead of using actors, we may be tempted to use typed actors. However, just like actors, typed actors run in isolation and don't provide transactional coordination—we'll have to use coordinating typed actors for that.

Akka makes it really simple to make a typed actor a coordinating typed actor; we simply have to mark the corresponding interface methods with a special Coordinated annotation. To indicate that a sequence of calls should run under a coordinated transaction, simply wrap the calls into a coordinate() method. This method by default waits for all the methods we invoked within to commit or roll back before proceeding further.

There is one limitation; only void methods can be marked with the special Coordinated annotation. Void methods translate to one-way calls, and these can participate in transactions. Methods that return values translate to two-way blocking calls and so can't participate in free-running concurrent transactions.

Let's implement the transfer of money sample that we have played with so many times now, in Section 8.10, *Using Transactors*, on page 202.

Coordinating Typed Actors in Java

Typed actors use a pair of interface and implementations, so let's start with the two interfaces we'll need, the Account and AccountService interfaces:

```
favoringIsolatedMutability/java/coordtyped/Account.java
public interface Account {
  int getBalance();
  @Coordinated void deposit(final int amount);
  @Coordinated void withdraw(final int amount);
}
```

```
favoringIsolatedMutability/java/coordtyped/AccountService.java
public interface AccountService {
  void transfer(final Account from, final Account to, final int amount);
}
```

The @Coordinated annotation marking is the only thing special in the Account interface. By marking the methods, we indicated that these either should run in their own transaction or participate in the transaction of the caller. The method in AccountService is not marked with the annotation since the implementor of this class will be managing its own transaction. Let's take a look at the implementation of the Account interface now:

favoringIsolatedMutability/java/coordtyped/AccountImpl.java

```java
public class AccountImpl extends TypedActor implements Account {
  private final Ref<Integer> balance = new Ref<Integer>(0);

  public int getBalance() { return balance.get(); }

  public void deposit(final int amount) {
    if (amount > 0) {
      balance.swap(balance.get() + amount);
      System.out.println("Received Deposit request " + amount);
    }
  }

  public void withdraw(final int amount) {
    System.out.println("Received Withdraw request " + amount);
    if (amount > 0 && balance.get() >= amount)
      balance.swap(balance.get() - amount);
    else {
      System.out.println("...insufficient funds...");
      throw new RuntimeException("Insufficient fund");
    }
  }
}
```

By extending TypedActor, we indicated that this is an actor. Instead of using simple local fields, we're using the managed STM Refs. We don't write any code specific to transactions here; however, all the methods in this class will run within a transaction since the relevant interface methods are marked with @Coordinated. The deposit() increases the balance if amount is greater than 0. The withdraw() method decreases the balance if sufficient money is available. Otherwise, it throws an exception indicating the failure of the operation and the encompassing transaction. The methods will participate in their own transaction if one is not provided. In the case of transfer, however, we want both the operations of deposit and withdraw to run in one transaction. This is managed by the AccountServiceImpl, which we write next:

favoringIsolatedMutability/java/coordtyped/AccountServiceImpl.java

```java
public class AccountServiceImpl
  extends TypedActor implements AccountService {

  public void transfer(
    final Account from, final Account to, final int amount) {

    coordinate(true, new Atomically() {
      public void atomically() {
```

```
        to.deposit(amount);
        from.withdraw(amount);
    }
  });
  }
}
```

The transfer() method runs the two operations, deposit and withdraw, within a transaction. The code to run within a transaction is wrapped into the atomically() method, which is a method of the Atomically interface. The coordinate(), which is statically imported from the akka.transactor.Coordination class, runs the transactional block of code in atomically(). The first parameter, true, tells the method coordinate() to wait for its transaction to complete (succeed or roll back) before returning. The methods invoked within the transaction are one-way messages, however, and the coordinate() method does not block for their results but only for their transactions to complete.

The code to use these typed actors should not look any different from code that uses regular objects, except for the creation of these objects. Rather than using new, we use a factory to create them, as shown next:

favoringIsolatedMutability/java/coordtyped/UseAccountService.java
```java
public class UseAccountService {

  public static void main(final String[] args)
    throws InterruptedException {

    final Account account1 =
      TypedActor.newInstance(Account.class, AccountImpl.class);
    final Account account2 =
      TypedActor.newInstance(Account.class, AccountImpl.class);
    final AccountService accountService =
      TypedActor.newInstance(AccountService.class, AccountServiceImpl.class);

    account1.deposit(1000);
    account2.deposit(1000);

    System.out.println("Account1 balance is " + account1.getBalance());
    System.out.println("Account2 balance is " + account2.getBalance());

    System.out.println("Let's transfer $20... should succeed");

    accountService.transfer(account1, account2, 20);

    Thread.sleep(1000);

    System.out.println("Account1 balance is " + account1.getBalance());
    System.out.println("Account2 balance is " + account2.getBalance());
```

```java
    System.out.println("Let's transfer $2000... should not succeed");
    accountService.transfer(account1, account2, 2000);

    Thread.sleep(6000);

    System.out.println("Account1 balance is " + account1.getBalance());
    System.out.println("Account2 balance is " + account2.getBalance());

    Actors.registry().shutdownAll();
  }
}
```

The actions of the previous code are the same as the example in Section 8.10, *Using Transactors*, on page 202. The output from this example is:

```
Received Deposit request 1000
Account1 balance is 1000
Received Deposit request 1000
Account2 balance is 1000
Let's transfer $20... should succeed
Received Deposit request 20
Received Withdraw request 20
Account1 balance is 980
Account2 balance is 1020
Let's transfer $2000... should not succeed
Received Deposit request 2000
Received Withdraw request 2000
...insufficient funds...
Account1 balance is 980
Account2 balance is 1020
```

As we'd expect, the output produced by the coordinating typed actor version is similar to the output produced by the transactor version—any changes made within a failing transaction are discarded.

Coordinating Typed Actors in Scala

Let's translate the Java version to Scala. Scala uses traits instead of interfaces, so that's the first difference we'll see:

favoringIsolatedMutability/scala/coordtyped/Account.scala
```scala
trait Account {
  def getBalance() : Int
  @Coordinated def deposit(amount : Int) : Unit
  @Coordinated def withdraw(amount : Int) : Unit
}
```

favoringIsolatedMutability/scala/coordtyped/AccountService.scala
```scala
trait AccountService {
  def transfer(from : Account, to : Account, amount : Int) : Unit
}
```

The implementation of the Account trait is a direct translation from the Java version:

favoringIsolatedMutability/scala/coordtyped/AccountImpl.scala

```scala
class AccountImpl extends TypedActor with Account {
  val balance = Ref(0)

  def getBalance() = balance.get()

  def deposit(amount : Int) = {
    if (amount > 0) {
      balance.swap(balance.get() + amount)
      println("Received Deposit request " + amount)
    }
  }

  def withdraw(amount : Int) = {
    println("Received Withdraw request " + amount)
    if (amount > 0 && balance.get() >= amount)
      balance.swap(balance.get() - amount)
    else {
      println("...insufficient funds...")
      throw new RuntimeException("Insufficient fund")
    }
  }
}
```

Likewise, let's implement the AccountService class:

favoringIsolatedMutability/scala/coordtyped/AccountServiceImpl.scala

```scala
class AccountServiceImpl extends TypedActor with AccountService {
  def transfer(from : Account, to : Account, amount : Int) = {
    coordinate {
      to.deposit(amount)
      from.withdraw(amount)
    }
  }
}
```

In the Scala version, the call to coordinate(), which defines the participants of the transaction, is much simpler than the Java version. By default the coordinate() method waits for its transaction to complete (succeed or roll back) before returning. The methods invoked within the transaction are one-way messages, however, and coordinate() does not block for their results but only for their transactions to complete. We may pass an optional parameter like coordinate(wait = false) {...} to tell the method not to wait for the transaction to complete.

Finally, let's write the sample code to use the previous code:

favoringIsolatedMutability/scala/coordtyped/UseAccountService.scala

```scala
object UseAccountService {

  def main(args : Array[String]) = {
    val account1 =
      TypedActor.newInstance(classOf[Account], classOf[AccountImpl])
    val account2 =
      TypedActor.newInstance(classOf[Account], classOf[AccountImpl])
    val accountService =
      TypedActor.newInstance(
        classOf[AccountService], classOf[AccountServiceImpl])

    account1.deposit(1000)
    account2.deposit(1000)

    println("Account1 balance is " + account1.getBalance())
    println("Account2 balance is " + account2.getBalance())


    println("Let's transfer $20... should succeed")

    accountService.transfer(account1, account2, 20)

    Thread.sleep(1000)

    println("Account1 balance is " + account1.getBalance())
    println("Account2 balance is " + account2.getBalance())

    println("Let's transfer $2000... should not succeed")
    accountService.transfer(account1, account2, 2000)

    Thread.sleep(6000)

    println("Account1 balance is " + account1.getBalance())
    println("Account2 balance is " + account2.getBalance())

    Actors.registry.shutdownAll
  }
}
```

The Scala version behaves just like the Java version, as we see from the output:

```
Received Deposit request 1000
Received Deposit request 1000
Account1 balance is 1000
Account2 balance is 1000
Let's transfer $20... should succeed
Received Deposit request 20
Received Withdraw request 20
Account1 balance is 980
```

```
Account2 balance is 1020
Let's transfer $2000... should not succeed
Received Deposit request 2000
Received Withdraw request 2000
...insufficient funds...
Account1 balance is 980
Account2 balance is 1020
```

8.12 Remote Actors

In the actor examples we have written so far, the actors and their clients were all within a single JVM process. One camp of developers believes actors should really be used for interprocess communication, like in Erlang. The other camp of developers uses actors for intraprocess communication like we saw. Scala and Akka cater to both camps.

Using remote actors in Akka is much like using in-process actors; the only difference is in how we get access to the actors. Under the covers, Akka uses JBoss Netty and Google Protocol Buffers libraries to make the remoting happen seamlessly. We can pass any serializable message and references to any actor to the remote actors across process boundaries. Akka provides both programmatic and configuration options to configure the hostname, port number, message frame size, security settings, and so on. Refer to the Akka documentation for these details; we'll simply use the defaults in the examples in this section.

In addition to creating an actor, we need to register it for remote access. This binds the actor to a name or an ID that the clients will use to identify the actor. The client will use the registered ID, the hostname, and the port number to request an actor. It can then send one-way or two-way messages to the actor much like how it would interact with local actors.

Let's create an example using remote actors. In my past life, I used to be a systems administrator. Various details about systems like available disk space, performance, CPU utilization, and so on, are information that an administrator often needs at his or her fingertips. Depending on the sensors connected, we often monitored details such as room temperature, humidity levels, and so on, to ensure that the high-performance computing labs were operational at all times. It would be great to have an application that can collect these details from all of the remote machines, so let's create one. We'll let a Monitor actor receive system information from remote clients. Clients on various machines can decide when to send this information to the monitor. In this example, they'll send a few pieces of data each time they're run.

Let's start with the Monitor, which is the remote actor that the clients will interact with:

favoringIsolatedMutability/java/remote/monitor/Monitor.java

```java
public class Monitor extends UntypedActor {
  public void onReceive(Object message) {
    System.out.println(message);
  }

  public static void main(final String[] args) {
    Actors.remote().start("localhost", 8000)
      .register("system-monitor", Actors.actorOf(Monitor.class));

    System.out.println("Press key to stop");
    System.console().readLine();
    Actors.registry().shutdownAll();
    Actors.remote().shutdown();
  }
}
```

The way we create a remote actor is no different from the way we create an in-process actor—we extend UntypedActor and implement the onReceive() method. We could generate a sophisticated report with tables and graphs if we desire, but let's keep the focus on actors here. We'll simply print the message received.

In the main() method, we first start the remote service by indicating the hostname and the port number. Then we register the actor for remote access using an ID system-monitor. When it's time to shut down the monitor service, we invoke the methods that'll help us terminate the remote service. That's all the code we needed in the monitor service. Let's now create the client code:

favoringIsolatedMutability/java/remote/client/Client.java

```java
public class Client {
  public static void main(final String[] args) {
    ActorRef systemMonitor = remote().actorFor(
      "system-monitor", "localhost", 8000);

    systemMonitor.sendOneWay("Cores: " +
      Runtime.getRuntime().availableProcessors());
    systemMonitor.sendOneWay("Total Space: " +
      new File("/").getTotalSpace());
    systemMonitor.sendOneWay("Free Space: " +
      new File("/").getFreeSpace());
  }
}
```

To gain access to the remote actor, the client indicates the ID, the hostname, and the port number where the remote actor resides. Once we get a reference to the ActorRef, we send messages to it with the appropriate information, as Strings in this example.

Let's open two command windows to run the monitor in one and the client in another. Let's first start the monitor and then the client. Each time we run the client, the monitor will print the information sent to it, as shown next:

```
Press key to stop
Cores: 2
Total Space: 499763888128
Free Space: 141636308992
```

To compile and run the monitor and the client, we'll have to include a few additional JAR files: akka-remote-1.1.2.jar, protobuf-java-2.3.0.jar, netty-3.2.3.Final.jar, and commons-io-2.0.1.jar.

Let's not let the ease of creating remote actors deceive us. We still need to ensure that messages are immutable (and serializable) and that our actors don't modify any shared mutable state.

8.13 Limitations of the Actor-Based Model

The actor-based model makes it easy to program with isolated mutability, but it does have some limitations.

Actors communicate with each other through messages. In languages that do not enforce immutability, we must be very careful to ensure the messages are immutable. Passing mutable messages can lead to thread-safety concerns and eventually the perils of shared mutability. Tools may evolve to verify that the messages are immutable; until then, the onus is on us to ensure immutability.

Actors run asynchronously but coordinate by passing messages. The unexpected failure of actors may result in starvation—one or more actors may be waiting for messages that would never arrive because of the failure. We must program defensively and handle exceptions within the actors and propagate error messages to actors awaiting a response.

Actors do not prevent deadlocks; it's possible for two or more actors to wait on one another for messages. We have to design carefully to ensure that the coordination between actors doesn't fall into a deadlock state. Also, we should use timeouts to ensure we don't wait endlessly for a response from an actor.

Actors can handle only one message request at a time. So, both action messages and messages requesting a response or state run sequentially. This can result in lower concurrency for the tasks that are interested only in reading the value. It is better to design applications with coarse-grain messages instead of fine-grain messages. Also, we can reduce waits by designing with one-way "fire and forget" messages instead of two-way messages.

Not all applications are well-suited for an actor-based model. Actors serve well when we can divide the problem into parts that can run quite independently and need to communicate only sporadically. If frequent interaction is required or the parts or tasks need to coordinate to form a quorum, the actor-based model is not suitable. We may have to mix other concurrency models or consider significant redesign.

8.14 Recap

Actors are single-threaded and communicate with each other by passing messages.

We learned that actors do the following:

- Make it easy to work with isolated mutability

- Eliminate synchronization concerns at its root

- Provide efficient one-way messaging but also provide the less efficient send-and-wait facility

- Are very scalable; while being single-threaded, they efficiently share a pool of threads

- Allow us to send messages but also provide typed versions (in Akka) backed by interfaces

- Allow us to coordinate with other actors using transactions

Although actors provide a powerful model, they also have limitations. There is potential for actor starvation and also deadlock if we're not careful in designing with them. Also, we have to ensure that the messages are immutable.

In the next chapter, we'll learn how to use actors from a variety of JVM languages.

CHAPTER 9

Actors in Groovy, Java, JRuby, and Scala

We worked with actors in the previous chapter. We will learn how to program with them in some of the popular JVM languages in this chapter.

Erlang popularized the interprocess actor-based model. Scala brought an Erlang-style model to intraprocess communication. Clojure does not directly support actors—Rich Hickey expresses his reasons for that at http://clojure. org/state#actors. Clojure supports agents that represent shared mutable identities but with asynchronous, independent, mutually exclusive updates. We will discuss Clojure agents in Appendix 1, *Clojure Agents*, on page 249.

We could use Akka actors from Groovy; instead, we'll use GPars, which is a concurrency library with close ties to Groovy. We'll then look at using Akka actors from the other languages we consider.

Sending messages to actors does not seem like a big deal; the real concern is about creating actors—this involves extending from classes and overriding methods in some languages. There are some minor issues we'll run into, but nothing someone who has survived this far into this book can't handle.

Focus on the sections related to languages you're interested in and feel free to skip the others.

9.1 Actors in Groovy with GPars

To create actors, we have at least as many options in Groovy as in Java.

We can implement Akka actors in Groovy by extending Akka UntypedActor. Groovy allows us to extend from classes written in other JVM languages, so it's a direct override of the onReceive() method of UntypedActor. Within this method, we can check for the message type and perform appropriate actions.

We may also use one of the other actor frameworks available for Java. However, in this chapter we'll use a concurrency library geared more toward Groovy—GPars.

GPars is a library written in Java that brings the love of programming concurrency to Groovy and Java. The Java's performance and the sheer elegance of Groovy shine in GPars. It provides a number of capabilities—asynchrony, parallel array manipulations, fork/join, agents, data flow, and actors. I won't discuss GPars in its entirety here. I'll show how we can implement some of the examples we saw earlier using GPars actors. For a comprehensive discussion on GPars, refer to the GPars documentation.

First, the actors in GPars take care of the fundamentals: they cross the memory barrier at appropriate times, allow for only one thread to run their receiver methods at any given time, and are backed by message queues. GPars has different flavors of actors and allows us to configure various parameters such as fairness of thread affinity. The API for creating and using actors is fluent, as we'll see next.

Creating Actors

To create an actor in GPars, we extend from DefaultActor or simply pass a closure to the actor() method of Actors. We use the latter if we have a simple message loop. If we have more complex logic or want to call into other methods of our actor class, then we should take the route of extending DefaultActor.

We must start an actor before it can accept messages; any attempt to send a message before that will result in an exception. Let's create an actor first using the DefaultActor class and then by using the actor() method.

Let's create an actor that will receive a String message and respond by simply printing the message. We extend DefaultActor and implement its act() method, as shown in the next code. This method runs the message loop, so we invoke a never-ending loop() method and call react() to receive a message. When our actor runs into react(), it blocks without holding a thread hostage. When a message arrives, a thread from the thread pool is scheduled to run the closure we provide to the react() method. Once the thread completes the block of code provided to the react(), it reruns the containing loop(), placing the actor again on the message wait queue. In the example, we simply print the message received plus the information on the thread that's processing the message:

polyglotActors/groovy/create/createActor.groovy
```groovy
class HollywoodActor extends DefaultActor {
  def name

  public HollywoodActor(actorName) { name = actorName }

  void act() {
    loop {
      react { role ->
        println "$name playing the role $role"
        println "$name runs in ${Thread.currentThread()}"
      }
    }
  }
}
```

We create an instance of an actor much like how we create an instance of any class, but remember to call the start() method. Let's create a pair of actors:

polyglotActors/groovy/create/createActor.groovy
```groovy
depp = new HollywoodActor("Johnny Depp").start()
hanks = new HollywoodActor("Tom Hanks").start()
```

The actors are now ready to receive messages, so let's send a message to each actor using the send() method:

polyglotActors/groovy/create/createActor.groovy
```groovy
depp.send("Wonka")
hanks.send("Lovell")
```

Instead of using the traditional Java-style method call, we can also use the overloaded operator << to send a message. If that's too much noise, we can simply place the message next to the actor, as in the next example:

polyglotActors/groovy/create/createActor.groovy
```groovy
depp << "Sparrow"
hanks "Gump"
```

The actors, by default, run in daemon threads, so the code will terminate as soon as the main method completes. We want it to live long enough for us to see the messages being processed, so we can add a delay to the end or use the join() method with a timeout. The join() method will wait for the actors to terminate; since we did not use the terminate() call, they will not die, but the timeout will get the main thread out of the blocking call.

polyglotActors/groovy/create/createActor.groovy
```groovy
[depp, hanks]*.join(1, java.util.concurrent.TimeUnit.SECONDS)
```

Let's take this example for a ride, run groovy, and provide the GPars JAR in the classpath, like so:

```
groovy -classpath $GPARS_HOME/gpars-0.11.jar createActor.groovy
```

The actors respond to the messages by printing the role we asked them to play. The two actors run concurrently, but each of them processes only one message at a time. At different instances, different threads from the thread pool may run the actors' method in response to the messages sent. Each time we run the code, we may see a slightly different sequence of calls in the output because of the nondeterministic nature of concurrent executions. Coincidentally, in one of the outputs I managed to capture, we see two actors share the same thread at different instances and also an actor switching threads between messages.

```
Johnny Depp playing the role Wonka
Johnny Depp runs in Thread[Actor Thread 3,5,main]
Tom Hanks playing the role Lovell
Tom Hanks runs in Thread[Actor Thread 3,5,main]
Tom Hanks playing the role Gump
Tom Hanks runs in Thread[Actor Thread 2,5,main]
Johnny Depp playing the role Sparrow
Johnny Depp runs in Thread[Actor Thread 3,5,main]
```

If we want to process messages indefinitely or until an actor is terminated, we use loop(), as we saw in the previous example. If we want to run the loop only a finite number of times or until some condition is met, we can use variations of the loop() method that give us more control. To run for a finite number of times, use loop(count) {}. If we'd like to specify a condition, use loop ({-> expression }), and the actor will repeat the loop as long as the expression is true. We can also provide an optional closure to run when the actor terminates, as we'll see in the next example.

Let's create an actor this time using the Actors' act() method. We'll call the act() method and send the message loop to it as a closure. In the previous example, we used loop() with only the closure—the message-processing body with a call to react(). In this example, we pass two additional parameters to the loop(). The first parameter can be a condition or a count. Here we pass 3 to tell the actor to respond to three messages and then terminate. The second parameter, which is optional, is a piece of code (given as a closure) that's executed when the actor terminates.

polyglotActors/groovy/create/loop3.groovy
```
depp = Actors.actor {
  loop(3, { println "Done acting" }) {
    react { println "Johnny Depp playing the role $it" }
  }
}
```

The actor is programmed to receive only three messages. Let's send one additional message than it's expecting in order to see what happens:

```
polyglotActors/groovy/create/loop3.groovy
depp << "Sparrow"
depp << "Wonka"
depp << "Scissorhands"
depp << "Cesar"

depp.join(1, java.util.concurrent.TimeUnit.SECONDS)
```

When we run the previous example, we'll see the actor received three messages and then terminated. The last message to the actor is ignored because the actor has already terminated by this point.

```
Johnny Depp playing the role Sparrow
Johnny Depp playing the role Wonka
Johnny Depp playing the role Scissorhands
Done acting
```

We saw the flexibility that GPars offers to create actors and control the message loop. Let's now look at the options for two-way messaging.

Sending and Receiving Messages

In addition to one-way messages, GPars allows us to send messages and receive responses. We can make a blocking sendAndWait() with an optional timeout, or we can use the nonblocking sendAndContinue(), which accepts a closure that is to be called when the reply arrives. This nonblocking version will make it easier for us to message multiple actors and then wait for their responses.

To facilitate sending a reply to the message sender, the Actor provides a convenient sender property. We'll call the send() method on the sender to send a reply, as in the next example:

```
polyglotActors/groovy/create/fortune.groovy
fortuneTeller = Actors.actor {
  loop {
    react { name ->
      sender.send("$name, you have a bright future")
    }
  }
}
```

The fortuneTeller actor receives a name and replies with a lame fortune message. From the user of the actor's point of view, we'd call the sendAndWait() to send a name and block for a response:

polyglotActors/groovy/create/fortune.groovy
```
message = fortuneTeller.sendAndWait("Joe", 1, TimeUnit.SECONDS)
println message
```

Although it's simple, the sendAndWait() method won't help if we want to send multiple messages at once. We can send multiple messages using the non-blocking sendAndContinue(), but once we send the messages, we need a way to block for all the responses to arrive. We could use CountDownLatch for that. When replies arrive, we can count down on that latch. The main thread that blocks on the latch can continue when all responses arrive. If the timeout happens before that, we can handle that case from the return value of the await() method:

polyglotActors/groovy/create/fortune.groovy
```
latch = new CountDownLatch(2)

fortuneTeller.sendAndContinue("Bob") { println it; latch.countDown() }
fortuneTeller.sendAndContinue("Fred") { println it; latch.countDown() }

println "Bob and Fred are keeping their fingers crossed"

if (!latch.await(1, TimeUnit.SECONDS))
  println "Fortune teller didn't respond before timeout!"
else
  println "Bob and Fred are happy campers"
```

The output from a run of the example is shown next:

```
Joe, you have a bright future
Bob, you have a bright future
Bob and Fred are keeping their fingers crossed
Fred, you have a bright future
Bob and Fred are happy campers
```

We can see the Groovy expressiveness along with the closure convenience play nicely in GPars for two-way messaging. Let's move now beyond simple String messages and look at sending other types of messages.

Handling Discrete Messages

Messages are not restricted to the simple String used in the GPars examples so far. We can send any object as a message, but we need to ensure they're immutable. Let's create an example actor that mimics stock trading; it would handle a couple of different types of messages. But first we need to define the messages. We can make use of the Groovy-defined annotation Immutable to ensure the message is immutable. This annotation not only ensures all fields are final; it also throws in a constructor (plus a few more methods).

polyglotActors/groovy/multimessage/stock1.groovy
```groovy
@Immutable class LookUp {
  String ticker
}

@Immutable class Buy {
  String ticker
  int quantity
}
```

The LookUp holds a ticker symbol and represents a message that requests price for a stock. The Buy class holds a ticker and the number of shares we'd like to buy. Our actor needs to take different actions for these two messages. Let's get to that now:

polyglotActors/groovy/multimessage/stock1.groovy
```groovy
trader = Actors.actor {
  loop {
    react { message ->
        if(message instanceof Buy)
          println "Buying ${message.quantity} shares of ${message.ticker}"

        if(message instanceof LookUp)
          sender.send((int)(Math.random() * 1000))
    }
  }
}
```

When the actor receives a message, we check whether the message is an instance of one of the message types we expect using runtime type identification's (RTTI's) instanceof. We take the necessary action based on the message type or ignore the message if it's something we didn't expect; alternately, we could throw exceptions if we receive an unrecognized message. In this example, if the message is a Buy, we simply print a message, and if it is a LookUp, we return a random number representing price of the stock.

There's nothing special in using an actor that takes different types of messages, as we can see here:

polyglotActors/groovy/multimessage/stock1.groovy
```groovy
trader.sendAndContinue(new LookUp("XYZ")) {
  println "Price of XYZ sock is $it"
}
trader << new Buy("XYZ", 200)
trader.join(1, java.util.concurrent.TimeUnit.SECONDS)
```

The output from the code is shown next:

```
Price of XYZ sock is 27
Buying 200 shares of XYZ
```

It was simple, but the way our actor handled the message can be improved. Rather than using conditional statements to check the type, we can leverage Groovy's typing system to do the branching. For this we'd use DynamicDispatchActor as the base actor class, as shown here:

polyglotActors/groovy/multimessage/stock2.groovy
```
class Trader extends DynamicDispatchActor {
  void onMessage(Buy message) {
    println "Buying ${message.quantity} shares of ${message.ticker}"
  }

  def onMessage(LookUp message) {
    sender.send((int)(Math.random() * 1000))
  }
}
```

We extended the actor from DynamicDispatchActor and overloaded the onMessage() method for each type of message our actor handles. The base class DynamicDispatchActor will check the message type and then dispatch the appropriate onMessage() of the actor. Since we defined a separate class, we must remember to call start() to initialize the actor message loop, as we see next:

polyglotActors/groovy/multimessage/stock2.groovy
```
trader = new Trader().start()
trader.sendAndContinue(new LookUp("XYZ")) {
  println "Price of XYZ sock is $it"
}

trader << new Buy("XYZ", 200)

trader.join(1, java.util.concurrent.TimeUnit.SECONDS)
```

To provide discrete message handlers, we're not forced to create a separate class. Instead, we can pass a closure that handles a chain of methods to the constructor of DynamicDispatchActor, as we see next:

polyglotActors/groovy/multimessage/stock3.groovy
```
trader = new DynamicDispatchActor({
  when { Buy message ->
    println "Buying ${message.quantity} shares of ${message.ticker}"
  }

  when { LookUp message ->
    sender.send((int)(Math.random() * 1000))
  }
}).start()
```

The closure that we send as the constructor parameter has a nice fluent syntax where each type of message is presented in a when clause. At first glance, this appears much like the conditional if statements, but there are some significant differences. First, we don't have the bad taste of RTTI. Second, each of these when clauses transforms into a specific message handler under the covers. Invalid or unhandled messages result in exceptions, whereas in the case of explicit conditional statements, we had to write code to handle that.

Using GPars

We got the hang of creating and coordinating GPars actors. Let's put that knowledge to use to rewrite the file size program. We discussed an actor-based design for that program in Section 8.6, *Coordinating Actors*, on page 182, and we saw the implementations using Scala and Java before. Let's see how the Groovy and GPars implementation of that design compares.

The file size program design asked for two actors, SizeCollector and FileProcessor. Each FileProcessor will receive as a message a directory and send as a message the size of files and list of subdirectories in that directory. SizeCollector is the main actor, the mastermind. We need to define the message types, so let's start with that first:

polyglotActors/groovy/filesize/findFileSize.groovy
```
@Immutable class RequestAFile {}
@Immutable class FileSize { long size }
@Immutable class FileToProcess { String fileName }
```

We defined the messages types RequestAFile, FileSize, and FileToProcess as immutable classes.

Next, we need to create FileProcessor. We'll extend DefaultActor to give that class the actor capabilities. This actor needs to register with the SizeCollector actor for receiving the directories. We can do this in the afterStart() method. GPars provides event methods such as afterStart() and afterStop() just like Akka's preStart() and postStop() methods. The afterStart() is called right after the actor is started but before the first message is processed. Let's implement the FileProcessor actor:

polyglotActors/groovy/filesize/findFileSize.groovy
```
class FileProcessor extends DefaultActor {
  def sizeCollector

  public FileProcessor(theSizeCollector) { sizeCollector = theSizeCollector }

  void afterStart() { registerToGetFile() }

  void registerToGetFile() { sizeCollector << new RequestAFile() }
```

```groovy
    void act()  {
      loop {
        react { message ->
          def file = new File(message.fileName)
          def size = 0
          if(!file.isDirectory())
            size = file.length()
          else {
            def children = file.listFiles()
            if (children != null) {
              children.each { child ->
                if(child.isFile())
                  size += child.length()
                else
                  sizeCollector << new FileToProcess(child.path)
              }
            }
          }
          sizeCollector << new FileSize(size)
          registerToGetFile()
        }
      }
    }
}
```

The SizeCollector will receive three different types of messages as it communicates with the FileProcessors. Since we have three distinct type of messages, we can avoid the switch statement and write three separate methods if we extend from the DynamicDispatchActor to implement this actor. Just like the previous implementations of this design, we maintain a list of files to process, a list of idling file processors, a count of files pending to be visited, and the most important total file size being computed. As files are received and file requests arrive, we dispatch them to idling FileProcessors. Let's look at the code for the SizeCollector:

polyglotActors/groovy/filesize/findFileSize.groovy
```groovy
class SizeCollector extends DynamicDispatchActor {
  def toProcessFileNames = []
  def idleFileProcessors = []
  def pendingNumberOfFilesToVisit = 0
  def totalSize = 0L
  final def start = System.nanoTime()

  def sendAFileToProcess() {
    if(toProcessFileNames && idleFileProcessors) {
      idleFileProcessors.first() <<
        new FileToProcess(toProcessFileNames.first())
      idleFileProcessors = idleFileProcessors.tail()
      toProcessFileNames = toProcessFileNames.tail()
```

```
    }
  }

  void onMessage(RequestAFile message) {
    idleFileProcessors.add(sender)
    sendAFileToProcess()
  }

  void onMessage(FileToProcess message) {
    toProcessFileNames.add(message.fileName)
    pendingNumberOfFilesToVisit += 1
    sendAFileToProcess()
  }

  void onMessage(FileSize message) {
    totalSize += message.size
    pendingNumberOfFilesToVisit -= 1
    if(pendingNumberOfFilesToVisit == 0) {
      def end = System.nanoTime()
      println "Total size is $totalSize"
      println "Time taken is ${(end - start)/1.0e9}"
      terminate()
    }
  }
}
```

When the pendingNumberOfFilesToVisit falls to zero, the actor prints the total files size and the time taken. It then terminates itself. It's time to put these actors to use, and that's the job of the main code:

```
polyglotActors/groovy/filesize/findFileSize.groovy
sizeCollector = new SizeCollector().start()
sizeCollector << new FileToProcess(args[0])

100.times { new FileProcessor(sizeCollector).start() }

sizeCollector.join(100, java.util.concurrent.TimeUnit.SECONDS)
```

The main code sets one SizeCollector and 100 FileProcessors in motion and waits, with a timeout, for the SizeCollector to terminate. The output from running the code for the /usr directory is shown next:

```
Total size is 3793911517
Time taken is 8.69052900
```

The file size reported by the Groovy–GPars version is the same as the result from the other versions, and the time taken is pretty comparable. The Groovy version enjoys a comparable level of conciseness in syntax with the Scala version as well. Overall, that's pretty groovy.

Data Flow

Data-flow programming was all the rage a couple of decades ago. Companies were eager to build data-flow processors to exploit parallelism in applications, unconstrained by programming constructs. Computations would be carried out by these processors as soon as the data needed for them becomes available. Rather than a von Newmann–style instruction execution, the data flow through the application would decide the set of instructions to execute. Even though data-flow processors never took off, data-flow programming is grabbing attention again.

In a data-flow program, computations or tasks block for data and run as soon as all the data they depend on becomes available. There is no synchronization or locking. As long as we keep the tasks pure (that is, they're idempotent, don't have side effects, and don't alter any data; in other words, they're functional in style), data-flow programs, as we'll see, are quite easy to write. Akka provides API for data-flow programming, but in this section we'll use the fluent GPars API for data-flow programming.

We're tasked with fetching content from different websites and reporting the size of the content in each site. The code to print or report the content size must run sequentially, because it involves updating the console or a GUI that often is single-threaded. However, we can fetch the data from the websites concurrently. The code to print the information can run as soon as the data is available. Let's write the code for this first and discuss the details right after that:

polyglotActors/groovy/dataflow/dataflowvariable/dataflow.groovy
```
def fetchContent(String url, DataFlowVariable content) {
  println("Requesting data from $url")
  content << url.toURL().text
  println("Set content from $url")
}

content1 = new DataFlowVariable()
content2 = new DataFlowVariable()

task { fetchContent("http://www.agiledeveloper.com", content1) }
task { fetchContent("http://pragprog.com", content2) }

println("Waiting for data to be set")
println("Size of content1 is ${content1.val.size()}")
println("Size of content2 is ${content2.val.size()}")
```

A DataFlowVariable class in GPars is a write-once variable that can be read any number of times. The first read will block, if necessary, until the data is available. Subsequent reads will return the prewritten value. The variable is bound to a value on first write, and any attempt to write to a bound variable will result in an exception. Since the read blocks until data is bound, there is no need for synchronization to get the data from a DataFlowVariable.

In the example, the fetchContent() method receives a URL and a DataFlowVariable content as parameters. It fetches the content of the website by using the elegant combination of toURL() and text calls. It then writes the content to the DataFlowVariable class using the << operator.

After defining the method, we create two data-flow variables to hold the content of two sites we'll visit. We then use the task() method of the DataFlow class to create two data-flow tasks. Each of these tasks runs concurrently. While the websites are being accessed from these two tasks, we invoke the val property of the first DataFlowVariable content1. This will block the execution until the data becomes available. Once data is available, we print the size of the contents, as we can see from the output next:

```
Waiting for data to be set
Requesting data from http://pragprog.com
Requesting data from http://www.agiledeveloper.com
Set content from http://www.agiledeveloper.com
Size of content1 is 2914
Set content from http://pragprog.com
Size of content2 is 13003
```

Even though the example is quite simple, it exposes the nature of a data-flow program. The execution sequence is purely dictated by the availability and flow of data.

DataFlowVariable eliminates the need for synchronization; however, its write-once nature is quite restricting. GPars provides alternatives such as DataFlowQueue to stream data. It allows us to connect multiple readers or a single reader for each data value in the stream—refer to the GPars documentation for various options.

We used task to create asynchronous tasks. This is convenient for a small number of tasks, but if we need to create a large number of tasks, we'd want to manage the threads for these tasks using a pool of threads. GPars provides DefaultPGroup, a thread group class, just for that. Instead of calling the DataFlow's static method task(), we'll use the group's instance method with the same name.

Let's rewrite the file size program using the data-flow API, as shown next:

polyglotActors/groovy/dataflow/filesize/fileSize.groovy

```groovy
class FileSize {
  private final pendingFiles = new DataFlowQueue()
  private final sizes = new DataFlowQueue()
  private final group = new DefaultPGroup()

  def findSize(File file) {
    def size = 0
    if(!file.isDirectory())
      size = file.length()
    else {
      def children = file.listFiles()
      if (children != null) {
        children.each { child ->
          if(child.isFile())
            size += child.length()
          else {
            pendingFiles << 1
            group.task { findSize(child) }
          }
        }
      }
    }

    pendingFiles << -1
    sizes << size
  }

  def findTotalFileSize(File file) {
    pendingFiles << 1
    group.task { findSize(file) }

    int filesToVisit = 0
    long totalSize = 0
    while(true) {
      totalSize += sizes.val
      if(!(filesToVisit += (pendingFiles.val + pendingFiles.val))) break
    }

    totalSize
  }
}

start = System.nanoTime()
totalSize = new FileSize().findTotalFileSize(new File(args[0]))
println("Total size $totalSize")
println("Time taken ${(System.nanoTime() - start) / 1.0e9}")
```

We create two instance of DataFlowQueue, one to keep a tab of file visits that are active and the other to receive the size of files and subdirectories. We'd like to run our tasks in a pool of threads, so we create a DefaultPGroup.

In the findSize() method, we total the size of all files in the given directory and set that value into the sizes DataFlowQueue using the << operator. For each subdirectory we find under the given directory, we create a new task to explore that directory using the call to group.task.

We push a 1 into the pendingFiles before we start a task, and we push a -1 onto it when a task is completed. This will allow us to keep track of when all tasks to explore directories are complete.

In the findTotalFileSize() method, we create a task to explore the given file/directory. We then receive the file sizes from the task and from all the subtasks that are created as each subdirectory is explored. The loop terminates when we determine there are no more pending directories to explore. We finally return the total file size from this method.

The last bit of code is to execute and time these functions. Let's run the code and observe the output:

```
Total size is 3793911517
Time taken is 9.46729800
```

The file size program lends itself really well to the data-flow approach. The code is remarkably simple, and the performance is quite comparable to the other solutions.

9.2 Java Integration

We have a handful of choices for actor-based concurrency in Java, as we discussed earlier. We get to pick from ActorFoundary, Actorom, Actors Guild, Akka, FunctionalJava, Kilim, Jetlang, and so on. We used Akka fairly extensively in Chapter 8, *Favoring Isolated Mutability*, on page 163. Akka was written in Scala, but they've done a fairly decent job of exposing convenient interface for us to use in Java. To use Akka, refer to the Akka documentation and the examples given in this book. For one of the other libraries, refer to their respective documentation.

9.3 JRuby Akka Integration

To use Akka in JRuby, we'll follow along the same lines as we did in Java. The main difference is we'll be able to benefit from JRuby conciseness. We're already familiar with the capabilities of Akka and its powerful API from Chapter 8, *Favoring Isolated Mutability*, on page 163. Let's jump right into implementing the design in Section 8.6, *Coordinating Actors*, on page 182 for the file size program in JRuby. Remember, we need a bunch of message types, two actor types, and some main code to exercise these. Let's start with the message types first:

polyglotActors/jruby/FileSize.rb

```ruby
class RequestAFile; end

class FileSize
  attr_reader :size
  def initialize(size)
    @size = size
  end
end

class FileToProcess
  attr_reader :file_name
  def initialize(file_name)
    @file_name = file_name
  end
end
```

These message-representing classes are a direct translation of the respective classes from the Java version we saw earlier. Writing the FileProcessor actor involves a little bit more effort. When we extend a Java class, JRuby does not allow us to change the constructor signature. The Akka actor-based class UntypedActor has a no-argument constructor, but our FileProcessor needs to accept a parameter for SizeCollector. If we proceed to write an initialize() method in this class, we'll run into runtime errors. The trick is to invoke super()() with a parenthesis to get around this problem. Except for that, the rest of this class is a simple translation of the Java code to JRuby:

polyglotActors/jruby/FileSize.rb

```ruby
require 'java'
java_import java.lang.System
java_import 'akka.actor.ActorRegistry'
java_import 'akka.actor.Actors'
java_import 'akka.actor.UntypedActor'

class FileProcessor < UntypedActor
  attr_accessor :size_collector

  def initialize(size_collector)
    super()
    @size_collector = size_collector
  end

  def preStart
```

```ruby
      register_to_get_file
  end

  def register_to_get_file
    @size_collector.send_one_way(RequestAFile.new, context)
  end

  def onReceive(fileToProcess)
    file = java.io.File.new(fileToProcess.file_name)
    size = 0
    if !file.isDirectory()
      size = file.length()
    else
      children = file.listFiles()
      if children != nil
        children.each do |child|
          if child.isFile()
            size += child.length()
          else
            @size_collector.send_one_way(FileToProcess.new(child.getPath()))
          end
        end
      end
    end
    @size_collector.send_one_way(FileSize.new(size))
    register_to_get_file
  end
end
```

Next let's get the second actor SizeCollector ready. When we create an instance of this actor using one of the versions of UntypedActor's actor_of() method, we'll get an error that this class lacks the create() method. So, let's provide that factory method. Except for this addition, the rest of the code is a direct translation of the Java version to JRuby:

polyglotActors/jruby/FileSize.rb
```ruby
class SizeCollector < UntypedActor
  def self.create(*args)
    self.new(*args)
  end

  def initialize
    @to_process_file_names = []
    @file_processors = []
    @fetch_size_future = nil
    @pending_number_of_files_to_visit = 0
    @total_size = 0
    @start_time = System.nano_time
  end
```

```ruby
  def send_a_file_to_process
    if !@to_process_file_names.empty? && !@file_processors.empty?
      @file_processors.first.send_one_way(
        FileToProcess.new(@to_process_file_names.first))
      @file_processors = @file_processors.drop(1)
      @to_process_file_names = @to_process_file_names.drop(1)
    end
  end

  def onReceive(message)
    case message
      when RequestAFile
        @file_processors << context.sender.get
        send_a_file_to_process

      when FileToProcess
        @to_process_file_names << message.file_name
        @pending_number_of_files_to_visit += 1
        send_a_file_to_process

      when FileSize
        @total_size += message.size
        @pending_number_of_files_to_visit -= 1
        if @pending_number_of_files_to_visit == 0
          end_time = System.nano_time()
          puts "Total size is #{@total_size}"
          puts "Time taken is #{(end_time - @start_time)/1.0e9}"
          Actors.registry().shutdownAll()
        end
      end
  end
end
```

As the last step, let's write the code that will exercise these two actors:

polyglotActors/jruby/FileSize.rb
```ruby
size_collector = Actors.actor_of(SizeCollector).start()
size_collector.send_one_way(FileToProcess.new(ARGV[0]))

100.times do
  Actors.actor_of(lambda { FileProcessor.new(size_collector) }).start
end
```

The Actors class provides a few flavors of the actor_of() or actorOf() method in Java lingo. We use the version of this method that expects a factory with a create() method to create an instance of the actor SizeCollector. The static create() method we provided in SizeCollector gets used here. Since we need to set a parameter at construction time into the instances of FileProcessor, we use the version of actor_of() that accepts a closure that internally creates an instance of the actor. JRuby allows us to fluently pass lambdas where closures are expected, so we took advantage of that here. The rest of the code is a simple translation from the Java version to JRuby.

Let's take this JRuby version of the file size program for a ride across the /usr directory:

```
Total size is 3793911517
Time taken is 9.69524
```

We had to jump through some small hoops to implement the JRuby version. Once we figured out how to get around the inheritance restriction of JRuby, we were able to make use of the Ruby conciseness and fluency.

9.4   Choices in Scala

We have a few options for actor-based concurrency in Scala; one of them is the scala.actor library that's provided with the Scala installation. Akka library provides better performance and is better suited for enterprise applications (see Akka benchmarks in Appendix 2, *Web Resources*, on page 255). To use the Scala actor library, refer to Scala's documentation, *Programming in Scala* [OSV08], or *Programming Scala* [Sub09]. To use Akka, refer to Akka's documentation and the examples provided in Chapter 8, *Favoring Isolated Mutability*, on page 163.

9.5   Recap

We can program concurrency in any language on the JVM. In this chapter, we learned the following:

- The Akka Java API can be readily used from multiple JVM languages including JRuby.

- GPars brings Groovy elegance and Java performance to programming concurrency.

- Pattern matching messages is not the only option; we can overload the message handler methods based on the message types in GPars.

- When mixing APIs, we'll run into a few language-level integration issues but nothing that's insurmountable.

- While we program concurrency, we can continue to enjoy the expressive and conciseness syntax of these modern JVM languages.

We've come a long way! In the next chapter, we'll wrap up with recommendations for programming concurrency.

Part V

Epilogue

To understand a new idea, break an old habit.

    Jean Toomer

Zen of Programming Concurrency

I wish you well for the exciting journey across the sea of concurrency. Doing it right can help you safely reach the destination—delivering high-performing, responsive applications that make good use of multicore processors.

Programming concurrency is not about the methods we call or the parameters we pass. It's more about the approaches we take, the effort we put in, and the set of libraries we opt to use. We have to make the right choices to arrive at a clear concurrency solution.

The coding journey is not all about surviving the perils; it's about succeeding and having fun doing that. We have to decide on the number of threads to use and how to divide applications into concurrent tasks. The number of threads depends on the number of cores an application will have available at runtime and how much time the tasks will spend being blocked vs. in active computations. Dividing the application into tasks takes effort. We have to understand the nature of the application and how to partition into tasks with uniform workload. Choosing the right number of threads and a uniform workload across the parts will help better utilize the cores throughout the application runtime, as we discussed in Chapter 2, *Division of Labor*, on page 15.

10.1 Exercise Your Options

Few things affect concurrency and correctness as much as the approach we take to deal with state; you can choose from shared mutability, isolated mutability, and pure immutability. Exercise your options and choose wisely.

Shared mutability is the fail-boat we want to avoid. The minute we refuse to get on it, a number of concurrency issues disappear. It takes some effort and discipline to avoid the all-too-familiar shared mutable style of programming; however, those efforts will soon pay back.

Get on board the boats of isolated mutability and pure immutability (where possible) to set on a smooth sail to realize the goals. These approaches remove the concerns at the root. Rather than spending valuable time and effort preventing race conditions, these approaches completely eliminate them so we can focus on the application logic.

Even in problems where there is significant state change, we can use isolated mutability and pure immutability, as we saw in Chapter 3, *Design Approaches*, on page 35.

10.2 Concurrency: Programmer's Guide

Upgrade to the modern JDK concurrency API as the first step to programming concurrency. Reduce the use of the old multithreading API that shipped with the first versions of Java. The java.util.concurrent API is such a breath of fresh air. We can easily manage a pool of threads, have better control over synchronization, and also benefit from high-performing concurrent data structures, as we saw in Chapter 4, *Scalability and Thread Safety*, on page 47. Several libraries now make use of this modern API, and concurrency libraries (such as Akka and GPars) provide a layer of abstraction on top of this modern API.

If your job responsibilities include "mutable state wrangler," you know the frustrations of ensuring thread-safety and achieving concurrent performance. We saw the tools and techniques to cope with these concerns in Chapter 4, *Scalability and Thread Safety*, on page 47 and Chapter 5, *Taming Shared Mutability*, on page 73. Make use of the ExecutorService class to graciously manage a pool of threads and the concurrent data structures to coordinate between threads/tasks. Utilize the Lock interface and related facilities for fine-grained synchronization, improved concurrency, and better control on lock timeouts.

Make fields and local variables final by default and relent only as an exception. Avoid shared mutability. After reasonable efforts, if there is no clear way to avoid mutability, then favor isolated mutability instead of shared mutability. It's much better to avoid concurrency concerns by design than to struggle to handle those issues in your code.

Take the time to learn and prototype solutions using STM and the actor-based model.

The examples in Chapter 6, *Introduction to Software Transactional Memory*, on page 89 and Chapter 7, *STM in Clojure, Groovy, Java, JRuby, and Scala*, on page 141 will help you create prototypes and gain you experience with somewhat limited but very powerful ways to deal with shared mutability. If an application has frequent reads and infrequent write collisions but has significant shared mutability, we may find solace in Software Transactional Memory (STM). The trick here is we must ensure the state values are immutable and the mutation is performed only on managed references.

We can eliminate the problem at the root and isolate mutable states within actors. Actors are highly scalable because they make effective use of threads. As active objects, they internally sequence operations and therefore eliminate concurrency concerns. Spend time creating prototypes using the examples in Chapter 8, *Favoring Isolated Mutability*, on page 163 and Chapter 9, *Actors in Groovy, Java, JRuby, and Scala*, on page 221.

If an application does not allow for such clean isolation but has isolated tasks with interleaved coordination, explore options to mix the two models together, as we saw in Section 8.9, *Mixing Actors and STM*, on page 201.

Some of these approaches may be new to you, so there may be a bit of a learning curve. Remember the first time you learned to ride a bike? It took time and effort, but once you got proficient, it helped you get around much faster than on foot. That's exactly how these unfamiliar techniques are. When we start, they may take us out of our comfort zone and require some time and effort. Once we learn and master them, we can avoid the perils of concurrency and devote more of our time and effort where it's really deserved, on application logic.

Programming with actors and immutable message passing takes some effort and learning. It also involves some unlearning of the ways we've gotten used to in OO programming. Not only do we have to pick up the new APIs, but we have to get comfortable with a different way to design applications. So, take the time to refactor your design skills.

10.3 Concurrency: Architect's Guide

Concurrency and performance are most likely two issues that you have to contend with quite extensively. Fortunately, there are some good options to influence the design and architecture of applications to deal with these issues effectively.

It's much better to eliminate concurrency concerns than tackle them. There's an easy way to achieve that; we can eliminate mutable state. Design applications around immutability or at least isolated mutability.

The two challenges we'll face as we move away from shared mutability are design and performance. We're so used to designing with shared mutability that it takes a good amount of practice and effort to do it differently. Look toward persistent and concurrent data structures for better performance.

Another area of influence you may have is the language choice. This generally is a touchy issue when we have developers who are quite attached to the languages they're comfortable with. If we're not convinced that a particular language is better, then it's hard for us to convince teams and managers. The same applies to concurrency approaches. The approach that's well known and widely used in teams may or may not be the right solution. It's hard to convince others if we're not convinced ourselves. If we're convinced that one approach is better than the other for an application, then we have a chance to convince others.

So, as the first step, we should convince ourselves about these choices on hand. Take the time to prototype and create small yet significant parts of applications using the language or the concurrency model most suitable for the application. Don't tackle the language choice and the concurrency choice at once. This may not help you or your team see a clear distinction. So, take them in turn and be objective in comparisons.

Once we're convinced, we'll find it easier to lead teams. Teams may have to slow down as they pick up a new approach, but once they get proficient, they'll be able to benefit from the improved efficiency. The time they had spent in ceremonial activities, like managing shared mutable state or language constraints, can now be devoted to solve real problems. The examples using different concurrency models and different languages in this book will help you compare the effectiveness of one over the other. They will help you decide whether the approach you want to consider is better than the one that your team may currently be using in practice.

10.4 Choose Wisely

Programming concurrency on the JVM has come a long way; we're no longer confined to one prescribed model. We have the freedom to choose from the models that make the most sense for each application we create.

We can choose from at least three options:

- The beaten path of synchronize-and-suffer model
- The software transaction memory
- The actor-based concurrency

No one option provides a perfect solution for all applications; each one of them has its strengths and weaknesses. We have to judiciously pick the solution with the most pros and the least cons for the application on hand.

The Modern JDK Concurrency API

The modern JDK concurrency API is baked right in, so everyone using JDK 1.5 or later will be able to use it. This API makes it easy to create and manage pool of threads and schedule concurrent tasks. There are a wealth of data structures, from managing concurrent collections to blocking queues to take care of exchanging data between threads. The newer Lock interface allows locks to be composed easily and provides an API that can time out instead of falling into deadlocks or starvation.

The main drawback is not at the surface of this API but at the root of how we use it. To make proper use of this API, we still have to know about the memory barrier, where to lock, for how long, and so on. The model is complex and error prone, so it is quite difficult to get it right for any nontrivial application, as we discussed in Chapter 4, *Scalability and Thread Safety*, on page 47 and Chapter 5, *Taming Shared Mutability*, on page 73.

The Software Transactional Memory

This is a bold step to deal with shared mutability. Its key is in the separation of mutable identity from immutable state values. STM was popularized by Clojure where states are immutable and managed identities are mutable only within the confines of STM's transactions. This brings predictability and deterministic behavior to mutating identity while providing explicit lock-free programming.

There are two main drawbacks to STM. If we're programming in languages other than Clojure, we have to use extreme caution to ensure that the state we're dealing with is immutable and that only managed identity is mutable. We don't get support for this from most of the languages on the JVM. Also, we must ensure that the code within transactions is idempotent and has no side effects. STM is suitable where the write collisions are infrequent. STM will repeat the transactions in case of write collisions. This is OK when such collisions are infrequent; however, it may lead to poor performance under extreme conditions. In general, however, if we can carefully deal with managed shared mutability, STM can provide at most concurrency. This comes at a price of exercising greater discipline when there's no language support to rely upon.

The Actor-Based Model

This model removes the synchronization issues at the root by promoting isolated mutability. Actors run independently, communicate using efficient asynchronous messages, and guarantee that simultaneous messages sent to them are processed in sequence.

The main drawback of this approach is that all communication between the concurrently running tasks has to happen through messages, which includes reads. So, readers who are interested in getting a fairly consistent value of state are forced to interleave their requests. The way we design applications using the coordinating actors is significantly different from the way we design an OO application. We have to ensure that the messages are immutable and that the actors are fairly coarse-grained so they can accomplish significant tasks independently. We should avoid designing actors in a way that they require chatty communication that may result in actors spending time waiting on each other instead of solving the problem on hand.

We saw throughout this book that the concurrency model we choose is not forced upon us by the language we program in. It's decided by the nature of the application, the design approaches we take, and the willingness of teams to adapt to the model that's the right fit. Choose wisely and enjoy your journey.

Bon voyage.

Clojure Agents

Clojure agents[1] represent a single identity or location in memory. Recollect that STM's refs manage coordinated synchronous changes to multiple identities. Agents allow independent asynchronous changes to the individual identities they manage. The changes are expressed in the form of functions or actions that are applied to that location asynchronously. Multiple independent concurrent actions are run in sequence, one after the other. Upon successful completion of an action, an agent is changed to the new state returned by the action. This new state is used for subsequent reads or subsequent actions on the agent.

The calls to run actions on an agent return immediately. The action is then applied on the agent using a thread from a Clojure managed thread pool. If we expect an action to be mostly CPU bound, then we use the send() method to run it. If IO blocking is possible within the function, we use send-off() instead of send() to prevent agents from starving for threads while some agents are blocked.

Let's see agents in action with an example—create a Hollywood actor and ask him to play different roles. We'll execute multiple roles to play concurrently on different actors. While the actions run concurrently, we'll see that multiple actions sent to a single agent are run sequentially.

Let's first create a function that will ask an actor to play a role and add the role to the list of roles played. In the code shown next, the act() method receives two parameters: actor and role. The actor is a tuple with two elements: the name of the actor and a list of roles played. We print the actor's name and the given role. Then, after a simulated delay to show the sequencing of concurrent calls to the same agent, we return the new state for the actor,

---

1. See http://clojure.org/agents.

the name, and a new list of roles. We don't modify anything in the action. The agent will take as its new state the value we return from the action.

```
(defn act [actor role]
  (let [[name roles] actor]
    (println name "playing role of" role)
    (. Thread sleep 2000)
    [name (conj roles role)]))
```

The let statement binds name and roles to the first and second elements in the actor tuple, respectively. The last line of code returns a tuple with name as the first element and the new list as the second element. The new list contains the roles in the given list plus the new role that was sent as the parameter to the act() method.

We saw the method that acts on an agent, but we haven't seen any agent yet, so let's get to that now. Agents are quite simple; they don't need any fanfare. In the code shown next, we define two agents, each representing a famous Hollywood actor. All that these agents contain is a tuple with the name of the actor and an empty list. We use the keyword agent to define them.

```
(try
  (def depp (agent ["Johnny Depp" ()]))
  (def hanks (agent ["Tom Hanks" ()]))
```

Our agents are geared up to receive messages, so let's send a few messages to them, asking the two actors to act on some roles, as shown next. The send() method takes the agent as the first parameter followed by the function to invoke. The first parameter this function takes is the agent that preceded it in this call list. If the function takes additional parameters, like role in this example, we place it after the function name.

```
(send depp act "Wonka")
(send depp act "Sparrow")
(send hanks act "Lovell")
(send hanks act "Gump")
```

The call to send() is nonblocking. If we want to wait for the agent to respond to all messages sent from the current thread, we can use the await() or the civilized version of it, await-for(), which accepts a timeout, as shown next. The await-for() takes the timeout in milliseconds as the first parameter followed by any number of agents we'd like to wait for. We break off from this blocking call when the agents complete the calls or the timeout occurs, whichever comes first.

```
(println "Let's wait for them to play")
(await-for 5000 depp hanks)
```

To dereference the agents, we simply prefix the agent with an @ symbol, as shown next:

```
(println "Let's see the net effect")
(println (first @depp) "played" (second @depp))
(println (first @hanks) "played" (second @hanks))
```

One last details to remember is that we must terminate the agents since they run in nondaemon threads. Remember to perform this operation within the finally block to ensure release even in the face of exceptions, as shown next:

```
(finally (shutdown-agents)))
```

Let's put all that together so we can see the complete sequence of code:

polyglotActors/clojure/clojureagent.clj
```
(defn act [actor role]
  (let [[name roles] actor]
    (println name "playing role of" role)
    (. Thread sleep 2000)
    [name (conj roles role)]))

(try
  (def depp (agent ["Johnny Depp" ()]))
  (def hanks (agent ["Tom Hanks" ()]))

  (send depp act "Wonka")
  (send depp act "Sparrow")
  (send hanks act "Lovell")
  (send hanks act "Gump")

  (println "Let's wait for them to play")
  (await-for 5000 depp hanks)

  (println "Let's see the net effect")
  (println (first @depp) "played" (second @depp))
  (println (first @hanks) "played" (second @hanks))

  (finally (shutdown-agents)))
```

Let's run it and observe the output. The output sequence may slightly vary each time we run since the agents are running concurrently and the exact ordering is nondeterministic.

```
Johnny Depp playing role of Wonka
Tom Hanks playing role of Lovell
Let's wait for them to play
```

```
Johnny Depp playing role of Sparrow
Tom Hanks playing role of Gump
Let's see the net effect
Johnny Depp played (Sparrow Wonka)
Tom Hanks played (Gump Lovell)
```

It's clear from the output that the calls to send() are nonblocking. Each of the agents executed the first message sent to them. The second messages to the agents are delayed because of the induced delay in the first messages. The main thread, in the meantime, awaits for the agents to handle these messages. When done, the roles played by the actors represented by these agents are printed.

Let's compare the Clojure agents with Akka actors. Agents don't have any specific methods or messages that they respond to. We can schedule arbitrary functions to run on agents. In contrast, Akka actors have designated onReceive() or receive() methods and have predefined messages that they respond to. The sender of the messages has to know which messages are supported. In comparison, both actors and agents serialize calls to them, allowing only one thread to run on them at any time.

By default agents don't run in any transaction. Recall that transactional code should have no side effects since they can be rolled back and retried several times. What if we do want to perform some actions or send messages to agents from within these transactions? Clojure tactfully handles this by grouping all the message sends to agents within a transaction and dispatching them only if the transaction commits.

Let's send messages to an agent from within transactions to see this behavior. In the code shown next, the sendMessageInTXN() method will send an act message to the given actor to play a given role. This message is sent from within a transaction delineated by the dosync() method. The transaction is forced to fail if the shouldFail parameter is true. If the transaction fails, the message send will be discarded; it will be dispatched otherwise. We create an agent depp and send a transactional message to play the role "Wonka" first. Then, within a failed transaction, we send a message to play the role "Sparrow" next. Finally, we wait for the messages to be processed and then print the roles played by depp.

```
(defn act [actor role]
  (let [[name roles] actor]
    (println name "playing role of" role)
    [name (conj roles role)]))

(defn sendMessageInTXN [actor role shouldFail]
```

```
(try
  (dosync
    (println "sending message to act" role)
    (send actor act role)
    (if shouldFail (throw (new RuntimeException "Failing transaction")))))
  (catch Exception e (println "Failed transaction")))))

(def depp (agent ["Johnny Depp" ()]))

(try
  (sendMessageInTXN depp "Wonka" false)
  (sendMessageInTXN depp "Sparrow" true)
  (await-for 1000 depp)
  (println "Roles played" (second @depp))
  (finally (shutdown-agents)))
```

We expect to see the first message being delivered to the agent, but the second message will be discarded, as shown in the output:

```
sending message to act Wonka
Johnny Depp playing role of Wonka
sending message to act Sparrow
Failed transaction
Roles played (Wonka)
```

The sequence in the output may vary slightly each time we run; we have to remember that actions sent to agents run asynchronously in a separate thread and the sends are nonblocking.

When bound by a transaction, messages sent to agents are grouped and dispatched only when the transaction succeeds. We can contrast this with the Akka transactors where we mixed actors with transactions. The Clojure solution is very concise and does not have some of the drawbacks of transactors we discussed earlier in Section 8.10, *Using Transactors*, on page 202.

Web Resources

- *Akka*

  http://akka.io

  Jonas Bonér's Akka is a Scala-based scalable concurrency library that can be used from multiple languages on the JVM. It provides both STM and actor-based concurrency.

- *Clojure Data Structures*

  http://clojure.org/data_structures

  This page discusses various data structures in Clojure, including the persistent data structures.

- *Values and Change—Clojure's approach to Identity and State*

  http://clojure.org/state

  Rich Hickey discuses the Clojure model of separating the identify and state and his approach to balance the imperative and functional styles of programming.

- *Designing and Building Parallel Programs*

  http://www.mcs.anl.gov/~itf/dbpp/book-info.html

  This is the online version of the book by Ian Foster with the same title.

- *The Dining Philosophers Problem*

  http://www.cs.utexas.edu/users/EWD/ewd03xx/EWD310.PDF

  This is the original paper by Edsger W. Dijkstra, "Hierarchical Ordering of Sequential Processes" Acta Informatica, 1971.

- *GPars*

  http://gpars.codehaus.org

  Started by Vaclav Pech as GParallelizer, GPars is a Groovy-based concurrency library for use with Groovy and Java.

- *Ideal Hash Trees*

  http://lamp.epfl.ch/papers/idealhashtrees.pdf

  This is Phil Bagwell's paper that discusses persistent *Tries*.

- *The Java Memory Model*

  http://java.sun.com/docs/books/jls/third_edition/html/memory.html

  This is the Java Language Specification discussing Java threads and the Java Memory Model.

- *The JSR-133 Cookbook for Compiler Writers*

  http://g.oswego.edu/dl/jmm/cookbook.html

  Doug Lea explains memory barriers in this article.

- *The Lock Interface*

  http://download.oracle.com/javase/1.5.0/docs/api/java/util/concurrent/locks/Lock.html

  This is the javadoc for the Lock interface introduced in Java 5.

- *The Meaning of Object-Oriented Programming*

  http://userpage.fu-berlin.de/~ram/pub/pub_jf47ht81Ht/doc_kay_oop_en

  In an email exchange, Alan Kay discusses the meaning of OOP.

- *Multiverse: Software Transactional Memory for Java*

  http://multiverse.codehaus.org/overview.html

  Multiverse, founded by Peter Veentijer, is a Java-based implementation of STM that can be used from multiple languages on the JVM.

- *Polyglot Programming*

  http://memeagora.blogspot.com/2006/12/polyglot-programming.html

  This is Neal Ford's vision of "Polyglot Programmers."

- *Test Driving Multithreaded Code*

http://www.agiledeveloper.com/presentations/TestDrivingMultiThreadedCode.zip

These are my notes and code from my presentation entitled "Test-Driving Multithreaded Code."

Bibliography

[Arm07]   Joe Armstrong. *Programming Erlang: Software for a Concurrent World*. The Pragmatic Bookshelf, Raleigh, NC and Dallas, TX, 2007.

[Bec96]   Kent Beck. *Smalltalk Best Practice Patterns*. Prentice Hall, Englewood Cliffs, NJ, 1996.

[Blo08]   Joshua Bloch. *Effective Java*. Addison-Wesley, Reading, MA, 2008.

[FH11]   Michael Fogus and Chris Houser. *The Joy of Clojure*. Manning Publications Co., Greenwich, CT, 2011.

[Goe06]   Brian Goetz. *Java Concurrency in Practice*. Addison-Wesley, Reading, MA, 2006.

[Hal09]   Stuart Halloway. *Programming Clojure*. The Pragmatic Bookshelf, Raleigh, NC and Dallas, TX, 2009.

[Lea00]   Doug Lea. *Concurrent Programming in Java: Design Principles and Patterns*. Addison-Wesley, Reading, MA, Second, 2000.

[Mey97]   Bertrand Meyer. *Object-Oriented Software Construction*. Prentice Hall, Englewood Cliffs, NJ, Second, 1997.

[OSV08]   Martin Odersky, Lex Spoon, and Bill Venners. *Programming in Scala*. Artima, Inc., Mountain View, CA, Second, 2008.

[Pag95]   Meilir Page-Jones. *What Every Programmer Should Know About Object-Oriented Design*. Dorset House, New York, NY, USA, 1995.

[Sub09]   Venkat Subramaniam. *Programming Scala: Tackle Multi-Core Complexity on the Java Virtual Machine*. The Pragmatic Bookshelf, Raleigh, NC and Dallas, TX, 2009.

[VWWA96] Robert Virding, Claes Wikstrom, Mike Williams, and Joe Armstrong. *Concurrent Programming in Erlang.* Prentice Hall, Englewood Cliffs, NJ, Second, 1996.

Index

Learn a New Language This Year

Want to be a better programmer? Each new programming language you learn teaches you something new about computing. Come see what you're missing.

If you're a Java programmer, if you care about concurrency, or if you enjoy working in low-ceremony language such as Ruby or Python, *Programming Clojure* is for you. Clojure is a general-purpose language with direct support for Java, a modern Lisp dialect, and support in both the language and data structures for functional programming. *Programming Clojure* shows you how to write applications that have the beauty and elegance of a good scripting language, the power and reach of the JVM, and a modern, concurrency-safe functional style. Now you can write beautiful code that runs fast and scales well.

Stuart Halloway
(304 pages) ISBN: 9781934356333. $32.95
http://pragmaticprogrammer.com/titles/shcloj

Scala is an exciting, modern, multi-paradigm language for the JVM. You can use it to write traditional, imperative, object-oriented code. But you can also leverage its higher level of abstraction to take full advantage of modern, multicore systems. *Programming Scala* will show you how to use this powerful functional programming language to create highly scalable, highly concurrent applications on the Java Platform.

Venkat Subramaniam
(250 pages) ISBN: 9781934356319. $34.95
http://pragmaticprogrammer.com/titles/vsscala

Welcome to the New Web

The world isn't quite ready for the new web standards, but you can be. Get started with HTML5, CSS3, and a better JavaScript today.

CoffeeScript is JavaScript done right. It provides all of JavaScript's functionality wrapped in a cleaner, more succinct syntax. In the first book on this exciting new language, CoffeeScript guru Trevor Burnham shows you how to hold onto all the power and flexibility of JavaScript while writing clearer, cleaner, and safer code.

Trevor Burnham
(136 pages) ISBN: 9781934356784. $29
http://pragmaticprogrammer.com/titles/tbcoffee

HTML5 and CSS3 are the future of web development, but you don't have to wait to start using them. Even though the specification is still in development, many modern browsers and mobile devices already support HTML5 and CSS3. This book gets you up to speed on the new HTML5 elements and CSS3 features you can use right now, and backwards compatible solutions ensure that you don't leave users of older browsers behind.

Brian P. Hogan
(280 pages) ISBN: 9781934356685. $33
http://pragmaticprogrammer.com/titles/bhh5

Be Agile

Don't just "do" agile; you want *be* agile. We'll show you how.

The best agile book isn't a book: *Agile in a Flash* is a unique deck of index cards that fit neatly in your pocket. You can tape them to the wall. Spread them out on your project table. Get stains on them over lunch. These cards are meant to be used, not just read.

Jeff Langr and Tim Ottinger
(110 pages) ISBN: 9781934356715. $15
http://pragmaticprogrammer.com/titles/olag

Here are three simple truths about software development:

1. You can't gather all the requirements up front. 2. The requirements you do gather will change. 3. There is always more to do than time and money will allow.

Those are the facts of life. But you can deal with those facts (and more) by becoming a fierce software-delivery professional, capable of dispatching the most dire of software projects and the toughest delivery schedules with ease and grace.

Jonathan Rasmusson
(280 pages) ISBN: 9781934356586. $34.95
http://pragmaticprogrammer.com/titles/jtrap

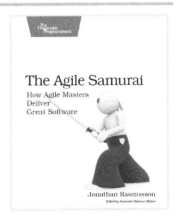

Advanced Ruby and Rails

What used to be the realm of experts is fast becoming the stuff of day-to-day development. Jump to the head of the class in Ruby and Rails.

Rails 3 is a huge step forward. You can now easily extend the framework, change its behavior, and replace whole components to bend it to your will, all without messy hacks. This pioneering book is the first resource that deep dives into the new Rails 3 APIs and shows you how to use them to write better web applications and make your day-to-day work with Rails more productive.

José Valim
(180 pages) ISBN: 9781934356739. $33
http://pragmaticprogrammer.com/titles/jvrails

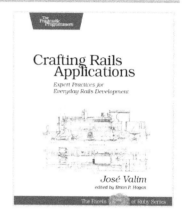

As a Ruby programmer, you already know how much fun it is. Now see how to unleash its power, digging under the surface and exploring the language's most advanced features: a collection of techniques and tricks known as *metaprogramming*. Once the domain of expert Rubyists, metaprogramming is now accessible to programmers of all levels—from beginner to expert. *Metaprogramming Ruby* explains metaprogramming concepts in a down-to-earth style and arms you with a practical toolbox that will help you write great Ruby code.

Paolo Perrotta
(240 pages) ISBN: 9781934356470. $32.95
http://pragmaticprogrammer.com/titles/ppmetr

Pragmatic Guide Series

If you want to know what lies ahead, ask those who are coming back. Our pragmatic authors have been there, they've done it, and they've come back to help guide you along the road. They'll get you started quickly, with a minimum of fuss and hand-holding. The Pragmatic Guide Series features convenient, task-oriented two-page spreads. You'll find what you need fast, and get on with your work

Need to learn how to wrap your head around Git, but don't need a lot of hand holding? Grab this book if you're new to Git, not to the world of programming. Git tasks displayed on two-page spreads provide all the context you need, without the extra fluff.

NEW: Part of the new *Pragmatic Guide* series

Travis Swicegood
(168 pages) ISBN: 9781934356722. $25
http://pragmaticprogrammer.com/titles/pg_git

JavaScript is everywhere. It's a key component of to-day's Web—a powerful, dynamic language with a rich ecosystem of professional-grade development tools, infrastructures, frameworks, and toolkits. This book will get you up to speed quickly and painlessly with the 35 key JavaScript tasks you need to know.

NEW: Part of the new *Pragmatic Guide* series

Christophe Porteneuve
(150 pages) ISBN: 9781934356678. $25
http://pragmaticprogrammer.com/titles/pg_js

Testing Is Only the Beginning

Start with Test Driven Development, Domain Driven Design, and Acceptance Test Driven Planning in Ruby. Then add Shoulda, Cucumber, Factory Girl, and Rcov for the ultimate in Ruby and Rails development.

Behaviour-Driven Development (BDD) gives you the best of Test Driven Development, Domain Driven Design, and Acceptance Test Driven Planning techniques, so you can create better software with self-documenting, executable tests that bring users and developers together with a common language.

Get the most out of BDD in Ruby with *The RSpec Book*, written by the lead developer of RSpec, David Chelimsky.

David Chelimsky, Dave Astels, Zach Dennis, Aslak Hellesøy, Bryan Helmkamp, Dan North
(448 pages) ISBN: 9781934356371. $38.95
http://pragmaticprogrammer.com/titles/achbd

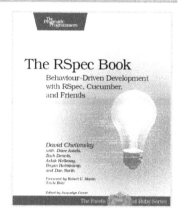

Rails Test Prescriptions is a comprehensive guide to testing Rails applications, covering Test-Driven Development from both a theoretical perspective (why to test) and from a practical perspective (how to test effectively). It covers the core Rails testing tools and procedures for Rails 2 and Rails 3, and introduces popular add-ons, including RSpec, Shoulda, Cucumber, Factory Girl, and Rcov.

Noel Rappin
(368 pages) ISBN: 9781934356647. $34.95
http://pragmaticprogrammer.com/titles/nrtest

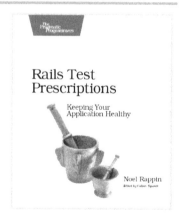

Pragmatic Practices

Pragmatic Programmers *think* about their practices and improve them. Start here.

Software development happens in your head. Not in an editor, IDE, or design tool. You're well educated on how to work with software and hardware, but what about *wetware*—our own brains? Learning new skills and new technology is critical to your career, and it's all in your head.

In this book by Andy Hunt, you'll learn how our brains are wired, and how to take advantage of your brain's architecture. You'll learn new tricks and tips to learn more, faster, and retain more of what you learn.

You need a pragmatic approach to thinking and learning. You need to *Refactor Your Wetware.*

Andy Hunt
(288 pages) ISBN: 9781934356050. $34.95
http://pragmaticprogrammer.com/titles/ahptl

Do you ever look at the clock and wonder where the day went? You spent all this time at work and didn't come close to getting everything done. Tomorrow, try something new. Use the Pomodoro Technique, originally developed by Francesco Cirillo, to work in focused sprints throughout the day. In *Pomodoro Technique Illustrated*, Staffan Nöteberg shows you how to organize your work to accomplish more in less time. There's no need for expensive software or fancy planners. You can get started with nothing more than a piece of paper, a pencil, and a kitchen timer.

Staffan Nöteberg
(144 pages) ISBN: 9781934356500. $24.95
http://pragmaticprogrammer.com/titles/snfocus

The Pragmatic Bookshelf

The Pragmatic Bookshelf features books written by developers for developers. The titles continue the well-known Pragmatic Programmer style and continue to garner awards and rave reviews. As development gets more and more difficult, the Pragmatic Programmers will be there with more titles and products to help you stay on top of your game.

Visit Us Online

This Book's Home Page
http://pragprog.com/titles/vspcon
Source code from this book, errata, and other resources. Come give us feedback, too!

Register for Updates
http://pragprog.com/updates
Be notified when updates and new books become available.

Join the Community
http://pragprog.com/community
Read our weblogs, join our online discussions, participate in our mailing list, interact with our wiki, and benefit from the experience of other Pragmatic Programmers.

New and Noteworthy
http://pragprog.com/news
Check out the latest pragmatic developments, new titles and other offerings.

Save on the eBook

Save on the eBook versions of this title. Owning the paper version of this book entitles you to purchase the electronic versions at a terrific discount.

PDFs are great for carrying around on your laptop—they are hyperlinked, have color, and are fully searchable. Most titles are also available for the iPhone and iPod touch, Amazon Kindle, and other popular e-book readers.

Buy now at *http://pragprog.com/coupon*

Contact Us

Online Orders:	*http://pragprog.com/catalog*
Customer Service:	*support@pragprog.com*
International Rights:	*translations@pragprog.com*
Academic Use:	*academic@pragprog.com*
Write for Us:	*http://pragprog.com/write-for-us*
Or Call:	+1 800-699-7764